VLADIMIR PEREVERZ[...] [...]ed
in Russia on fraudulent cha[...] [...]ion
when he refused to give [...] [...]ner
Mikhail Khodorkovsky. H[...] [...]ost
notorious prisons and labour camps, including two of the penal
colonies political prisoner Alexei Navalny has been held in.
Vladimir now lives in Berlin and campaigns for human rights.

ANNA GUNIN is a translator from Russian. Among her
translations are Svetlana Alexievich's *Chernobyl Prayer* (with Arch
Tait), Oleg Pavlov's award-winning *Requiem for a Soldier*, and
Mikail Eldin's *The Sky Wept Fire*, which won an English PEN
award. Her translations of Pavel Bazhov's fairy tales appear in
Russian Magic Tales from Pushkin to Platonov, which was shortlisted
for the 2014 Rossica Prize.

THE PRISONER

BEHIND BARS IN PUTIN'S RUSSIA

Vladimir Pereverzin

Translated by Anna Gunin

First published in the UK in 2024 by Gemini Adult Books Ltd,
part of the Gemini Books Group

Based in Woodbridge and London

Marine House, Tide Mill Way,
Woodbridge, Suffolk IP12 1AP

www.geminibooks.com

Text © 2024 Vladimir Pereverzin
English translation © 2024 Anna Gunin

Paperback ISBN 9781802472516
eBook ISBN 9781802472523

A CIP catalogue record for this book is available
from the British Library.

Every reasonable effort has been made to trace copyright-
holders of material reproduced in this book, but if any have
been inadvertently overlooked the publishers would be glad to
hear from them.

Printed in the UK
10 9 8 7 6 5 4 3 2 1

CONTENTS

1

FREEDOM

In a south-west suburb of Moscow, inside a 1970s tower block. It is early morning. 'Bzzzzz …' A shrill ringing breaks in on my dream. I try to work out where the sound is from. My mobile is off, and I didn't set my alarm clock. For the past seven years, I have woken each morning to a wailing siren and the yell of 'Everybody up!' It takes me some time to realise where I am. The sound is from my landline phone, which I rarely use – I don't even know the number. 'Hey, you're flooding my apartment,' says a woman's angry voice. 'Can't you hear? There's water bucketing down!'

I rush in a panic to check the radiators, which were replaced a day ago. There is a puddle on the floor: water is trickling from a radiator. Grabbing a cloth and basin, I try to do battle with the elements. I phone the plumber; earlier in the morning he connected the radiators to the water supply, and now I have a leak. But the problem is quickly solved: it turns out yesterday's fitters just forgot to tighten a nut. We go downstairs to the neighbour's flat to check the damage. We press on her bell for ages, but there is no answer. 'Oh, to hell with her!' the plumber says. 'It can't be that bad if she won't even bother to open up.'

The plumber leaves, and I go back to my apartment. The telephone starts ringing again; it is the downstairs neighbour. She is yelling into the receiver. I speak politely, trying to defuse the situation: 'I just came down to your flat with the plumber, but you wouldn't come to the door.'

'I was in the shower.'

'Well, I can come back down now.'

'What for?'

'To examine the damage and pay you for it.'

'No, I won't let you in. It's terrifying having you as a neighbour, I never know what might happen,' she says.

I have been away from home for seven years and two months. For all that time, I was living in a foreign country. In a different reality, a parallel world, separated from this one by barbed wire.

There are no regrets. I don't regret a thing I did – nor anything I didn't do. If I could turn back the clock, I would do it all the same. My actions were shaped by my values; they were preordained by how I was brought up. Now I can look my son in the eye without shame. And if only he hadn't died during the trial, if he'd lived to see my release, I could have looked my father in the eye as well. I believe that nothing ever vanishes into thin air; no one ever gets off scot-free. There will come a time when we will pay for our sins. If you won't pay, then your children surely will. Or your grandchildren …

The past few years lasted a whole lifetime. How can you put a price on the seven years and two months stolen from me? Is it even possible? My father died; my son grew up fatherless. How can you work out the cost of a broken life, wrecked health, a career in tatters?

I am a lucky man; fate has been kind to me. I spent seven years and two months behind bars, but it was my good fortune to be freed. There were moments when I believed I'd never get out.

People often ask me how I came to be put on trial with Khodorkovsky. Not without irony, I always say, 'Sheer luck!'

After seven years of being locked up, I'm now home.

Free at last! After being robbed for seven years of the simple human pleasures that in ordinary life we take for granted, I now see things through fresh eyes. For all those years, having a shower or bath was a distant dream. Now the smallest things, the slightest trifles, fill me with delight. The sheer pleasure of being able to wear ordinary clothes, of lounging about on a bed covered in proper bed linen. In Russian penitentiaries, for some strange reason, there is a strict ban on blanket covers. I go for a ride on the underground, pop into a café, order coffee and ice cream. The pleasure from visiting an ordinary shop overwhelms me.

And, to my surprise, there are no claps of thunder, bolts of lightning do not smite my oppressors, the sun doesn't turn black. It is all rather grey and mundane. The cars race heedlessly past, people hurry along on their way, indifferent to me.

I want to shout to the world: 'Hey, everyone, look! They've set me free!' My heart is exploding, I want to laugh and cry. It still hasn't sunk in – I cannot quite believe I've been released. Right up till the last moment, I just couldn't believe they would let me out. After all that had happened to me behind bars, I was ready for dirty tricks and set-ups. And, sure enough, they didn't pass up the chance to mess with me a little, one last time.

Here is how prisoners are normally released. At around ten in the morning, they take you to the main office, along with your belongings, then lead you to the checkpoint, where your identity is verified to make sure the right man is being let out. At this point, friends and family are arriving to meet you at the gates. This is the moment you've spent years waiting for: that joyous reunion, longed for and emotional.

That was not how things went for me. At six in the morning, I was woken by none other than the head of the prisoner unit himself. 'Get your belongings and go to the office!' he said. 'Get ready for your release.' I instinctively tensed up. Asking one of the prisoners to accompany me, I headed for the office with all my things packed into a bag. From there, an officer led me towards the checkpoint. The heavy door separating the two worlds swung open, and there I was before another officer. 'Name? Surname? Date and place of birth? Place of residence? Date of registration of your marriage?' Questions rained down on me. 'Face the front, now sideways.' The officer checked me against my photos. Once he was satisfied that it was me – that I wasn't an imposter being let out under my identity – he handed over a certificate of release, my passport, my belongings and the cash in my prison account. I walked out into the street. It was dark. The time was 6.15 a.m. A case officer, the deputy head of operations for the penal colony and some unknown man in plain clothes were all waiting for me. They politely suggested I get in the car. This threw me into a panic! Where were they going? Could they be about to bring new charges against me? Or were they planning to bump me off and dump my corpse? But there was no way out; I had nowhere to go. So I meekly got in the car.

'Where would you like to go? The railway station or the bus terminal?' the case officer asked.

I chose the bus terminal. They let me call my relatives. And so I found myself standing at the Pokrov town bus terminal in my prison-camp outfit: a ghastly padded jacket with my name tag sewn on the chest, an equally hideous cap and trousers and prison-issue boots, along with my bag. To avoid alarming the passers-by, I tore the tag off the jacket, removed the cap and hid it, then went into a roadside café, which was empty at this early hour. A good thing I had some cash. I should mention: the Russian state shows a touching concern for its convicts, issuing them a sum of 800 roubles upon their release.[1] I ordered a coffee, some cake and an ice cream. I sat and wondered what to do next. I decided to take a taxi. Twenty minutes later, a silver Renault Megane bearing the words 'Pokrov Town Taxi' was ferrying me to the long-awaited reunion with my loved ones. We met on the Vladimir–Moscow road, in the village of Obukhovo. There were tears of joy and embraces. I'm not ashamed to admit I cried. They'd stood by me all those years: my friend Leonid Belenky, my son Dennis and my wife Irina. I changed into ordinary clothes. We folded the camp uniform, put it in a bag and burnt it at the side of the road. We drank champagne – my first champagne in seven years and two months. Hurray! This wasn't a dream; I truly was free. My new life had begun.

It is 15 October 2012. I am sitting with Vladimir Malakhovsky in a small café near Park Kultury metro station. A week has passed

---

1   Worth roughly £16 at the time.

since he was released. This is our first meeting on the outside. Until now, we have only ever seen each other in the courts, which is where we first met. We sit and sip coffee. Welling up with emotion, I feel like getting to my feet and shouting: 'Hey, look at us! They locked us away for embezzling thirteen billion dollars and laundering eight billion! Can you believe that?' No doubt they would have taken us for nutters. When we've finished our coffee, we walk to the metro and go our separate ways. We each wander off on our own business. Vladimir will take the Radial line, and I'll leave on the Circle line. 'Sheer insanity!' you might say, and you'd be right. There were no billions of dollars, just as there was no embezzlement. But the years spent in prisons and camps, they were real. The years squandered for the benefit of someone's private agenda and ambitions, the years stolen from us, never to be returned.

I remember vividly the day my life was turned upside down. It was 16 December 2004, the day of my arrest. The day my life was split in two: into life before and life after. At the time, I could scarcely believe it was happening to me. And now, I can barely believe that it's all over. As I pen these lines, I am haunted by the feeling that it is not me I'm writing about, but some other man who lived through it all. It is as though I was watching a film about him, reading a book on him. And here is that book.

2

THE JOURNEY BEGINS

I was born in Moscow into an ordinary family. My childhood and teen years were spent in Chertanovo district, in the city suburbs. Life for me differed little from the lives of many of my peers. I went to an ordinary district school and attended a Sambo-70 sports club. The idea of a career in sports appealed.

After leaving school, I stood at a crossroads, considering whether to apply to Moscow's Institute of Physical Education. But I chose an economics degree. After graduating, I did a brief stint in the Moscow Regional Executive Committee, then found a job in the USSR State Committee for Sport, working in the Department for Foreign Activity.

The year was 1991. Our work involved handling the accounts for the various sports federations. For instance, when Soviet skaters won the World Figure Skating Championship, we would receive the prize money. The winnings would go into a pool to be allotted for the upkeep of sports federations that weren't earning anything. I worked in the planning department for the convergence of foreign currency – merging all the revenue streams. The sports federation chairs and famous sportspeople would visit our department. The job was prestigious and the pay was good. But weighing heavy on my conscience was the sense that I was part of a redundant superstructure leeching off the talents of the sportspeople.

So when I came across a newspaper ad – 'Commercial bank seeks specialists in foreign economic affairs' – I lost no time in applying. The job was with the Commercial Innovation Bank of Scientific-Technical Progress, later renamed as Menatep. My career in banking began with the post of specialist in international settlements – in other words, I was an ordinary teller. The bank was thriving and expanding fast, and in the process it launched my career. I became senior teller, deputy head of international settlements, head of department … Slowly surmounting the obstacles, I moved up the career ladder.

In 1994 I took a break, leaving to study on a British Council scholarship at the University of Leeds. After a year, I returned to Russia, going back to work at my old home, Menatep Bank, where I headed the main currency section. One year on, the bank opened a subsidiary in Cyprus, and I moved out to work there. I was in Cyprus for about a year. When the 1998 financial crisis hit, the bank went bust.

But I didn't stay jobless for long, soon landing work with the Yukos Oil Company. When Yukos decided to open a subsidiary in Cyprus, I was the obvious candidate. The company's financial director, Michel Sublen, filled me in on my mission and its terms and conditions, and next thing I was packing my bags and flying out to Cyprus. For Yukos I was a godsend, and the minute I stepped off the plane, I buckled down to work. Six months later, the company had a well-staffed and fully operational office on the island, where I stayed on in my job. My boss Michel Sublen quit Yukos without saying goodbye and without honouring his commitments and obligations. When I raised my complaints at a meeting with Bruce Misamore, the US citizen who was replacing him, Misamore looked at me in surprise and told me frankly that if things at Yukos weren't to my liking, I was free to leave.

I had not yet met the accomplices with whom, as it later transpired, I was busy stealing oil. For that matter, I still hadn't met Khodorkovsky, and, bearing in mind my role in the company, I could not even theoretically have met him, as my job grade would not have allowed it. Lebedev, as far as I recall, wasn't even working for Yukos at the time. The best thing for it was to follow Misamore's advice, so I resigned without severance pay. I couldn't sit idle for long, though, and within a few months I was deputy chairman of another bank and Yukos seemed a distant memory. But fate would decree otherwise; it was to bind me to the company for life.

December 2004. Platon Lebedev and Mikhail Khodorkovsky were under arrest. At the time, I thought the arrest had to be some sort of mix-up. It was an event so remote that I couldn't imagine it might affect me. I'd quit Yukos in 2002 and was now deputy chairman of another bank. Life was going swimmingly, with no signs of trouble ahead. I've often asked myself what I might have done if I'd known in advance what was coming. Would I have gone in for questioning? At the time, there was no reason for alarm, because I was as clean as the driven snow. But I don't know the answer. Everything just happened the way it did. I have no regrets.

Different fates awaited those who decided not to go in for questioning. For some, everything came to grief. Although others, despite the odds, pulled off a lucky escape.

When I was arrested, my lawyer asked Artyom Butovsky, who'd replaced me in Cyprus, for some documents about the workings of the company. Butovsky lost no time in demanding a fat sum for the paperwork. I didn't have that sort of money, and after discussing it with the lawyer, I decided to drop the idea and do without the documents. Artyom was a strange fellow. An ordinary employee, just as I had been; two years before my arrest, he had arrived in Cyprus to take over from me when I resigned. Before leaving the island, I handed everything over to him: the office, paperwork, company car, apartment, even the mobile phone. When that mobile received a text message intended for me, saying, 'A beautiful blonde is waiting for you at the bar,' Artyom raced there on his beloved motorbike. And he could just as easily have taken my place in the dock. The investigators for the Prosecutor-General's Office certainly weren't fussy about who they threw behind bars.

I still had friends and acquaintances working at Yukos, and from time to time I dropped in on their office on Dubininskaya Street. We usually met in the staff café. Once, I ran into a friend there. I was reading an article in *Kommersant* that seemed totally unconnected to me – little did I know – about the embezzlement of Yukos oil and the arrest of a man called Vladimir Malakhovsky. I turned to Boris in bewilderment. 'How on earth could anyone steal anything at Yukos? The whole place is under the tightest control. It's all tied up in paperwork and procedures. There's an endless stream of approvals, internal audits, external audits, security checks ...'

'I really don't know.' Boris shrugged.

'And who is this Malakhovsky?'

'No idea,' he said.

Later on, it emerged that Malakhovsky was my 'accomplice', though, by a curious turn of events, I only ever met him during the trial. Credit is due to my friend Boris, who appeared in court as a witness for the defence and told them this story. And what if Malakhovsky and I had known each other, would it have mattered? We were working in the same organisation: two employees carrying out our jobs. There was no more to it. In our case, it so happened we'd never set eyes on each other. But that was not enough to stop us being found guilty of stealing all the oil produced by Yukos over the course of the company's existence and landing monstrous sentences. The court effectively ruled that we were doing nothing in Yukos but pilfering oil and the company's entire activity was illegal. By that logic, Yukos would have been paying billions of illegal dollars in taxes into the Russian state treasury. What else can one say if they used my employment-record book and the company's official tax and financial records as evidence of criminal activity? I was convicted for the mere fact that I'd worked at Yukos. Remarkable as it may sound, any random Yukos employee could just as easily have taken my place. Fate, however, picked me.

3

ARREST

It was November 2004. My father rang me from the apartment where I was officially registered. 'Volodya, you've got a subpoena here for questioning by the Prosecutor-General's Office.' Later, while I was in remand prison, my father died. He didn't live to hear my sentence: eleven years in a strict-regime penal colony.

I collected the subpoena from my father and naively went along to the Prosecutor-General's Office, taking a lawyer with me. The first interview was in a gloomy building on Tekhnichesky Lane. They asked some standard questions. On the advice of the lawyer, who was provided by Yukos, I refused to give evidence, citing Article 51 of the Russian Constitution.[2] With the benefit of hindsight, I now see this was a fatal mistake. But at the time, in late November 2004, I left the building and blithely resumed my usual routine. The interrogation cost me my position as deputy chairman of the board: the bank's shareholders politely asked me to step down. I walked into the building of the Prosecutor-General's Office unemployed, burning with ambitions and hopes for a bright future. And I emerged from the building in the same breezy mood. There was plenty to keep me occupied. Some part of me was even glad to be free from the shackles of being a company manager; at long last I'd be able to focus on projects of my own.

New Year's Eve was fast approaching. In a flurry of activity, everyone shopped for presents and prepared for the holidays. We had already bought our tickets and paid for a hotel. We'd decided the whole family would see in the New Year in Prague. I was snowed under with things to do. The date was 16 December 2004; I was in a restaurant called Noah's Ark. Over a business lunch, I was chatting pleasantly with the chair of one of the banks, an agreeable lady. Suddenly my phone rang. An unknown voice was on the other end.

'Mr Pereverzin?'

'Speaking.'

'Investigator Asadulin here. Could you please come to Bolshaya Pionerskaya, Building No. 20?'

'Can't make it today,' I said. 'But I'll be there tomorrow.'

The investigator stood firm. 'No, you must come today. It'll take around twenty minutes.'

My heart did not lurch. There was no voice in my head saying, 'Run, Volodya, run!' Khodorkovsky and Lebedev were

---

2 Article 51 of the Russian Constitution states, 'No one is obliged to testify against himself, his spouse or his close relatives.'

already under arrest. The mysterious Malakhovsky whom I'd read about in *Kommersant* had been arrested too. Feeling guilt-free and blameless before the law, I thought, 'Okay, I'll go today. Otherwise they'll give me no peace.' At the time, I had no idea those twenty minutes would stretch into seven years and two months ...

So I finished lunch and headed for the address given. It turned out to be a building in the Russian Ministry of Internal Affairs: the Department for High-Security Facilities. A kind of state within a state, with its own bureau of investigations, complete with wiretapping, surveillance and other covert activities. How many of these secret departments with concocted functions lurk buried in Russia's magic kingdom? And they don't just sit there, doing nothing. No, they need to keep busy, tackling urgent problems. So they hatch problems, and then they solve them. It gives them all something to do. But it would be better all round if they simply did nothing. The way it works is they spend our money on putting us behind bars, and they rob us blind into the bargain. The whole system in Russia is topsy-turvy; we've all forgotten who should be serving whom. If everyone could just do what they were meant to do, life would be so much better. But this is Russia ...

Having reached the Department for High-Security Facilities, I asked at the reception for the investigator – and fell into a trap! They were lying in wait. The time was 2.15 p.m. They swooped and surrounded me, then handed me a subpoena for an interrogation at 3 p.m. in the Prosecutor-General's Office, Building 2, on Tekhnichesky Lane. They offered to take me there in a police van marked 'State Traffic Inspectorate'. I was genuinely baffled by what was going on and asked, 'Why all the game-playing? Why not just hand me the subpoena for interrogation and be done with it?' My words hung in the air. Later, I discovered they'd placed me under surveillance after the first interview. But on that same day they'd lost me, and so they decided to lay their cunning trap. That was how they ensnared me. I shouldn't be surprised if someone somewhere won a medal or promotion for this 'special op'.

These brave officers of the Department for High-Security Facilities valiantly delivered me to Tekhnichesky Lane for questioning at precisely the prescribed time. In other words, it was a plain old police abduction. They drove me to the building, and we went up to the third floor. We walked into an office where some unknown people were pacing back and forth. Later, I discovered their surnames: Karimov, Khatypov, Alyshev, Rusanova, Ganiev ... I declined the offer of a lawyer. They presented me with a warrant to search my apartment, which was the entire party's next stop. Nobody was home. They rustled up some witnesses. I rang my close friend Leonid and asked him to come over urgently. They searched high and low, turning the place inside out: they broke open ceiling panels in the bathroom, trawled through all the closets, climbed under the bathtub, rifled through our things. I had no idea what they were looking for. I don't think they knew themselves. Nothing went missing. After the search, we headed back to the Prosecutor-General's Office. Again they questioned me – without a lawyer since I'd turned down the offer of one. They produced an arrest warrant. Investigator Khatypov kindly allowed me to call my wife and tell her I was under arrest. By now it was around midnight.

'Ira, I've been arrested.' I choked the words out.

'Come on, stop messing me around!'

She wouldn't believe me.

'No really, I'm under arrest,' I insisted, though the words sounded just as implausible to me. I passed the phone to the investigator.

'This is Special Cases Investigator Khatypov of the Prosecutor-General's Office.'

My wife still refused to believe it, and I heard her say, 'Come on, Leonid, that's enough of your games.'

She'd mistaken the investigator for my close friend, but, catching the chilly tone in his voice, she now realised this was serious. For a long time, I could not shake off the sensation that someone was playing a cruel prank on me. It felt as though any moment now the doors would swing open, it would all be over and I could get back to my humdrum existence. But it was to stretch on and on for years …

The first night began. They took me from the Prosecutor-General's Office to the Department for High-Security Facilities on Bolshaya Pionerskaya Street. A peculiar detail caught my attention: the officials in this mysterious department introduced themselves with fake names and surnames. I was offered a choice: I could be moved to a detention centre or stay put and wait for some general to turn up who'd question me to assess whether to keep me in custody. Grasping at my last chance, I chose the latter. If you check the paperwork, from the moment of my arrest at 11.50 p.m., 16 December, until 3 p.m. on 17 December, when I was logged at the detention centre, I vanished without trace.

I sat ensconced in a shabby armchair in the corridor, trying to make sense of what was going on. Nearby sat my guards: three young policemen. A tall, drunken man in plain clothes wandered out of an office. 'What's this, eh, detainees with no handcuffs on?' he said, slurring his words, and he walked right up to me. I rose calmly and looked him in the eye. He stood a good 15 centimetres taller than me, getting on for 1 metre 90. I was smothered in a cloud of boozy fumes. Grabbing the collar of my jacket, he yanked it down my back – effectively pinioning my arms. 'If he punches me, I'll use my legs to fight back,' I thought, continuing to stand calm. I shifted into position, feet apart and trunk at a slight angle. He picked up on my intention and dithered. Realising that things were hotting up, one of the guards ran to fetch someone senior, and they led the bastard away. The next morning, an official who introduced himself as Vasily (although, curiously, his colleagues called him Alexander) apologised for the incident.

Presumably to avoid a repeat of this incident – for who knows how many more drunken thugs were lurking in those rooms –

they led me to the office of one of their principals, Office No. 3. A small reception desk served two rooms – for the chief and deputy chief of the Eighth Division, Colonel Florinsky and Lieutenant Colonel Zelepushchenkov. I spent the rest of the night in the latter's office. My guards sat there too, keeping a beady eye on me. During the night, another plainclothes officer dropped in, wanting to know about my life. He told me the general would arrive soon and decide what to do. This general was clearly taking his time. Then I heard some noises and commotion: footsteps, the sound of doors slamming. The long-awaited comrade must have arrived. A rather plain-looking man of medium height walked into the office and greeted us. The guards departed, and we were alone in the room. My visitor introduced himself as the head of a team providing operational support for the case. He grandly announced his rank and presented his ID. He did so in rather an odd manner: keeping hold of the card, he hid the surname with his little finger. The photo indeed showed a man wearing the uniform of a major general. This wasn't an official interrogation; rather, we were having a chat. He strongly advised that I confess. Without the foggiest idea what I was to confess to, I decided he must be crazy.

'Ah, you have no idea what we've got on you!' he said, pulling some paper from his briefcase. It turned out to be a CV I'd once sent to some job agencies.

'That's it, he's a nutcase,' I thought.

'We're not interested in you,' this character continued. 'Give us a statement against Brudno, Lebedev and Khodorkovsky, and you can go home and get on with your life. All you need do is confess.'

I genuinely couldn't follow what I was meant to confess to.

The mysterious general persisted.

'Listen, you'll get twelve years, with no chance of parole. By the time you get out, your son will be fully grown and he'll tell you to eff off, and your wife will have left you …'

I was desperate to sleep, but here I was, listening to this drivel, unable to make sense of it all. Twelve years? Whatever for? What on earth was this idiot jabbering on about? When was this going to end? What did these strange people want from me?

The general was called Yurcheko, he was entirely sane and his words were anything but drivel. In fact, he proved clairvoyant and knew precisely what he was saying. After two years and eight months spent in various remand prisons, I would get eleven years in a strict-regime penal camp. They wouldn't release me on parole. I'd serve my full sentence. But all that lay ahead ...

The conversation continued for hour after hour. He cajoled me, threatened me, tried winning me over. But I had nothing to confess. I possessed no secret knowledge, had nothing juicy to tell them.

Neither side understood the other; we were talking at cross purposes, and both of us were flagging. At last, our 'friendly chat' was wound up. We went our separate ways. The general left on his heroic business, while I was led to the detention centre, which was nearby on Shchipok Street, concealed by a gate bearing the inscription 'Fire Station'. They searched me, confiscated my belt, shoelaces, watch, cash and ID, and led me to a dingy cell measuring 2 metres by 3. Attached to the wall was a broad wooden plank-bed designed to sleep several men. There was also a pedestal with a hole in it for answering the call of nature and a tapless sink. The taps could only be turned on by the guard from outside the cell, for which you had to knock on the door. The walls wore what was known as a fur coat: a shaggy concrete coating that had accumulated dirt in the recesses.

I sat on the bunk and sank deep into thought. For the first time in twenty-four hours, I was alone. I hadn't slept or eaten the entire time; the whole thing felt like a dream. I tried pinching myself, opening and closing my eyes, shaking my head in the hope I'd wake up and find myself some place else. But, sadly, nothing changed.

The bolts rattled, the door swung open and a cultured-looking man entered the cell. Here was a fellow victim of fate. He'd apparently been arrested for financial fraud, as he was eager to tell me. Drawn in by his candour, I spilled out my own story. The moment I mentioned the word 'Yukos', he broke in: 'I was at school with Brudno's brother. You don't happen to know him, do you?' I had met Mikhail Brudno, one of the company's shareholders, a few times at work, but we weren't on good enough terms for me to know about his family, let alone the existence of a brother. It was becoming apparent that this 'fellow victim' – he must have had at least the rank of major – had been planted on me for some special purpose.

Again, I heard the clank and clatter of metal; the door opened and I was ordered to leave the cell. They had come for me. I was handcuffed, plonked on the back seat of an unmarked Lada Riva and driven away for questioning at the Prosecutor-General's Office. So I was back in that gloomy building. We went up to the same office as before, where the investigators were waiting for me. There were quite a few of them. I was offered a lawyer but firmly refused one. I asked to make a call, but they wouldn't let me. Our conversation began. Somebody came in, somebody else went out; one played bad cop, another played good cop. They advised me to confess and give a statement while there was still time. The conversation was clearly not going to be pleasant. One of the investigators, a short and scrawny man dressed in a grey suit with a tie and white socks, let rip. With spit flying, he yelled, 'Ivanovich! Look, you're a Russian! What do you want with all those Jews, all those Borisoviches?' The man was deranged, a danger to society.

I felt unmoved by the threats and couldn't take in the reality of what was happening. It was as though I'd stumbled into a nuthouse. I consented to being questioned on tape without a lawyer present. I told them the whole truth: my life story, how I'd landed a job at Yukos, who I knew there, what I did in the company. But the truth clearly wouldn't satisfy them. They led me to another room to see the 'good-cop' special cases investigator whom I'd already met, Mr Khatypov. He officially made me an offer to testify to events that hadn't happened. The whole thing felt like a bad dream, or a scene from a low-budget movie.

The team of investigators on our case had been mustered from every corner of our vast country. The finest professionals had been drafted in. Or maybe the provincial offices had decided to pawn Moscow off with their worst workers. Some men from Bashkortostan formed the core of the group. There was the Head of the Investigation Team Karimov, his deputy Khatypov, plus Ganiev. There were also men from Volgograd, Belgorod, Kursk and even Michurinsk. They had come to conquer Moscow and launch their meteoric careers.

I genuinely could not work out what the charges against me were. The 'good-guy' investigator Khatypov kindly offered me tea, honey from Bashkortostan, cured horse sausage, and enticed me with the prospect of release. I was not at all hungry. Nor did I feel like sleeping. Inventing memories of something that had never happened didn't appeal, and neither, for that matter, did the horse sausage. Clearly the conversation was going nowhere.

So I returned to the cell without discovering what Bashkir honey tasted like. To my delight, my cellmate had vanished. I was left in the cell all alone with my thoughts. I lay on the plank-bed and tried to doze off. This was my second day without sleep, but sleep just wouldn't come. It felt as though I'd merely closed my eyes for a moment when the door clanked open again and they took me for interrogation. I didn't return to the cell that day. The forty-eight hours for which they had the right to detain me were up. They were now faced with two options: let me go home or press charges and resolve the problem of my pretrial detention in court. Oh yes, they would *resolve* it. While in the prosecutor's office, I overheard a conversation between two investigators.

'We just need to warn Fairy Godmother.'

'Oh, I've already phoned her, it's all taken care of,' the other said casually.

Later, I learnt that this was their pet moniker for the presiding judge of the Basmanny District Court. On that day, I first encountered the court that spawned the term 'Basmanny-style justice'. In that courtroom, I first set eyes on Mr Lakhtin, who lied brazenly and cynically about the risk I'd abscond and the need to lock me up. My assertion that I'd come in for questioning of my own free will and had no intention of hiding from anyone fell on deaf ears. The judge quickly and perfunctorily gave her ruling on my detention. She delivered the judgement as though glugging on a glass of cold water. 'Due to the heightened danger and risk of absconding, I order the suspect to be remanded in custody.' The End. It all felt like some kind of nasty stunt or bad joke.

'Eh? Prison?' My mind refused to take in what was happening. 'But I've already bought our air tickets, I've paid for the hotel, my son's been so excited about this trip!' I kept believing that any moment now everything would stop, it would all go back to normal, but the bad joke dragged on.

They handed me the provisional charge sheet, later reissuing it in an amended version. The charges were totally unintelligible. In prison slang, this document is known as a 'fuck-over', and with good reason. That's precisely the point. Apologies for the language, but there really is no other word for it. I was offered a lawyer called Mr Yartykh, and I asked him, in all seriousness, to explain what the charges meant. I wrote on the charge sheet, 'These charges are incomprehensible.' Later, I declined the services of this lawyer, who, by a strange coincidence, within a few years would be representing my 'nocturnal visitor': the General, who by that time had been fired from the Interior Ministry.

Each of us forms our own mental picture of the world, which sometimes falls wide of reality. When the two pictures don't match up, a serious clash can arise. In my – no doubt naive – conception, the Prosecutor-General's Office and the courts were the pinnacle of law and justice, and I was pinning my hopes on justice, on them putting things right and any moment now releasing me. This naivety helped to pull me through all that happened. I was forever waiting for something. First, I waited for the court hearing, where they would once again consider whether to extend my detention, and I hoped to make my way home from the courthouse. Then I waited for the trial to end and to hear the verdict, hoping I'd be acquitted. And then I waited for the cassation proceedings at the Moscow City Court, then the supervisory appeal at the Moscow City Court and the Supreme Court ... I've already served my sentence, and I'm still waiting. I pleaded not guilty, refused to accept the sentence. My appeal against the sentence has been waiting its turn in the European Court of Human Rights for six years ...

4

WELCOME TO BUTYRKA

From the courthouse they took me in a police van to Butyrka Prison. I jumped out of the van. Built in the reign of Catherine the Great and more fit for a museum, the prison building was bleak and imposing. The gates were huge and the ceilings soared. The jangle of locks opening and the sound of doors slamming echoed down the vast corridor. It conjured up a gut feeling that the entire machinery was dangling over you, weighing you down, ready to come crashing down on your head with all its might, making you ill at ease.

They took me for processing to a room where they could keep you as long as they liked before allocating a cell. There were six of us. One by one, we were led out for something resembling a medical examination: we were photographed – 'to capture the moment' – and fingerprinted. For a long time afterwards, the dense black ink wouldn't wash off our hands. We were all of us fresh from the outside, brought here by an array of circumstances. The usual conversation sparked up, with everyone sharing impressions and confiding their woes. A young guy of around twenty proudly told us his story and even bragged that the investigator had complimented him on his good taste. He'd shoplifted a bottle of wine that cost more than the maximum penalty, and so he was facing time inside rather than an administrative fine. As for me, I had nothing to say, let alone to boast of.

I had no idea what they were charging me with, and I'd spent a long time racking my brains over it. They were talking about stolen oil. When I worked in Yukos's subsidiary in Cyprus, I didn't sign a single payment instruction.

Several oil companies fell within the company's structure, any of which might, in theory, have sold oil independently. But since all these companies came under one owner, a centralised structure had been set up in the holding company to handle oil sales for the production companies belonging to Yukos. To this end, special trading companies had been created, one of which I worked for. The trading companies bought the oil from the production companies – from Yuganskneftegaz, say – and sold it on to the end user. This offered substantial savings for the shareholders by keeping down costs (as there was no need for each oil company to have its own sales team), leaving the profit netted by the traders for the shareholders themselves, since all these companies operated under the same holding company, Yukos. There was nothing novel in this set-up: it was how all the major companies worked at the time and how they still work now.

The company I'd been working for purchased oil from Yukos. Since I was not involved with payments and wasn't even authorised to access the accounts from which all the payments came, an idea occurred to me, which I instantly dismissed: 'What if they hadn't actually paid for the oil?' A specialist financial company in Switzerland had been set up that handled all the payments and managed the accounts. 'No, that wouldn't have been possible!' I thought it through desperately. 'I personally requested all their account statements, all their contracts for our auditors. Everything was checked!' I thought, comforting myself. 'Stealing oil? Impossible!' Much later, it all started to click, but for a long time, I just couldn't fathom the idea of this oil theft. It turned out the prosecution's allegation was that the oil was stolen from the production companies. 'How much?' you might ask. The entire output over all the years of Yukos's existence! Why not think big?! And even a little extra on top. When was it stolen, and where? The theft allegedly took place at the precise moment that, for example, Yuganskneftegaz sold the oil to the trading company and the money for the oil purchased – that is to say, for the 'stolen' oil – entered Yuganskneftegaz's account.

'What a load of guff! How could that be possible?' you might ask. Oh, but you'd be surprised! These monstrously absurd ravings from someone's fevered brain formed the basis of our conviction and were set firmly in concrete through the rulings of one court after another.

But as I waited to be allotted a cell, I had no inkling of all that.

5

MY PRISON EDUCATION

I was handed a grotty mattress, a blanket, some shabby old prison-issue sheets and aluminium eating utensils, then led to my cell. It was a four-person cell with a broken window. Two men were already in there, one of whom had just arrived. We introduced ourselves. Gena was an old-timer, aged thirty-four, and he was to be the first instructor in my prison education. He wouldn't say exactly what he was in for, but he chatted eagerly and volubly. The other cellmate was a first-timer, like me. He was a young lad, studying law at Moscow University. Originally from Ivanovo, he'd won a government scholarship place. He was a National Bolshevik activist. They had arrested him for occupying a room in the Presidential Administration. The lads had entered the building; then, using a nail gun, they'd barricaded themselves into one of the offices and hung a poster from the window saying 'Down with Putin'. They now faced cooked-up charges of 'attempting an armed overthrow of the government', carrying a maximum sentence of twenty-five years! How do you explain that? The work of an overzealous and apparently crazy investigator? Or the desire of some bumbling idiot to win a promotion? At the time, I still knew nothing of my own theft of thirteen and a half billion dollars and laundering of eight and a half billion, so when I was asked what I was in for, I couldn't come up with a meaningful answer. The story of the armed overthrow of the government had a happy ending – relatively speaking. The guys were convicted of disorderly conduct and got off with light sentences.

Vova and I listened keenly to our mentor. We were in the cell known as the 'boiler room', the nerve centre of the prison. A pulley system of threads linked virtually all of the cells in Butyrka. They were used for shuttling items: coffee, tea, cigarettes and clandestine letters. Old-hand Gena was a masterful manipulator of these threads. He would receive letters through this prison mail service, sort them, reassigning a few, then forward them on to their intended recipients in another wing of the prison. He worked without a moment's break, catching up on his sleep during the day, when the system shut down. I was entranced by this spectacle, viewing it all as a mini adventure.

The night flew by. We realised it was morning when the food hatch clattered open and our simple breakfast appeared: a piece of bread, some liquid purporting to be tea, and gruel. I tried to eat some of the prison glop, but just couldn't do it. This was my third day without sleep or food. I heard the sound of metal clinking on metal. It was the warden bashing his key against the iron door. He called my name and said, 'Bring your belongings with you and wrap up warm.' I was led to the Prosecutor-General's Office for the same old cautionary talk – this time, without a lawyer. There is a song by Mashina Vremeni called 'Marionettes' with the words 'their faces erased and paint faded' that perfectly captures my condition by that point. I must have looked like someone sleepwalking or who'd slipped into an altered state of mind. I have memories of a glass of tea being drunk and a sandwich eaten.

At that moment, my lawyer and all my loved ones were in a panic verging on shock. All they knew was that I'd vanished again. The Prosecutor-General's Office had told my lawyer that I was in Matrosskaya Tishina Prison. After queuing for ages, he was surprised to discover I was not there. He went back to the Prosecutor-General's Office, where they claimed it was an error, before deceiving him a second time. The lawyer made his way to Butyrka Prison. But at that very moment, I was being transferred to Matrosskaya Tishina. Imagine my lawyer's bewilderment and my family's horror at finding I wasn't there either.

The torturous session in the Prosecutor-General's Office didn't last long. When they realised the hazy state I was in, the investigators released me – back to prison. I had three police guards and the whole car to myself: a Lada 1600. I sat handcuffed in the back and, with a heavy heart, observed the pedestrians hurrying about their business. I gazed at the faces of passing drivers, stared at the festive preparations in Moscow and the freshly fallen snow. We were on our way to Matrosskaya Tishina. The huge metal gates appeared and the security checkpoint, where the guards handed in their weapons. There were dogs barking. We entered the grounds.

The prison felt bleak and oppressive. The guards were clearly not thrilled by my arrival. After a brief dispute, some papers were signed and they handed me over. The prison took me in. It was a strange place: a sinister site of grief and mourning, of evil, pain and desperation, where all human vices were tangled into one. I have always been astonished at the dubious celebrations held by employees in the Russian Penitentiary Service. Recently, they commemorated with great fanfare the centenary of Vladimir Central Prison. Having invited a large number of guests and journalists, the screws proceeded to boast that the mystic Daniel Andreyev, the singer Lidia Ruslanova and other famous victims of the repression had been imprisoned on the site. My goodness! You'd expect them to be ashamed, rather than proud.

6

MATROSSKAYA TISHINA

They brought me to an inner courtyard of the prison, where I was left to wait and wait. I had lost track of time. Watches, for some obscure reason, were a prohibited item; mine had been confiscated while I was still in Butyrka, and they had 'forgotten' to return it. I waited for what seemed an eternity. They led me into the prison and locked me in the 'glass' – a dark little room with standing space only. Well, there was the semblance of a bench: a 10-centimetre-wide board, fixed to the wall, and clearly not intended for seating but as a joke. I'm convinced some specialist in the Research and Development Department for the Russian Penitentiary Service – a department that really exists! – wrote at least a doctoral thesis on the topic. 'The effect of inhuman custodial conditions on crime-solving rates,' perhaps. And, sure enough, many of the men longed to quit the prison for the penal colony. I too was no exception – but more on that later.

For an interminably long time, I was left standing in the 'glass'. Then I was taken for a medical, where a long-faced clinical worker with a giant syringe, complete with blunt needle, drew blood from my vein for HIV testing. He took a good look at me, and for some reason chose to confide his troubles.

'I don't like working here, there's a bad vibe,' he said broodingly.

'Where did you work before?' I asked.

'In the morgue,' he said, heaving a sigh.

They took more 'capturing the moment' mugshots for my file, and I was fingerprinted again. I was issued a mattress, some sheets, a spoon, a mug and a bowl and led to my cell. It was a small-sized 'deluxe unit', cell number 412. I vividly remember the moment: it is burnt in my brain. This time, here was real prison. The door opened, and I walked into the cell. The stench, the dingy light, the cords criss-crossing the cell hung with things that, because of the overcrowding, had no chance of drying and were merely soaking up the odours. The battered walls. Men everywhere, filling the entire space. I stepped in as though entering a crowded bus. Some people were sitting, some were standing, some were lying down. It was like a disaster scene. I'd never seen anything like it, not even in the movies.

Crammed into the cell were eight double-bunk iron beds for forty men. The shortage of places meant the inmates took turns at sleeping. I moved forward, said hello and asked who was the elder. This is the inmate responsible for compliance with the prison code of life – not the system imposed by the authorities, by the 'pigs', but by the 'thieves in law'. We made our introductions. Zhenya – 'the Artist' – was a veteran jailbird, a junkie who had HIV. On the outside, he worked as an art restorer, having undergone professional training. He'd been arrested under Clause 158 for theft. When he discovered this was my first time inside, he gave me a crash course in prison mores. Never shake hands with an untouchable (a category of pariah among the prisoners); never take anything from their hands; never use the toilet when somebody's eating. The rules were clear and simple enough.

I told him about myself – who I was and where I came from. A letter was sent from our cell across the entire prison via the pulley system. It stated: Volodya Pereverzin from Chertanovo has arrived, a first-timer arrested for Articles 160 and 174.1. This routine is followed in every Russian prison, enabling a prisoner's past sins and transgressions to come to light and be punished. The prison community lives by its own honour-based – and at times more just – rules of life. In prison, there is nothing you can hide. Under the beady eye of your fellow inmates for twenty-four hours a day, you become an open book to those around you. I settled into prison life. They offered me a bunk, somewhere to rest. I didn't feel drowsy, despite being on my fourth day without sleep. Zhenya and I got into a long talk. I found him agreeable and interesting. He drew sketches for the entire prison. The men respected him, and there was demand for his work. The inmates showed their gratitude by sending him cigarettes and tea through the pulley postal system. In here, each man had a role. There was the 'postman' who operated the pulleys and was in charge of the unofficial prison organisation. Gradually, I met the other occupants of the cell.

Viktor claimed to have studied directing at the Gerasimov Institute of Cinematography. An erudite guy and an alcoholic, arrested under Article 319 for failure to obey a police officer – a highly respected offence in the prison. Put simply, he had smashed a neighbourhood cop in the face and been arrested for it. Viktor was a master of the written word and wrote flowery missives for his fellow cellmates, which they then posted under their own names to their sweethearts on the outside.

Everything was in short supply in the cell. There was not enough air, food, space, tea or cigarettes. There were no books, no newspapers, no television, and radios were forbidden. The one thing we had in abundance was spare time. Everyone tried to keep themselves occupied in some way or other, to while away the hours. There were endless conversations, at times totally empty and meaningless, but they could also be deeply absorbing. I was chatting casually with one guy when he brought up his friendship with a man who'd been in the cell before me. He mentioned his surname: Malakhovsky. It was a name I'd already come across, although I hadn't met the man in person. The thought occurred that I might have seen him somewhere in

Yukos, for instance at a nearby table in the cafeteria. I asked how old this Malakhovsky was. He told me roughly what age he was and confided they'd become friends and he knew which cell he'd moved to. And he just happened right then to be writing him a letter, and kindly offered to add a message from me. For one brief moment, I had a crazy idea: 'Wouldn't it be funny to write out of the blue to a total stranger who's been named as one of your accomplices – it makes for a great excuse to get acquainted.' Reason got the better of me, and I didn't go through with it. Later, I found myself in a similar situation, and more than once. I was in a cell that Pichugin had occupied before me. I crossed paths with men who'd shared a cell with Kurtsin. Only now do I realise what thin ice I was skating on. The most mundane office contact with any of those men could have added years to all of our sentences.

Eight years later, in November 2012, we would all meet as free men and women: Svetlana Bakhmina, Vladimir Malakhovsky, Alexei Kurtsin and me. 'So, the entire gang has convened,' somebody joked bitterly. Between the four of us, we had spent a combined thirty-odd years behind bars …

I began settling into the cell. My lawyer finally found out where I was. That same day, a parcel of necessities came. There was soap, a toothbrush, toothpaste, a change of underwear, tea, coffee, something sweet … Sorting through these goodies, I caught my cellmates eyeing me with envy, and I welled up with a remarkable feeling of pride and joy, a sense of confidence in the future. I understood that I was not alone, that people supported me, they cared for me. And I carried that feeling through all those years.

Life began to pick up. In prison, you're expected to share things. If you get a parcel, you hand it over. The cell elder will divide it among the needy, meaning most of the inmates. For the first time, I slept soundly, slumping into total oblivion. From then on, I would sleep one day in three. The cell was filled with a burble of noise, swirling in an incessant hum, making it difficult to nod off. Only when you reached a state of total exhaustion could you slip away into slumber. The bedbugs and cockroaches crawling all over the place didn't bother me. But I watched in stunned bewilderment as my cellmates battled with a plague that was novel to me: body lice. Using a homemade kettle element, they boiled their undies in a tub, and applied burning matches to the seams on their clothes where the creepy-crawlies congregated. I hadn't watched for long before I felt something wriggling on me. Lifting my T-shirt, I was horrified to see dozens of insects grazing peaceably in my top, with plenty of eggs already laid. So I enthusiastically joined in the battle. Victory against the lice was impossible under the circumstances, but it was perfectly feasible to inflict serious damage on the enemy in localised conflict.

The New Year was approaching; soon it would be 2005. The cell was immersed in its own life. Once a week, we'd be taken to the showers, which for some reason were always referred to as the 'bathhouse'. The showers were unbelievably filthy. The walls were covered in some form of slime; deep puddles lurked on the floor. Some inmates wouldn't even bother leaving the cell. It was hard to know what was worse: staying grubby or risking contagion in the shower. Miraculously, I managed to escape both fates. Our prison routine included a daily hour-long walk. The detention facility slept by day, so only two or three guys would go on the walk. I leapt at the slightest chance to get away from the cell. It may only have been for an hour, but it was a change of scene. I could look at the sky, albeit through the bars, and inhale the fresh and frosty air. I no longer felt put off by the guards pacing along the perimeter fence that encircled the exercise yard. One sight stood out: a female warden with a freakish arrangement on her head. Her black hair was half-covered with a flame-red wig that had slid to one side and was topped, in turn, by her uniform cap. As a rule, the people employed in the prison came from other regions, travelling in for their shifts or living in purpose-built dorms.

Denis O. joined me on the walk. He was a committed National Bolshevik, willing to do time for his beliefs. I had already run into his fellow 'overthrower of the state'. Denis was a good guy, young and educated; he'd graduated from Kaliningrad University as a history teacher, and his political outlook inspired my respect. During the walk, he did push-ups and pull-ups, getting in shape for the ordeal ahead of him. At the time, he was facing up to twenty-five years behind bars! We talked. I was genuinely interested in what they hoped to achieve and how. A change of government, naturally enough. But what would come next? They had no programme, only slogans. 'Destroy this world down to the foundations.'[3] 'He who was nothing will become everything!'[4] Well, Russia's already been there and done that … The walk ended and we headed back to the cell. Tomorrow was New Year! It would be my first New Year behind bars. Some of the men in the cell got parcels. My family paid for a delivery from the prison shop, and so I received juice, sweets, chocolate, gingerbread and cured sausage. I still couldn't eat the prison glop; I was living on bread and tea and watching the pounds drop off. 'Great, I'm slimming down,' I told myself, trying to look on the bright side of my time in jail.

The cell was preparing to see in the New Year. Some basic grub had been split into portions, the *chifir* was brewed, sweets and chocolate shared out.[5] Everyone was quietly excited. Each inmate was hoping that the New Year would bring him luck, and it would be his first and last holiday spent in the clink. I still thought my imprisonment had to be some sort of mistake, and I remained quite sure that in a few months' time I'd be freed. The idea that I would see in seven more New Years behind bars

---

3   A slogan derived from line 5 of the Communist anthem, 'The Internationale'.

4   Last line of the first stanza of 'The Internationale'.

5   A highly concentrated tea with psychoactive properties drunk in Russian prisons and camps. *Chifir* is made with a whole packet of tea per mugful of water. Drinking *chifir* is a favoured pastime among Russian inmates.

was simply preposterous. It was this breeziness that saved me; my high hopes helped me plough on.

Time dragged ever so slowly. Then, through the bars on the broken window we heard the sounds of the New Year! There was the distant popping of fireworks, and, if you squinted, you could see them glittering beyond the bars. We felt happy. After 1 January, we'd have ten days of quiet. Those days were holidays on the outside, but dead days for the prison. It was a time when you received no parcels, no visits from your lawyer, no slender chance of good news.

Suddenly there was an inspection: the door opened and the guards swooped on the cell. We were all led into the corridor and shut in a cage. I looked on in amazement as forbidden items came flying out of the door. Homemade playing cards and shelves lovingly glued together by an inmate to cheer up our miserable prison existence were ruthlessly pulled down and chucked from the cell. The search ended abruptly and we went back in. Everything had been trashed and turned inside out. A mountain of belongings lay piled on the floor: the guards had emptied the contents of our bags into one big heap and mixed everything up. 'Bastards,' I said, beginning to sincerely hate the pigs. We spent a long time picking silently through the items, trying to find what was ours. The cell stayed quiet. It took a while to return to normal. And life went on.

I was to go through hundreds of such searches. There were times when the guards pilfered my things, casually helping themselves to T-shirts, pens or cigarettes. Occasionally, the search would be conducted in a civilised way. But I could never get used to those searches or keep calm. Right to the end, they always riled and revolted me.

Despite the poor sanitation and the rough living conditions, I didn't mope. We were all totally unalike, worlds apart. On the outside, I would never have encountered the men I was sharing a cell with. But in prison we got along, unified by our common interests and collective plight.

I heard the sound of iron clinking against iron. The warden called out my name. 'Don't bring your belongings,' he said. I left the cell, and we walked down the long, labyrinthine corridors of Matrosskaya Tishina. They locked me once again in the 'glass'. After a short wait, the door opened and they led me away. I could see other prisoners too. I asked the guard, 'Where are we going?'

'A quick visit,' he said curtly.

We were led into a shabby little room with a long table lined with telephones. In front of each phone was a chair. I sat on one and saw bars and a grubby-paned window in front of me. On the other side of the glass was an identical room lined with a table and phones. The door opened, and I watched people rush into the room and start searching frantically for their loved ones. Our time was limited. I saw my wife, then my father, who ran up to the phone opposite me. I could hardly hear a thing. There was a din, everyone shouting over each other. I didn't hear so much as lip-read his question: 'How are you?' Mustering all my strength, I tried to smile but looked lost. I had a lump in my throat; I couldn't speak … The meeting had ended. It felt like scarcely five minutes, though it had lasted for half an hour. I couldn't bear the pain, and felt physically unwell. 'What counts is that everyone's alive and healthy,' I tried to calm myself down. That was the last time I saw my father close up. He died during the trial; he didn't live to see me released.

Throughout our time behind bars, from the first day to the last, our loved ones were besieged with humiliation and harassment. The queues to hand over a parcel, the queues for the prison visits, the searches, the vast number of pointless hardships they were made to endure …

It took me a long time to recover from that first visit. Barely a few days had passed before they were sending me somewhere again – this time with my belongings. It was evening. I was being transferred to another cell. They gave me time to get my stuff together. It tore at my heart to leave those walls and those men whom I'd already grown close to. But there was no way out. I rolled up my mattress and collected my things. I said goodbye to the guys I'd been living with, cheek by jowl – quite literally – for over a month.

Once more, we walked down endless dingily lit corridors. Then we descended into some sort of underground tunnel that connected the wings of the building. We were on our way to Wing 6 of Matrosskaya Tishina. We reached cell number 601, on the fifth floor. My escorting warden couldn't find the guard with the key to the cell. I put my things down on the floor and sat on my mattress. Suddenly I saw Platon Lebedev coming down the corridor, escorted by a guard. He was being taken to the cell next to mine. He was wearing a tracksuit and seemed gaunt. I looked at him, trying to find something to say. We used to know each other, in the days before my job at Yukos. I hadn't seen him for around five years. He didn't recognise me that time. Neither Lebedev nor I knew at that point that we were 'partners in crime'. I only learnt of that in August 2010, when Khodorkovsky was put on trial in Khamovnichesky Court.

They had found the key to the cell. The door opened and I walked into a spacious, half-empty six-man cell. There were two people. One of them I already knew: Sergei had been with me in the 'deluxe unit', before being transferred to this cell. Here he was already performing chores for another prisoner, aged around fifty-five: Misha Dashevsky. He was washing the floor, making him tea – in a word, Sergei was his flunkey. Misha had been expecting me. It was obvious he was a collaborator, and he'd been told of my transfer by the prison management. Before my arrival, he'd stayed in the cell next door with Platon Lebedev. He talked a lot about Lebedev, while studying my reactions. And he kept probing me with questions. He made no attempt to conceal his connections with the investigators. For a fee, he offered to get me a mobile phone, bottles of vodka, whatever gourmet foods took my fancy. He bragged about the fun they'd had in here with some deputy minister celebrating the New Year. It was clear he wasn't lying. But none of this caught my interest; I was quite content with the stock in the prison shop. The cell contained an unimaginable luxury: a shower. I washed myself thoroughly and laundered all my clothes to get rid of the lice.

I spent a few days in the cell. We killed time playing cards. One evening, the warden told me to dress up warmly the next day. This meant they'd be taking me somewhere. I woke up, got dressed and was led from the cell. They put me in the 'glass' again. It was six in the morning. I stood inside for a long time, fretting and stewing. It was too cramped to sit down or pace about. All you could do was stand still. I tried squatting. That was uncomfortable too. I needed the toilet, knocked on the door – at first with my palm, then with my fist, then I kicked it. The door shuddered from my banging. But it was useless. No amount of bashing could grab their attention or get through to their consciences. Profound indifference was the prevailing mood. Towards eleven in the morning, the armed escort arrived and I was taken for interrogation at the Prosecutor-General's Office. Hurray – I saw white snow from the car window! I saw the sky and the sun!

Inside the building, my bliss soon ended. In the corridor, I ran into Svetlana Bakhmina. She was not walking so much as inching slowly forward, steadying herself against the wall. Her face was as pale as chalk, and her gaze was fixed on some point straight ahead. It was clear she was not taking anyone or anything in. Two policemen were supporting her arms so she wouldn't fall. Svetlana was mother to two young children at the time, and she was undergoing actual torture. I was brought to the same room as before for questioning by the same investigators. A conversation was had. We were back to these empty discussions. They asked me some strange questions: Had I ever been to Samara or Nefteyugansk?

Not following where this was leading, I told them truthfully that I hadn't. I was in luck. Any other answer would have served as 'evidence' of conspiracy to commit a crime. They tried persuading me to make a statement confessing my guilt. It was seemingly a doddle; all I had to say was: 'Yes, we knew each other. I was given instructions and followed them and deeply regret it,' and the whole nightmare would be over, they would leave me in peace. But none of what they were saying had any basis in reality, so I wasn't tempted by their inducements. I can't say how I might have acted if I'd been guilty of the crime, we'd known each other and I'd been given instructions. But on all three counts I was in the clear.

The investigators were none too pleased with my answers; they were plainly disappointed. Salavat Karimov looked in on us and uttered some words in broken Russian about me not being able to sit on the fence. He was the man in charge of this place, the one running the show. Investigator Rusanova took him the transcript of my interrogation. Returning after a while, she told me solemnly with a smile, 'Mr Karimov asked me to convey his regards and let you know you'll be getting twelve years.' The world went dark before my eyes. I no longer believed they were crazy, like the general who'd shown up on my first night. I realised these people had nothing remotely human inside, and they were capable of anything. I had no more to say to them, and, alas, I couldn't be of any help. It was my last interview without a lawyer.

7

A PRISON WITHIN A PRISON

They drove me back to Matrosskaya Tishina, taking the same route, with the same guards, in the same vehicle. We drove through the gates, along the familiar path. They signed some paperwork and handed me over to my jailers. We then went to the 'glass', which hardly thrilled me. I just wanted to get back into a cell. The guard opened the door, and there lay my neatly folded belongings, half of them missing. My cellmate Dashevsky had kindly 'taken care' of them …

They were transferring me to another prison. Meanwhile, I'd bought some supplies. I had a bag filled with food: instant hot cereal (you just add boiling water), Korean instant noodles, books and notepads, bed sheets, a blanket I'd purchased in the prison shop, laundry powder. We went out into the yard. A brand new GAZelle van marked 'Federal Penitentiary Service' was waiting for me. Changing hands yet again, I climbed aboard with my baggage. We pulled away. I barely had time to get comfortable before the vehicle stopped and I was asked to leave. We had been on the road for less than a minute. Wondering what was up, I got out. We had arrived. This was a 'prison within a prison'. Russian Federal Penitentiary Service Pretrial Detention Centre No. 99/1, located on the grounds of Russian Federal Penitentiary Service Pretrial Detention Centre No. 77/1 – otherwise known as Lefortovo, Wing 9. It was where I would spend the next two and a half years, and from where I'd set out on my journey to the prison camp.

Legends about this place abounded among the prisoners. I had heard many fantastical stories of swimming pools, cells with Jacuzzis and the like. In reality, it was a small prison designed for no more than a hundred people. This number of prisoners could be tightly controlled around the clock, ensuring maximum isolation from the outside world. Among ourselves we called this place the 'Laboratory'. You were under constant surveillance. The control really was total. Everything was being monitored and listened to. The peephole to the cell would be opened every five minutes. Its tinted glass changed colour whenever the warden raised the cover from the other side. The rules were rigidly adhered to. The guards here were well mannered and would address you with the polite form of 'you'.

We went up to the second floor and entered a small room designated for searches. My belongings were carefully combed through, not even the tiniest item escaping scrutiny. The officer made up a detailed inventory of all my property. A number of my things could accompany me to the cell, but the rest would be taken to the storage room, from where I could request them by filling out a form. It was already late, close to midnight. Finally, they finished the search – it had taken around an hour – and led me to the cell. The corridor was now laid with a carpet runner. It was used after lights out to muffle the steps of the guards as they approached the peepholes into the cells. I heard a strange noise resembling an alarm. It was the 'cuckoo'. They switched it on whenever an inmate was escorted along a corridor or the stairs. During this time, no one else would be led from the cells, eliminating the risk of chance encounters. You had no idea who was in the cell next door. In this place, there were no pulley postal systems, no logistics. When they called for you to leave the cell, the warden wouldn't announce your name from the corridor, he'd just use your initial: 'Surname beginning with P.'

We went up to the third floor. Cell 304. The door opened with a clang, and I stepped inside. The lights were already out, with a night light giving off enough of a glow for you to be spied on. It was a small four-man cell, and I found an empty top bunk. Everyone was sleeping, and my arrival woke them. One of the men got up to greet me: a red-headed muscleman who introduced himself as Oleg. He showed me where everything was, offered me tea and went back to bed, saying, 'We'll talk in the morning.' I lay down on the bed and tried to sleep. At six in the morning, it was time to rise, and the lights came on. We had to get up and make our beds. If you didn't make the bed, you'd be sanctioned for violating the daily routine. Later on, it could be raised as a pretext for denying you parole. Most people reached the prison camp with masses of violations from the pretrial detention, often without even knowing of their existence! How can they be allowed to issue sanctions to suspects before they're even convicted?

Everyone rose, got dressed and made their beds. Then you could go back to sleep in your clothes. The food hatch opened and breakfast was served. We took our bread, sugar and porridge. By prison standards, we were very well fed in this place. We drank our tea, chatted and got to know each other. A young guy called Andrei from Zelenograd was about to leave the cell for the courthouse, as he'd been informed the night before and reminded that morning. He'd been arrested under Article 105 for the murder of the mayor of Zelenograd. He would go to court and not return: the jury acquitted him. That happens very rarely; in a land where the presumption of innocence does not exist, as a rule the courts rarely acquit people. The only chance of that happening was with a jury. It is how our system works. If a crime takes place and you have ten suspects, then seven of them might be innocent. In Russia, they will throw the lot behind bars. It doesn't matter that innocent people will go to prison. All that's important is for the guilty to be punished.

The door opened and some guards entered the cell: an inspection. We all had to stand up. The cell's inmate-on-duty reported: 'We have four men in the cell. Duty-Inmate So-and-So.' The officer collected some forms, assigned the duty-inmate for the next day and left. 'What a strange ritual,' I thought. 'Isn't it obvious how many of us are here in the cell?' But this ritual was followed religiously. Anyone who refused to report was sanctioned. According to the unwritten prison rules, some prisoners weren't allowed to report: 'thieves in law' and those aspiring to be elevated to their ranks would refuse to take part. I didn't have any aspirations and complied with the orders.

We continued drinking our tea. My new cellmates told me about the prison, though I was already forming my own impressions. The cell had a TV and a fridge. The toilet was partitioned from the rest of the room by a wall and hidden away behind a curtain. I could see books and newspapers. Oleg told me there was a gym that you could go to if you turned down the walk. He pressured me to join them. If I chose the walk, then they couldn't use the gym. I yielded. There was a charge for using the gym, just as there was for the extra showers. You had to hand in a written request: 'Please debit my account with such-and-such an amount.' The gym cost 130 roubles a day per person. The shower cost sixty. One person would pay. It added up to quite a lot. But what bliss to get away from the cell – a change of scenery. This bliss didn't happen every day. We went to the gym two or three times a week. We were billed for the rental of the fridge and television; they cost thirty roubles a day. Once a month, we could use the prison shop, which stocked everything you needed and more.

The cell lived communally: we shared out all our food. In this cell, everyone had all they needed. We made our introductions. Oleg was from Murmansk. He was in for Article 105, Section 2 and Article 162, Section 4 – multiple murder and armed robbery. He was a genuine gangster and knew what he was in here for. I didn't much care for him, but we got along. My second cellmate was Andrei Kolegov – a far more heavyweight character. He was from Kurgan, the founder and leader of a notorious crime gang in his home town. He was here for murder, armed robbery and organising a criminal society. They worked hard and tough, killing when they needed to – and also when they didn't. Kolegov's victims included 'thieves in law'. In prison, that meant you'd had it. Your life was on the line. Kolegov was sentenced to twenty-four years. He'd been taken to Moscow from a prison camp in the Komi Republic, where he was serving his sentence. They'd transferred him so he could take part in the investigation of some other cases. They wanted to check out whether he was involved in the murder of Vlad Listyev and the notorious crime boss Sylvester. Andrei had been the last person to see Sylvester alive. Some time after their meeting, Sylvester's car was blown up on Tverskaya Street.

One year later, I would find myself back in a cell with them, and, a year on from that, I heard that Andrei was found hanging in his solitary-confinement cell in Tula Transit Prison, where they were holding him en route to Komi. They said it was suicide. But, knowing him personally, I don't believe it. He was self-assured and calm; used to speak in a very low voice. He'd look you straight in the eye, as if he were scanning you. He never broke his gaze. His eyes were tough and ruthless. He was erudite and educated; he'd graduated from a military academy. We whiled away the hours playing chess. Battles of the board took up almost our entire free time. Our games would keep gloomy thoughts at bay and save us from depression. We chatted about Alexei Pichugin, who'd been in this same cell before me. They told me about the time he was taken for questioning and brought back to the cell unconscious. He slept for over twenty-four hours and couldn't remember what had happened to him.

I didn't know Alexei Pichugin. Probably a good thing, too. Otherwise my eleven years in a strict-regime penal camp for the simple fact of having worked in Yukos would have looked like an unattainable dream compared to the life sentence I could have got for knowing him. Alexei Pichugin suffered more than any of us. They worked on him long and hard. They used their full arsenal of methods for putting the heat on someone, applying the entire monstrous experience gained during the Stalin years. He was the first person arrested, and, sad to say, he'll be the last one released. The investigators pinned their highest hopes on him, but he did not live up to their expectations. I take my hat off to this brave and strong-spirited man, whom they just couldn't break. I often thought of him, pondered his case and his fate.

'How on earth could all this have happened?' The number of times I have asked myself that.

It boggles the mind quite how far Russia lags behind the civilised world, where the justice system is the bedrock of a harmonious society. When each citizen can appeal against an official's action or inaction, this, in turn, ensures that the full rights, freedoms and equality of all members of society are upheld. In Russia, though, the justice system acts as an impregnable bulwark between the interests of the powers that be and everyone else, which is why the holders of power (in the narrower and broader sense) defend that bulwark so fiercely, clearly realising that if the fortress falls, it will spell the end of their rule.

How can that be possible in a country with such an intense history, in a country that experienced Stalin's Gulag and mass repressions? Why haven't we learnt from that experience? And therein lies Russia's tragedy. Meanwhile, the common folk dispense their pearls of wisdom: 'If you hew trees, the chips must fly.' 'Poverty and prison can befall any man.'

Well, I don't want to be a woodcutter's chip. Nor do I want my fellow citizens to become chips the next time they start hewing trees.

In 1878, 130 years ago, the head of the St Petersburg Circuit Court, Anatoly Koni, said, 'I wish to serve the law and not those persons above me.' On the eve of the trial of the young revolutionary Vera Zasulich, Minister of Justice Count Pahlen tried to guide Koni with the words, 'Now everything depends on you, on your ability and eloquence.' To which Koni replied, 'My dear Count! The ability of the court chairman lies in his impartial adherence to the law. I beg you not to expect anything more from me than the correct performance of my duties.' His principled stand ensured the acquittal of the revolutionary Zasulich. How relevant this is to Russia today! But sadly in our times the venerable Koni wouldn't have a hope of being made chairman of the Moscow City Court! It simply could not happen in a country where there is no presumption of innocence and the court system sets out to be punitive and underhand. It is evident in the paltry number of acquittals; to all intents and purposes, they are non-existent. This is despite Russia leading the planet in police numbers per capita, and when it comes to crime levels, Russia is hardly bottom of the league. In civilised countries, acquittals hover around the twenty per cent mark. How can that be? Are the Russian police so much better at their job than those, say, in Spain or in Germany? Not likely. It all comes down to the presumption of innocence. In the West, you have it, while in Russia, we don't. Of course it exists in Russia on paper, but not in practice. That's where the problem begins, and where it all gets scary … You can be charged with the most monstrous, unthinkable crime and be convicted without any evidence, as Pichugin discovered.

In this case, the terrible thing was that crimes really had taken place – horrific murders – which they decided to pin on Alexei Pichugin and Leonid Nevzlin. They administered a so-called truth serum to Pichugin, whereupon the investigators reliably discovered there had been no criminality in the Yukos security department. So their only option was to stick with their original charges based on false witness testimony and fabrications.

I was fated to share my time in prison with all manner of men. I shudder to think of the sheer numbers I found myself consorting with, some of whom could barely be called human. Sometimes it felt as though I was on a long-distance train journey. As time passed, my travelling companions would change, while I continued on my way … In the strict-regime penal colony in Melekhovo village, Vladimir Region, I'd be sent to the gruelling high-security third unit, which housed convicts with long sentences, convicts who posed an escape risk and also men transferred as punishment from other units throughout the camp. One day, I put a question to a man in the unit who'd been assigned to keep an eye on me. He didn't even bother hiding the fact he was working for the camp management. 'Roma,' I said. 'Imagine you have two men in plain clothes come up and offer a deal. You're doing time for double homicide and armed robbery, you've been given twenty-three years. Could you bring yourself to claim you've suddenly remembered who hired you? All you need is to say, "Yes, I did it, but it was a professional hit. I didn't speak before because I was frightened, but I've remembered now!" And they'll tell you what to say about the "mastermind"; they'll give you the story and point him out to you.' It took Roma all of a split second to answer in the affirmative, and he even perked up a bit, apparently picturing those plain-clothes miracle workers.

Some such miracle workers clearly paid a visit to Mr Korovnikov, convicted for five rapes, eight murders and a string of muggings and armed robberies. And that sorry excuse for a man did not let his chance slip away. The first case against Pichugin was built solely on the dubious testimony of that shady character. In the city of Tambov, a man had gone missing: a certain Mr Gorin, with whom Pichugin had been acquainted. And this murky case was pinned on Pichugin. There was no motive, not even a shred of evidence, nothing but speculation and Korovnikov's fishy testimony. And that was it. He was done for. *Guilty!* What came next was stark raving nonsense: the assault on Rosprom's managing director, Viktor Kolesov, and the attempted murder of Olga Kostina. It wasn't even clear whether murder had been attempted or if it was just a simulation. If it was attempted murder, then what stopped him from going through with it? There was no motive. Why would Nevzlin have wanted revenge on all those people in the first place? Why take revenge on Olga Kostina? When you study the case more closely, a vast number of questions leads you to the firm conclusion: nothing adds up. It's blindingly obvious Alexei Pichugin was framed.

The next episode was the murder of Valentina Korneyeva, the owner of a property on Pokrovka Street in Moscow. This is where it all got very strange. She had a property that Menatep Bank took an interest in. Some people from the bank visited Korneyeva and suggested she sell them the property for $350,000. She refused outright and asked for $500,000. According to the prosecution, Pichugin turned to Nevzlin, who allegedly gave the order to bump her off. But why? With what objective in mind? So they could negotiate the purchase of the property with Korneyeva's heirs and buy it for the same sum of $500,000? What kind of lunacy is that? On the basis of that lunacy, though, a man got a life sentence!

The murder of the mayor of Nefteyugansk, Vladimir Petukhov, on Khodorkovsky's birthday doesn't stand up to scrutiny. Here you are, Mr Khodorkovsky, your present from the security department! Can you take that idea seriously? The logical question arises: What did Yukos have to gain from the murder? Who benefited? Not Khodorkovsky, that's for sure! Did it reduce Yukos's tax bill? There was simply no motive. But the murder was real enough, and two men called Gennady Tsigelnik and Yevgeny Reshetnikov confessed to it; the charges against Pichugin rested entirely on their statements. Their former cellmates described to me how those men had behaved before the hearing: they were sharing with all and sundry their plans for life on the outside. It seems they'd been promised manna from heaven, and so they readily said a whole load of rubbish. And when they were given sentences of eighteen to twenty years, they wised up and confessed at the trial against Nevzlin, held in absentia, that they'd first heard the names of Pichugin and Nevzlin from the staff of the Prosecutor-General's Office. But it was too late. The judge based the ruling on their first statements, while ignoring the later ones as though they'd never happened.

What more can you say? To my mind, the whole thing is perfectly clear. Knowing how they fabricated cases, how the hearings were conducted, I don't doubt for a second that Alexei Pichugin is not guilty.

The clang of a door opening brought me out of my reverie, and I was back in Cell 304, Detention Centre 99/1. 'Inspection time,' the warden announced. This brief daily search lasted no more than ten minutes. Under the high-pitched shriek of the 'cuckoo', we were led out of the cell and locked in the 'box' – a small room with a bench attached to the wall that you could actually sit on. Meanwhile, the wardens searched the cell. We could hear the sound of wood against iron: they were knocking on the walls and beds with a mallet. They looked through our belongings. A short time later, we went back in. The cell was in perfect order, with nothing trashed; it was all nice and civilised. Within a few days, I would grow used to the procedure and pay it no attention. Then we sat down for tea. This was more of a ritual than a necessity. Yet another way to kill time. We heard the warden calling, 'Time for the gym.'

The gym was not far – it was right next door, in a large cell that was once used for its intended purpose. Now, though, it was a miniature sports club. There were wall bars, several pairs of dumbbells, a small barbell, some racks for the barbell, an exercise bench with an adjustable backrest. To say I was shocked would be putting it mildly. At first, I couldn't even focus and get down to proper exercise. I kept wandering from corner to corner, lifting the dumbbells, then having a go on the bar. Oleg and Andrei were doing bench presses. I was curious to see how much I could lift. Without straining, I managed 120 kilos, three times. My cellmates were amazed. It didn't surprise me, though. In my youth, I'd been into competitive wrestling, and had always kept in good shape. Sport helped me to survive. Behind bars, strength was respected and appreciated.

After an hour of exercise, we were led to the showers. We were legally entitled to shower just once a week. So the chance of an extra shower filled you with sheer delight. Sadly, this did not mean we could exercise regularly. If you made it to the gym twice in a week, you could count yourself lucky. We returned to the cell in high spirits. Another day in the detention unit and another pleasant surprise: the prison library. Once a week, a female warrant officer would call in on the cell with a catalogue of books. The choice blew me away. There were classics, detective stories, academic tomes, books in foreign languages, textbooks … There was a simple explanation behind this wide selection. You could apply to send your imprisoned relatives almost any book you liked, and after it was read, it would stay in the library. Those were the rules. After almost three years spent in that prison, I too left a decent legacy of books. There were times when the prison management had no need to do anything. All they needed was to keep out of the way. The men in the detention centre had still not been convicted, and in theory, they enjoyed exactly the same rights as a free person. But only in theory …

I pounced eagerly on the books. Later, I would often recount my time in the detention unit by quipping with bitter irony: 'Life was good. I did no work, had heaps of free time, ate whatever I liked and lived in central Moscow in a deluxe building with Khodorkovsky.'

I had been in the cell for two weeks. Before I'd had a chance to get used to my cellmates, I heard the supervisor calling, 'Surname P, bring your belongings.' I had no idea where they were taking me. This was already my third prison in three months. I collected my things, stuffed them into my bags, and donned my jacket. They took me from the cell and led me all the way to another on the same floor: cell No. 312. It was just like the last one, with the same daily routine that I'd been getting used to, but the men here were a sharp contrast. There wasn't the plentiful food that we'd had in the previous cell. These poor fellows were down on their luck, with no one supporting them on the outside.

My new cellmates and I made our introductions. Alexander from Krasnodar was a young guy of modest height, a bodybuilder wider in girth than in stature. He was charged with murder (Article 105) and supplying weapons (Article 222). He didn't seem the slightest bit ruffled. He laughed as he described how he'd been caught. He had got on an intercity coach. Dressed in a T-shirt and shorts, he was carrying two holdalls stuffed with hand grenades, pistols and the like. The police thought he looked suspicious, so they stopped him for a routine check. They opened the holdalls and gasped in surprise. And they discovered he was wanted on suspicion of a police colonel's murder. My second cellmate was Ruslan. He'd been arrested under the by now familiar Articles 105 and 162 (murder and armed robbery). Ruslan's shoulder was emblazoned with the tattoo: 'Pleasure to kill.' He had previous convictions and had done time in a juvenile detention centre.

After mixing with many men who'd been through these establishments, I concluded they should more correctly be called 'juvenile delinquent schools'. They were survival schools where deeply unchristian values were instilled. From a minute's conversation, I could immediately tell if someone had been in juvenile detention. There was a steady supply coming from the children's homes.

I was not exactly enamoured of my cellmates, but it couldn't be helped, and we socialised. We played chess, sat and read. My food supplies were demolished in two days. Porridge, instant noodles and instant mashed potatoes were put to work. This all took place between meals of prison gruel, which were also voraciously devoured. Alexander's appetite quite boggled the mind; Ruslan was far more restrained.

The long-awaited day when they opened up the prison shop was nearing. The cell received a price list. You'd put in an order and a few days later it would be brought to your cell. It took place once a month. My loved ones had already taken care of me. I had enough money in my account to indulge in anything I fancied. The store had a perfectly good selection. There were fruits and vegetables – tomatoes, cucumbers, cabbage – instant buckwheat and oat porridge. The kind you make up with boiling water and leave to stand. We had nowhere to cook, and nothing to cook on. A little later, I mastered the art of cooking rather decent soups inside an electric kettle. My birthday was approaching, and I spared no expense. As the saying goes, one leg of mutton helps down another. I ordered masses of sweet things, cigarettes, cereals, fruit and plenty of other stuff. We began feeling a delightful anticipation; we were all looking forward to it. Then the cell door opened, and the guards came in. There was going to be a search. A serious one. We collected our personal belongings in bags and left the cell. We entered a special room where searches were conducted and put down our things. We were locked up in the 'box', where everyone waited their turn. They examined and recorded the entire contents of our bags, pinching and peering at every last seam. Meanwhile, the cell was being searched. They looked high and low. Not a single plastic bag or box of cereal eluded their attention. They conducted these searches on a regular basis, but with unpredictable timing. Sometimes they'd happen twice in a week; sometimes we'd go a whole month undisturbed. The mood prevailing in this prison was of absolute, all-encompassing control. When you were led from the cell to see your lawyer, you were searched. When you went up to the visiting room for the meeting with your lawyer, you were searched again, but the search was conducted by a different guard. On your way back to the cell, it was the same procedure.

Our search took place without any losses or frayed nerves. We returned to the cell and put our things in order. We went back to our usual routine: drinking tea, discussing our prison life, dreaming about the future. Our dreams were starkly different. The other guys were dreaming of quick convictions, lenient sentences and leaving for the penal colonies. I was dreaming of imminent release, hoping to be acquitted. I whiled away the days in these dreams and hopes.

At last, the longed-for day of the prison shop arrived. They passed the goods we'd ordered through the food hatch into the cell, and we spent ages sorting through them all. A little later, we spent a good while polishing them off. We brewed the newly bought instant coffee and the party began. Everything tastes so much better in prison. The prison shop's wafer cake brought more unalloyed pleasure than the famous Sachertorte from Vienna's Café Sacher. In Russia, it goes by the name of 'Prague Cake'. The recipe was stolen from the West – always the same old story – and implanted to sweeten the bitter lives of Soviet citizens.

The cell was filled with food. Life lit up and became fun. For a long time, I hadn't wanted my cellmates to know of my upcoming birthday, but finally I'd succumbed. It's a sad celebration to hold in prison. I hadn't wanted to open up emotionally to strangers I found unappealing, to men whose way of life I condemned. But those guys threw me a genuine party, offering me a cake made with their own hands. They concocted cake layers from crushed biscuits mixed with butter, spreading this mixture on a sheet of paper and putting it in the freezer. Then, using an ordinary aluminium spoon, they whipped up the buttercream out of condensed milk and butter. Alexander spent half the day thrashing the spoon about the bowl to achieve the desired result. Coffee was sprinkled on the buttercream and blended in. The cake was lusciously filled with alternate layers of plain and coffee-flavoured buttercream. The cake top was coated in chocolate that had been melted in an aluminium bowl held over a boiling kettle. Emblazoned across the chocolate was a buttercream inscription piped from a polythene bag, reading: 'Happy Birthday!' They had spent two days toiling over their creation. The whole operation took a vast amount of time, patience and effort. I hadn't been allowed near this almost sacred activity. They let me be first to sample this miracle of the prison culinary arts. It was delicious.

Why did they do it? Why go to all this effort in a cell filled with food? I was deeply touched. In all my time behind bars, I saw a much more compassionate attitude from the prisoners, despite the crimes they were in for, than from the law-enforcement officers. In fact, 'law-debasement' would be a more accurate term for those officers. All the unpleasantness I encountered, all the foul play and deliberate provocations *always* came from the pigs, who, sadly, are unworthy of any other name.

The bolts clanked, the creak of metal cut through the silence and the door opened a little. For us prisoners, it never opened wide, only halfway – so that just one man could go in or out. We had an addition. A very chubby young guy walked into the cell. 'Archil,' he said by way of introduction. He was in for the same old murder, robbery and assault of security guards. Archil and his comrades had attacked a cash-in-transit van that was collecting the takings at a Kopeyka supermarket. The heist went wrong, and a shoot-out ensued in which a security guard was killed. The security guards wounded one of the attackers, who died during the escape. There was a car chase worthy of an action film. Archil's comrade, a policeman, was at the wheel of the Samara 2109. Just outside Ryazan, they were stopped by the traffic police. The driver showed his police ID, everything seemed to be going smoothly. But at the last moment, the traffic police noticed an arm sticking out of the boot. There followed a dialogue-free scene. The car took off. There was another shoot-out, another car chase. Archil hid in a haystack covered in snow. By tracing his footsteps, they found him and dealt sharply with him. In the cell, he bitterly rued his misfortune. 'Why didn't we just dump the corpse on the side of the road?' he asked himself rhetorically.

Archil was a charming man with a real lust for life. He fired his jokes off thick and fast. Witticisms, fun and laughter filled the cell, though I was in no mood for humour. The television never strayed from MTV, not even for a moment. I yearned for some peace and solitude, just wanting to be alone with myself. This was my second most burning desire, haunting me over the years. My first wish, naturally enough, being for freedom.

Despite his excess weight, Archil was constantly on the go. He was forever tidying the cell, cooking, making salads, deftly slicing the vegetables with his Perspex knife. The local prison management came up with this clever idea – a great little invention. Each cell was officially issued a piece of plastic, which was honed to a sharp edge with scissors. You ended up with something like a knife that could cut through bread, vegetables or cured sausage. So they could show a human face when they wanted to. The other prisons had no such luxury. People got parcels with cured pork fat, dried sausage and the like. But there was nothing to cut them with, and you could hardly use your fingers. It was why the convicts got up to their tricks, making sharp instruments from the materials to hand. But these were prohibited items, the possession of which was punishable by solitary. The police knew we had sharp instruments in the cells, but they didn't know how many. So you had a situation where the convicts were hiding them and the guards were searching for them. It kept everyone busy. But what sheer lunacy!

Archil stayed in our cell for about a week before he was taken away; a few minutes later, we heard the clang of another cell door on our floor. The prison was in constant motion. Faces changed, cells were swapped. People were forever being moved from cell to cell. You might stay in a cell for a week, or you might stay there for two whole months. There was no obvious rhyme or reason to it. A number of times, I met people I'd already shared a cell with. In the beginning, I was transferred between cells more often. It seems they were studying me. Later, when they began to work me out, they left me alone, though they took care that things didn't become too comfortable. The moment you got used to people, grew close to them, the moment you felt at ease, you'd be transferred. I spent time in many of the cells of that prison, with many of its inhabitants. There were men whom I'd never met in person, but I felt as though we knew each other. Because we'd both shared cells with the same cellmates.

A tanned, athletically built man of medium height entered the cell. It was obvious this stranger had just returned from a holiday. We introduced ourselves. I was surprised to learn that Andrei had spent the past two years in a Spanish prison. He'd been brought home in handcuffs on a regular scheduled passenger flight and escorted by guards. Spain had delivered him under an extradition agreement with Russia. He told us wonderful tales about that prison in Spain where he got his tan. I wanted to go to Spain …

His prison was on the outskirts of Madrid. Upon arrival, you're given a tracksuit, trainers and toiletries. At their expense, they allow you to call your relatives to put their minds at ease. The prison has a 50-metre pool for the inmates and two sports halls. If you want to practise yoga, you're free to do so. A female trainer visits the prison and holds classes. There are cookery courses. Andrei said that one of his friends spent a whole day at those classes and in the evening returned with a bag full of the goodies they'd made: biscuits, pastries and cakes. In the run-up to their release, the students on the culinary courses are let out at the weekends for work experience at a Madrid restaurant. Some ex-convicts get taken on to work there. Then there is the gardening club. The prisoners are paid 200 euros a month to work on planting the grounds. They grow flowers, plant grass and trees. Men from the former Spanish colonies – Colombia, Ecuador – like to do this work. Living an untroubled life with their needs taken care of, they send the cash home to their relatives. They also work as cleaners, sweeping the grounds. Feel like studying? Then take an English or Spanish language course. There is higher-education distance learning, free of charge. The Spanish prisoners live in two-man cells that resemble three-star hotel rooms. The rooms have showers and air conditioning. You get to choose your own cellmate. Feeling poorly? You can make use of the prison's medical care, free of cost. There are MRI scans to reveal hidden ailments and excellent doctors to cure you of a range of diseases. Dentistry is free; you only pay for prosthetic work. The less said on the topic of food, the better. Fruits, vegetables, yogurts, juices are all the norm. The diet is particularly varied and nourishing. I can't imagine this diet is drawn up and measured out by some Spanish penitentiary research institute – such institutes probably don't exist beyond Russia's borders.

Andrei pondered for a moment, and, after a pause, he said, 'I sincerely wish my parents could live out their Russian freedom the way I lived in my Spanish prison.' Indeed, in Russia, eighty per cent of the population on the outside live worse lives than the prison inmates of civilised countries.

In their own way, custodial conditions act as a barometer of a society's stage of development. Take Denmark, for example. The prisoners there live better than in Spain. And let's not even broach the subject of Switzerland. This is not about pampering and coddling criminals; rather, it's about showing a humane attitude. In Russia, around a million people are held in hellish conditions, suffering dreadful abuse and humiliation. Many of these people are entirely innocent. And most of the guys who serve out their sentence end up behind bars time and again. So the system is not working; it is not reforming their behaviour. The name 'correctional camp' does not live up to its meaning. The word 'correctional' could safely be replaced with 'abominable'. What word befits the men who sat Khodorkovsky behind a sewing machine and made him sew mittens? Was that the most dignified work they could put him to, the most beneficial to the camp's interests? Did they simply want to mock and degrade him? Then they failed. Those turnkeys succeeded in degrading only themselves.

I treasured this story about the Spanish prisons throughout my time inside, retelling it dozens of times.

Andrei P. was perfectly charming. He was pleasant company, an expert on history, and he doubled as the boss of the Medvedkovo criminal gang. He would be sentenced to twenty-five years – for murder, gangsterism and organising a criminal society. When, a year or so later, I found myself back in a cell with Andrei, boss of the Kurgan gang, the question naturally arose of who we'd run into or shared a cell with. I mentioned the Medvedkovo gang. To which Andrei casually replied, 'Oh, I know them well. They have their own cemetery.'

'What do you mean?' I asked, not catching his drift.

'I mean they have enough corpses to fill a whole cemetery,' he explained. He knew what he was talking about. They had known each other on the outside, moved in the same circles and carved up turf among themselves.

I shared cells with quite a few members of this gang. There was Oleg P., brother of Andrei, who would be sentenced to life imprisonment. I also knew Oleg's bodyguard Vladimir G., who struck a deal with investigators and gave evidence against them. When he found out I'd shared a cell with his former bosses, he began pouring out his story. Vladimir was a great big bruiser, almost 1 metre 95 tall, a Master of Sports in sambo and Champion of Russia in kickboxing. He was almost brought to tears as he told me what monsters those brothers had been: they had made him dress up in overalls and lug stones around at their villa in Spain. He told me an appalling story about the mores of their gang that gave me the creeps. Tough discipline ruled in the gang. They worked soberly and in grand style. As employees of a number of private security firms, the gang members could calmly and officially carry guns, though this did not stop them from using unregistered ones. The gang had former members of the KGB and the Ministry of Internal Affairs on their staff, and they had their own intelligence and counterintelligence. There were constant drills, training and shooting practice. They even invited some employees of the Federal Penitentiary Service to give a series of lectures on how to behave in the cells. The brothers had a house near Moscow – a place for showdowns with rivals and settling internal disputes. Once, at a routine workforce meeting that Vladimir was invited to, a colleague of his, a fellow bodyguard, was shot dead. They just killed him cold with a shot from a pistol for some misdemeanour or other. Meanwhile, they 'granted' Vladimir life, merely smashing his head to a pulp with a sledgehammer.

There was also a church in Medvedkovo that the whole gang attended regularly on Sundays to atone for their sins.

I couldn't say I found Vladimir likeable, or that we were friends. But we talked. One day, when he saw me holding a detective novel, he asked, 'What you reading those made-up stories for? You should read the charges against me instead. It's better than any detective story!'

Curiosity got the better of me, and I pored over the document. There were murders and an attempt on the life of Alexander Tarantsev (owner of the firm Russian Gold) that had been inspired by the film *The Jackal*. Shots rang out from a Zhiguli 2106 parked in front of Tarantsev's office, but the car was empty: the assault rifle was being remotely operated. The sight had moved out of alignment, though, and so the attempt failed.

The list of weapons went on for pages. You had an entire arsenal here, enough to equip a small army. In fact, they more or less had their own army. There were Kalashnikovs, Borz submachine guns (a Chechen-produced copy of the Israeli Uzi), TT pistols, Stechkin pistols, sniper rifles, grenades. These guys were ready for combat.

The gang controlled a number of companies and street markets. They levied tributes on businessmen, providing them with protection from rival gangs. Those were the wild days of the 1990s.

The gang was behind the murder of the legendary Alexander Solonik, otherwise known as the Macedonian. Solonik managed to escape from remand prison and go into hiding. But there was no escape from his own kind: the Macedonian was murdered in Greece, along with his girlfriend, a model called Svetlana Kotova. They didn't want to kill her too, but it had to be done. They couldn't leave any witnesses behind.

The endless killings, the corpses with the hands severed, the faces burnt with acid, making it impossible to identify the victim. My mind refused to take in this whole story; I felt physically ill from all this information, and I stopped reading. Vladimir, seeing my reaction, asked, 'What, didn't you like it?' Without answering his question, I sat down on the bed and stayed silent for a long time. Vladimir laughed.

The chances are he is free now. Coming under the witness protection programme, he will have begun a new life.

Andrei and I went for walks, just the two of us. We talked a lot. Our other cellmates did not venture out of the cell. If you were to rank the cellmates, then Andrei would come out somewhere towards the top.

I subscribed to some periodicals, and each weekday I was brought magazines and newspapers. For me, it was a blast of fresh air and an opportunity to all but return to freedom. I read up avidly on all that was happening in the world.

A week passed, and I was again moved to a new cell – with a search along the way. I collected my belongings, packed away my food. You never knew where you might end up. They could take you anywhere – to some half-starved prison. I was led to a special room for the search – such facilities are found on each floor. The guards routinely checked all my things, peered into every last packet of porridge or tea, made an inventory of my property and led me to the cell. It was empty. I took the lowest, most comfortable bunk, laid out the mattress and unpacked my things. The door clanked open, and a man came into the cell, then, after a while, another …

Changing cells, changing people. It all reminded me of a long-distance train. The train reached a stop. Passengers got on and off. The only unknown factor was my destination. I had no way of telling where I was going. Might it be Ivanovo, or Vladivostok? How long would my journey take? I had a long way yet to go.

Day after day, time dragged on endlessly. I remembered scenes from various films – the artistic device of leafing through entire years, allowing you to fast-forward to future events: 'Three years later …' My God, how I yearned to turn that page of my life and finish the story! And yet, as it later transpired, at that point I'd merely read a few pages of my book, having spent just six months inside. Six and a half years still lay ahead of me …

Meanwhile, prison life ground on. My lawyer painted a far from rosy picture. Hypothetically, I could be released on bail. But that was in theory, not in practice … At certain intervals, they took me to court to extend my pretrial detention. First, I went to Basmanny Court, then later, after I'd been in detention for over a year, it was Moscow City Court. I did not lose hope, each time preparing tenaciously, penning speeches. 'Why are you doing this?' I asked them. 'Why do you need to keep me in prison? I've done nothing wrong, I didn't go into hiding. I have a wife and child.' Each time, I earnestly tried to persuade the judge to let me go home. 'Your Honour!' I'd say. 'Judge for yourself. Let's say I am a criminal and I'm colluding with my accomplices.' I asked her to picture the scene. Malakhovsky, whom I've never met but who was marked down as my accomplice, is arrested. Next, the investigator calls me up and invites me to the department at Bolshaya Pionerskaya. 'And what do I do?' I desperately tried to get my point across to her.

The judge, clearly appreciating this comic situation, laughed, responding to my question: 'You go to Bolshaya Pionerskaya Street!' She understood it all perfectly. The prosecutor Lakhtin would stand up and crank out like a broken record, for the umpteenth time: 'Pereverzin is a menace to society. He might abscond; he might put pressure on witnesses.' He lied brazenly, cynically and endlessly. I heard all sorts of new and interesting things about myself. I couldn't grin and bear it; I couldn't acquiesce to the falsehoods. At each new hearing in the courthouse, when they turned to the matter of my pretrial detention, it would start all over again: my fiery speech, the prosecutor's lies, the judge's cynicism – and I would find myself returning to prison …

8

THE INVESTIGATION CONTINUES

The investigation was underway. Occasionally, I would be visited by investigators working on the case. My lawyer came regularly.

When it became clear that I would not be granted bail, a new phantom hope glimmered: I pinned my hopes on the court.

I suddenly learnt from the newspapers about a new 'accomplice' whom I'd never met. Antonio Valdés-García was descended from Spanish Communists who'd found refuge in the Soviet Union during the Second World War, and he had the good fortune to have dual citizenship. According to his story, he learnt from the newspapers that he was on Interpol's wanted list. And he decided to travel to Russia, following in his parents' footsteps, to clear his name. Life in Spain was not easy for him. He had to earn his living washing cars, delivering pizzas and newspapers. Things were no easier for him in Russia, where he worked as a dispatcher for Formula Taxi. This was the man they accused of stealing thirteen billion dollars! It remains a mystery why he even came to Russia. His investigators clearly pulled a fast one on him, removing him from the international wanted list to lure him to Russia. Quite plainly at the suggestion of the staff in the Prosecutor-General's Office, the story made a big splash. 'Khodorkovsky's partner and Fargoil director Antonio Valdés-García has voluntarily arrived from Spain to testify,' was how the papers painted it. He did indeed testify. To the great frustration of the investigators, he described everything as it really was. It turned out he was not Khodorkovsky's partner at all, just an ordinary employee of the company, no different to hundreds of others at Yukos.

Then strange things began to happen to him. The investigators may have removed him from the wanted list, but they decided to keep an eye on him and initially put him in a rural Interior Ministry property within a gated holiday complex. One day, he suddenly fell from a first-floor window. The guards took him to a local hospital, where they tried to blame his injuries on a traffic accident. It did not work. There was no official record of any traffic incident. So they were left with the story that he'd fallen from the window. The files for our case contain an extract from his medical records: 'Fractured jaw, fractured ribs, fractured hip, numerous bruises and abrasions on the body, the little toe on the right foot is fractured.' It would seem he fell from the window quite a few times. He picked himself up, climbed back to the first floor and fell again. And did so over and over …

The first time I saw Valdés-García was in court. I must say, he looked in a bad way. He had black eyes and was on crutches. When the prosecutor called for him to be given an eleven-year sentence, he managed to flee to Spain. Later, some interesting details emerged. From the safety of Spain, he wrote a number of criminal complaints against the investigators of the Prosecutor-General's Office and their henchmen, who'd smashed him up nicely while drawing out his testimony. The follow-up from those criminal complaints will hardly surprise you. The fact that a man had escaped from Russia by the skin of his teeth and been left disabled did not arouse the interest of Russia's investigative bodies. They did not set the dogs on anyone. Such were the adventures of a Spaniard in Russia – a man who came looking for justice. Poor, naive fellow! A good job he remains free and alive!

How lucky I was to be set free. How lucky to have our case drum up huge public interest and media attention; how lucky to have lawyers. Otherwise, they would simply have tortured me, beating the required testimony out of me. Nobody beat or tortured me physically, but they applied moral coercion and temptation. How many people have given themselves up, perjuring themselves, confessing their guilt to every mortal sin! Let's take, for example, one egregious case which – if you can put it that way – had a happy ending. A man confesses to the rape and murder of his own underage children. He is sentenced and thrown in a prison camp. My dear reader, you cannot begin to imagine what was done to him to knock that confession out of him. You just cannot imagine how the prisoners themselves punish men convicted for that sort of offence. But, some time later, our heroic police force catches a maniac who confesses to the very crimes for which that man was sentenced. He is lucky. He'll be freed and the investigators will even end up behind bars. But if they hadn't caught the real maniac, that martyr would have served out his entire term. And how many such cases are there throughout Russia? God alone knows. I'd hazard a guess that thirty per cent of all the prisoners are not guilty.

Another man gets sentenced for murder. He doesn't admit to his crime, and appeals against the court's decision. Four years go by. Then out of the blue, in another region, they catch a gang of killers who confess to the murder for which that guy was imprisoned. A good thing it happened in a different region. Had the gang been caught in his home town and ended up in the hands of the same investigators, no doubt the entire episode would have been hushed up, and he would have had to serve out his whole term. How lucky he was. The case was reopened, and he was released. The investigators got nothing – well, maybe some rapped knuckles, an official reprimand. The man received a million roubles in compensation for his four years in prison.[6] They made a film about him; it was shown a few years ago on television. He laments: 'How can you put a price on four years in prison? My father died, my wife left me. My career is over!' The scenes where they interviewed the prosecutor and the judge left me aghast. After all that had happened, when it was quite clear they'd imprisoned an innocent man, the prosecutor, a woman, instead of falling at his feet and begging forgiveness, would not let up: 'We carried out a reconstruction! He was sitting in the café at the birthday party with his friends, then slipped off to the toilet for a while, during which time he could have changed his clothes, reached the scene of the crime, committed the crime and returned to the café.' Could he really? No matter that he'd have had to run as fast as the record breakers at the World Athletics Championships!

---

6   Approximately £13,000.

But from my side of the barbed wire, I was to see plenty more of these 'wonders'. It would be funny if it weren't so depressing, as these were real events happening to real people.

On 6 April 2005, which happened to be my birthday, once again my detention period was due to run out. I was hoping that fate would grant me a birthday present and I'd be allowed home on bail. But it wasn't to be. I waited impatiently for the moment they'd take me to court. My last trip there had felt like a pleasant outing. That time, four policemen rode behind me in an unmarked Zhiguli 2106. I was shackled in handcuffs and put on the back seat between two plainclothes agents, then driven through the city streets to the Basmanny Court. I peered avidly into the passing cars and at the drivers' faces, keenly studying the buildings and houses, staring at the passers-by. The trip didn't take long. We were driven up to the courthouse, then went in at the main entrance. I saw my wife, friends and family in the corridor. They were standing near me. If I hadn't been handcuffed, I could have shaken hands with my loved ones. At that point, I became keenly, palpably aware of the finest fragile line between freedom and captivity. But the judge granted the prosecution's request to extend my detention, leaving me in prison. With the impressions and positive emotions from that trip fresh in my mind, I was looking forward to my next journey. It was spring outside, late March.

At six in the morning, the dim night light in the cell went out, and daylight took over.

'Surname P, we're leaving the prison,' I heard the guard say. I got up, made the bed, put on my clothes. My appetite had gone, but I forced down some porridge and drank a glass of strong tea. I waited. The television was working quietly. The bolts clanked, the door swung open and the guards came into the cell for an inspection. My cellmate reported, 'Four men are in the cell; Duty-Inmate Zagryadsky.'

'Surname P, you ready?' the guard asked me.

'I'm ready.'

The guards left. The doors of other cells clanged in the corridor. The inspection went on. Again I heard the jarring rattle of locks, and the door to our cell noisily reopened. 'They've come for me,' I thought. The officer led me away for a body search. I got undressed. The guard carefully checked and probed every last seam, painstakingly recording my simple outfit on paper: 'Black trousers, black shoes, black T-shirt, black puffa jacket, black cap.' I signed the receipt. Before I'd managed to get dressed, an unknown man came towards us. I noticed the badge on his army fatigues: 'Special Forces, Russian Federal Penitentiary Service.' He was a head taller than me, and broader in the shoulders. We left the building and went into the courtyard. Instead of the usual Zhiguli, two GAZelle vans were waiting for me, marked 'Russian Federal Penitentiary Service' and 'Special Forces, Russian Federal Penitentiary Service.' Five or so men were milling around nearby – burly guards in maroon berets. They bundled me into a van and we sped towards the Basmanny Court.

What I was seeing sent me into a panic. The truth is, the appearance of these guards made me tense up. They really made a strong impression. 'Has something happened? Are they going to kill me?' Feeling bewildered, I ran through the possible explanations of what was happening. 'Good Lord, what would they want with me?' I reassured myself. 'Whether I give testimony or not will hardly make much difference! To either of the sides.'

'But then why go to all this bother?' Questions kept popping into my head to which I could find no answers.

We arrived and found ourselves in the inner courtyard of the Basmanny Court. We got out of the van and went up towards the courtroom. The procession was headed by a 2-metre-tall commando with an assault rifle that had some unfamiliar kind of silencer. I was handcuffed to a guard. Men armed with assault rifles were behind me. We entered the room, and I was put in a cage. One of the armed guards stayed outside, the others took their places in the back row of seating. Flustered-looking relatives and my lawyer walked into the room. The lawyer came up to me and, seeing my state, asked, 'They haven't beaten you, have they?' My mouth was dry and I just shook my head and asked for some water.

The show did not go on for long. That lame old actor Lakhtin delivered his already familiar lie: 'Pereverzin wanted to abscond, to flee.' The lawyer filed a motion for bail with travel restrictions. I supported this request, but the prosecution vigorously opposed it.

Everything had been decided in advance. The trip to the court was a formality, carried out to produce a mere semblance of justice, while in reality it wasn't remotely related to it. In Russia, the judicial decisions are all made long in advance of the verdict.

So my birthday present wasn't happening. We headed back. Lost in thought, deaf and blind to my surroundings, I only snapped out of this state once I was back in the prison. There was a search, and I returned to the cell. I collapsed on the bunk and stared at the ceiling for a long time.

Investigations into particularly grave crimes can last for eighteen months. One of the charges against us was Article 174.1: 'Financial and other transactions involving money or property gained from the proceeds of crime.' Meaning that even before the trial takes place, you are adjudged a criminal. The rest is a mere formality, playing out as follows. A man has stolen a phone and is sentenced for theft. He sold the phone – and so, in accordance with Article 174.1, he gets another sentence. In this way, the man is tried twice for the same crime. Such a free interpretation of the law not only defies logic and common sense, it goes against basic legal principles and the Constitution of the Russian Federation. What's more, this article is universal and can be applied to any person to augment their sentence. Should the investigator wish to, he can tack on this article at will. Khodorkovsky's lawyers filed a motion to remove this article from the Penal Code for being unconstitutional. To no avail. The article hadn't been invented simply to be repealed! I feel quite sure this article was brought into the Penal Code in November 2002 for the express purpose of being used against Khodorkovsky.

Indeed, I got the impression that the Russian courts invoke the law solely for legalising their illegal decisions, to lend them the semblance of legitimacy, one might say. They often changed entire laws just for Khodorkovsky. In the first trial, he was convicted and sentenced. Of course, the question then arose of which penal colony to send him to. Prison life varies considerably from camp to camp, since it is determined not by the law but by the levels of despotism shown by the camp chief and his circle. In some camps, you can laze about with a mobile phone in your pocket, while in others you will spend your time chained to a shovel.

I can just picture the entire scene. The head of the remand prison meets with Mr Kalinin, then at the helm of the Russian Federal Penitentiary Service, and asks him: 'Where should we send Khodorkovsky?' Not the easiest of questions; get the answer wrong and you could find yourself out of a job. 'The hell out of here, the further the better!' Sheer genius! Next, this solution is taken literally. There's a map of Russia on the wall, with the penal territories marked. They take a ruler and start measuring away. Krasnokamensk, Chita Region. It's outrageously far. The journey there will take his relatives three days and three nights, while his lawyers won't even make it that far. 'Great! Fits the bill perfectly!' They chuckle like mischievous children, rubbing their hands with glee. But they'll need to iron out some details. The chosen camp is a 'black' one – controlled by the criminals – and so the convicts there live a free existence. To avoid Khodorkovsky having an easy time of it, the camp is quickly brought under the heel of law enforcement by maiming some of the prisoners. Now the camp is 'red'. One last niggle remains: the law. In their moment of joy, the authorities clean forgot about the law – or perhaps they were oblivious to it all along. The Penal Code of the

Russian Federation states: 'The convict shall serve his sentence in his home region or an adjacent region.' Khodorkovsky's lawyers bring a legal challenge against the plainly unlawful decision to send Khodorkovsky to Krasnokamensk. They file lawsuits and appeals. But some time later, the law is amended, getting rid of the offending clause. As though it had never existed.

Another well-known episode also relates to our case, and to Khodorkovsky in particular. There was a draft law on the way time spent in pretrial detention is offset against the total sentence length. It is clear enough that the conditions in pretrial detention are much worse than in the camps themselves. The bill proposed that two days in pretrial detention be treated as equivalent to three days in a general penal colony. Besides the humane considerations, adopting this law would have had the purely practical effect of relieving the overcrowding in the camps. The bill went through several readings, but it turned out they would have had to release Khodorkovsky, who had spent a long period in pretrial detention. As a result, the bill was shelved.

Gradually, my hopes of being let out on bail and attending court from the outside began to fade. In hindsight, I realise how lucky I was not to be released. Returning from freedom to prison upon sentencing would have been extremely painful and unpleasant. It was two years and eight months before the verdict was delivered!

With an unshakeable faith I'd be acquitted and released, I was impatient for the investigation to end and the trial to begin.

There was the clang of iron against iron. I heard the voice of a guard in the corridor. 'Surname P, leave with your paperwork.' I was being taken to my lawyer. Delighted at the chance to leave the cell, I got ready and gathered my notes. The door opened and I was led into the corridor. The 'cuckoo' began its monotone squeal while they searched me and looked over the paperwork I was taking to the lawyer. We were strictly prohibited from passing anything to or from our lawyers. We went up to the fourth floor. Another guard stood at the door to the room for meetings with lawyers, and he too searched me. On the way back to the cell, I'd go through exactly the same procedure, but in reverse order.

I was taken into a small, empty room with a table and chairs bolted to the floor. The door was closed, and I was left on my own. Bars covered the frosted window, but if you stretched up on tiptoes and peered through the small vent-window, you'd catch a glimpse of freedom. I could see an apartment block, a huge factory chimney in the distance; I heard the sounds of the city, the roar of cars. On Matrosskaya Tishina Street, life went on. I ravenously drank in the noise, the air. For that moment in time, I was on the outside. I was free. This was where Catherine the Great had once established a shelter for bachelor sailors, who, after many years of faithful service in the navy, found quietude, peace and serenity here.

'Get down from there!' The voice of a guard brought me back to the room. I'd become engrossed and had rested my knee on the window sill to get a better view. Everything in this place was being observed and monitored. And not just via the peephole. The door opened, and my lawyer appeared with the investigator. They'd brought me the indictment. Three volumes, each running to 400 pages of typed text. The First Deputy Prosecutor-General of Russia, Yury Biryukov, had graced the 'Approved' box with his signature. The executor was Vladimir Lyseiko, head of the special cases investigation department for the Prosecutor-General's Office, a State Counsellor of Justice, third class, thus ranked as a general. Had they read this document? I have no doubt the answer was no! They couldn't have given a monkey's about its contents. Never mind that there were a vast number of errors, slips of the pen and outright lies. The system would smooth things over.

After my release, I managed to confirm that First Deputy Prosecutor-General Biryukov had indeed signed my indictment without reading it. When he left the Prosecutor-General's Office, finding sanctuary in the Federation Council, he brought out a strange book called *Yukos: The Money Laundering*. Two-thirds of the book is made up of the rulings delivered in the Yukos case, along with a brief introduction where Biryukov systematically misleads the reader and distorts reality.

They were testing the prosecution scheme on us, setting a precedent for Khodorkovsky's second case. Had we pleaded guilty, it would have changed everything: we'd have seen a cruddy old spectacle under the direction of a bungling director. The script would have been crude and simplistic: penitent employees pointing the finger at their boss. Indeed, this performance would have gone down a storm among the rogues and phonies who elevate mediocrity, hypocrisy and soullessness to a cult. 'There, you see! They've confessed, meaning the theft must have been real!' those shameless cultists would have said. In their circles, ineptitude is all the rage, just so long as you're good at currying favour with the bosses. And the bosses never skimp on rewards: they lavish their grubby nonentities with medals and honours, gifts of cash and apartments.

But the production was pulled – because the actors refused to play their parts. And so the investigators decided to change the script mid-play. They artificially split our case into separate proceedings, and then our show trial began. To the staff of the Prosecutor-General's Office, it was a dress rehearsal for Khodorkovsky's second sentence.

Many of the documents showing the naked absurdity of the charges were later removed from the files and played no role in Khodorkovsky's subsequent trial.

9

THE CASE AGAINST ME

The indictment and case files that I'd soon begin reading were made available to the court. The investigation had ended; we were now entering a new stage, the beginning of a vast workload and challenge. I was faced with the task of scrutinising the case, line by line, in all its 161 volumes. Where had all these volumes sprung from? It turned out they'd been obligingly handed to the Prosecutor-General's Office from the tax office. So, first they convicted Khodorkovsky for not paying taxes on his plunder, and then for stealing from himself. The investigator and I negotiated a timetable for me to familiarise myself with the case, and I set eagerly to work.

This young and generally rather pleasant lad had been posted by the Belgorod prosecutor's office to the Office of the Prosecutor-General. His simple duties included monitoring me while I studied the case files. All he had to do was sit and watch me. What if I were to rip a page from the file and eat it? So he sat by my side for almost six months, every now and then asking me for leave. When he needed to travel to Belgorod for the New Year, he asked me to write a statement saying I felt unwell and wanted a few days' break from studying the files. I always played ball. Sometimes another employee would replace him. They both almost always brought lunch. The lad from Belgorod would offer me some of his grub. The other one would turn his back on me as he silently chewed on his food by the window.

Each weekday morning, the investigator would come to work at 9.10. He'd bring two or three volumes of the criminal case. I immersed myself in the task of reading them.

Those volumes set out the entire history of Yukos, and I learnt many interesting new details. While working at the Yukos office in Cyprus, I had only a rough idea of the company. Now I was being offered the chance to examine in minute detail how the company's work was arranged. The case files included the company's accounts, its founding documents, all manner of contracts. The investigator watching over me was polite and civil; he suggested I make copies of the items needed, which I did. It took me three days, but I managed to wade through two volumes. Then the investigator didn't show up for a few days. I waited a day, and once again I was led from my cell along the already familiar route, following the usual rituals, to the investigator's office. There, I found several investigators and my entire criminal case. All 161 volumes! My minder from Belgorod glumly explained that the period of access to the case files would start from today, as we – or rather, they – had not followed the proper procedure. It turned out that before I began reading the files, they should have presented me with all the volumes at once. This error had been picked up and promptly corrected by his immediate superior, the Deputy Head of Criminal Investigations, General Atmonyev.

I never ceased to marvel at the fanatical desire to comply with finicky details of the law while flouting its substance. I would come up against the same pompous zealotry time after time. When the verdict was announced, my wife was recovering from a recent operation, and so, rather than get up from the bench, she remained seated. This did not escape the beady eye of the lady prosecutor, whose entire 200 kilos quivered as she shrieked, 'Stand! The law says you must stand to hear the verdict!'

Everything went dark before my eyes. I had to strain every sinew to maintain my composure in court and keep from yelling, 'Hey, so you've suddenly remembered about the law, you snake? Where was your law when you were holding my trial? You weren't so quick with the law while demanding I get eleven years in a strict-regime prison camp!'

I carried on studying the case against me. The days flew by. Each morning I left the cell at 10.00 a.m. and came back around 5.00 p.m. – it was like going to work. I pored over the papers, copied extracts, analysed the material, did the maths. Finally, I figured out what I was accused of. On the weekends, I processed all the information, drawing up tables and charts. The work I did over that period should have earned me at least a master's degree. The longer I studied the case, the more my hopes of acquittal rose.

'But this bit's gibberish, and look at that – total rubbish, and this here is quite simply a brazen lie!' Engrossed in the work, I took to talking to myself. There were times when I could barely believe my eyes, perusing the text in amazement.

'Now what about this, the arbitration courts' rulings that led to extra tax being demanded from Yukos? It says here in black and white that the oil bought by Yukos from the oil companies had belonged to Yukos all along, and, as a matter of fact, that was exactly why the companies artificially charged additional taxes and penalties. Those penalties exceeded Yukos's profit margins over the same period! So, the idea was they wanted to ruin and bankrupt the company, and to get their claws into it,' I continued to think it through.

'But hold on, in my indictment, the Prosecutor-General's Office alleges that the oil from the oil companies was stolen! What? How would that have worked? One version contradicts the other. If there was a failure to pay taxes, it means there was no theft. If the theft took place, then you cannot level charges of failing to pay taxes on the stolen goods. It's either one or the other.' In my mind, I marshalled the facts into a logical argument. These documents essentially confirmed there was no evidence of a crime. The prosecutors realised as much during the court case, and these documents were conspicuously absent in Khodorkovsky's trial.

I often hear Russians whose knowledge of the Yukos case is sketchy and gleaned from hearsay opining: 'Over in America, Khodorkovsky would have got at least a 100-year sentence!' It is particularly astonishing to hear this from people well versed in law. What the devil is going on? Is it plain old stupidity? Even a cursory glance will show you the case was a stitch-up.

In America, they'd have put the investigators, the judges and everyone who was behind the case on trial. Alas, such a shamelessly dirty prosecution could only happen in a place like Russia – or Zimbabwe.

The investigators had been kind enough to include in the files a vast body of information proving precisely the opposite of what we were charged with. As I studied those materials, I began to appreciate how complex and well-oiled a machine Yukos had been.

The vertically integrated corporate group, made up of a range of different companies, ran as smoothly and flawlessly as a Swiss watch. The group included several oil firms. The single proprietor of the group created a centralised structure for selling oil. Why would each oil firm need a sales department of its own? They would end up duplicating each other's functions. So the proprietor optimised the company's management structure and kept costs down. However, this was what the investigators used against Yukos in court, where they argued: 'If the oil companies had sold their oil independently, they would have generated extra profit!' From a business perspective, this is unalloyed idiocy and basic ignorance.

Later, I learnt that some of the investigators found jobs with Rosneft. It should come as no surprise that Yuganskneftegaz's financial performance after the transfer to state ownership slumped sharply: their administrative costs rose significantly while profits fell. In court, this idiocy was voiced by the lawyer for the injured party, Rosneft, representing the interests of Yuganskneftegaz, which had been snatched through plain old fraud from the Yukos shareholders, including Khodorkovsky himself, and merged with the above-mentioned state-owned company. It's worth noting that even that lawyer was talking of another matter entirely, with not a word about any theft. The issue here was lost profits – a different category in law, a different article. The whole thing sounded like the spiel of a confidence trickster in a game of three-card monte!

Here is how it looked to me in simple terms. Suppose you're renting out an apartment that you own. A guy interested in relieving you of your property somehow conjures up a score that you must settle by handing over your flat. And then, in all seriousness, he brazenly sues you for damages, claiming he could have rented it out for more money! 'But that's insane!'

you might say, and you'd be quite right. In the courthouse, I often thought of Kafka and his famous *Trial*. Now, if he'd seen our trial, Kafka would have fled in horror. I remember what one of Khodorkovsky's lawyers said during the first trial. He was commenting on a public prosecutor decorated with an order: 'They were right to give him a medal! Anyone else in his shoes would have died of shame, but that fellow didn't bat an eyelid!'

At the well-staged sale of Yukos assets, Yuganskneftegaz went to Baikalfinansgrup, a newly registered and completely unknown company. The firm had been registered by lawyers for the company Surgutneftegaz with an address at some bar in the town of Tver! Whereupon the state-owned Rosneft acquired Yukos's core asset from this shell company. Now, that is where the prosecutor's office ought to have probed the legality of goings-on, as they were required by the law, but instead, all efforts were hurled into another activity – one diametrically opposed to the requirements of the law.

I studied extremely closely all the contracts for oil sales from Yuganskneftegaz to Ratibor, which was headed by my 'accomplice' Malakhovsky. I scrutinised all the payments. Here we had a contract, here was the delivery and acceptance paperwork, the money transfers, the account statements. I looked at the balance sheets and profit and loss statements for Yuganskneftegaz. The oil was reported at cost on the balance sheet. They produced a million tonnes of oil and sold that same million. The revenue came in, they deducted the oil sold from the balance sheet and received their profit. So where was the theft in all this? It was simply preposterous! The point of ownership transfer of the oil in accordance with the sales agreement was deemed theft!

The funniest part was that I had no connection whatsoever, even on paper, with all these events. Small wonder I was dubbed the most random prisoner in the case. At that time, I was quietly working in Cyprus, blissfully unaware of the existence of

Malakhovsky or Ratibor. I had quite different matters on my mind. I was one of five directors of Yukos's Cypriot subsidiary. When I was invited to join Yukos, those companies were merely registered on paper. I had to set up a fully-fledged organisation – to find an office and rent it, get all the relevant permissions from the Central Bank of Cyprus and the local authorities. My job, in short, was purely administrative.

The company was created for trading oil, and this served several purposes. The structure enabled the flow of goods and money to be managed more efficiently and meant loans could be obtained from Western banks on easier terms. There can be no doubt the attractive tax environment in Cyprus played no small part in it. Thus, the Cypriot firm where I worked bought oil from Yukos and other oil companies, pooled it and sold it on to other buyers. The case files contained contracts for the purchase of oil from Yukos by the Cypriot firm. There were also delivery and acceptance documents, customs declarations, transaction certificates stamped by the licensed bank, money transfers, bank statements. Everything added up, right down to the last cent. I wasn't involved in making the payments, and I was not even authorised to handle the accounts from which the oil purchases from Yukos were paid. At one point, the idea occurred: 'Maybe the company didn't pay for some of the deliveries?'

'No, out of the question! I personally discussed that topic with the auditors during one of the regular audits,' I remembered. The invoices for the shipped oil were handled by a specialist finance company created in Switzerland that managed all the money. It all added up, right down to the last cent.

'Then why did they throw me in jail?' A perfectly reasonable question.

Ha, for no special reason! They did it for the simple fact I'd worked at Yukos. For my failure to confess to crimes I hadn't committed. For refusing to give false testimony. The sad truth is that any one of the company's employees could have landed in my place. But I was the lucky man chosen.

I read a passage from my indictment. 'Through his actions, Pereverzin enabled the creation of an environment conducive to theft.'

Good Lord! Unable to believe my eyes, I continued examining the evidence of my 'criminal' activities. It turned out my guilt was proven by the following: my employment-record book; the telephone directories of employees of Yukos in Moscow; and some legal articles relating to the establishment of Yukos.

I was at a loss, and had no idea what to make of this drivel. I didn't know whether to laugh or cry. On my prison journey, I came across all sorts of men. Once I happened to share a cell with a Moscow University graduate who had a master's degree in physics and maths. Volodya had been charged with the attempted murder of an astronaut who headed a division in a large state-owned corporation. The case collapsed, and Volodya was acquitted. While in prison, we struck up a friendship, and, with his flair for maths, he helped me prepare for the trial, systematically ordering much of the material. Sometimes we'd simply laugh out loud at the patent nonsense contained in my indictment. Once he said to me, 'You know, if I hadn't seen all those gems with my own eyes, I would never have believed it was possible!'

The court date was approaching, and I awaited it with trepidation. Given all my knowledge and the evidence itself, I was sure they'd acquit me. My veteran lawyer, however, who had seen his fair share of trials, tried to bring me down to earth. 'Count yourself lucky if they release you with a guilty verdict and "time served"!' he told me.

There was no doubt in my mind that after the court case I'd be out of jail.

I heard from my lawyer the joyous news I was longing for: the court case would begin on Monday with a preliminary session.

10

IN THE DOCK

At six in the morning, the light came on in the cell. From the corridor I heard the guard's voice: 'Rise and shine, make your beds, and Surname P, get ready to leave.' I got up and quickly dressed myself. One of the big advantages of remand prison was that you could wear your own clothes. If your relatives put in the paperwork, you could have all the clothes you wanted. You could even wear a Brioni suit if you liked! The only items you weren't allowed were ties and belts, doubtless due to the risk of hanging. For that, you needed to improvise: men hanged themselves with sheets, trousers or other articles. There were inmates (I met some myself) who thought it showed great panache to go to court in a suit and white shirt. I was sent some black cords and a black sweater in advance, and I travelled to court in them right until spring.

For some time, I hadn't touched the prison slops and was surviving solely on food from the prison shop and parcels. I drank my coffee and ate some cheese and bread. I sat waiting.

'Surname P, you ready?' I heard the guard's voice.

'Ready,' I answered snappily, and picked up my things – a bag full of documents and my black puffa jacket.

The door opened, and I was taken to a room to be searched. You had to undress and squat down. The guards would check to see you hadn't hidden anything inside yourself. Then they'd make a detailed list of all the items on your person. Woe betide you if you came back with something not on that list! Once they found a packet of tissues on me that had somehow been missed off the list. What an almighty stink they raised!

After the search, I was locked in the 'box' – a little room that had become familiar, known in the other block as the 'glass'. My impression was that it wasn't a long wait, although no clocks or watches were allowed in there. After maybe twenty minutes, the chief guard came for me. We went out into the small prison yard, where an escort was waiting. As usual, there were the GAZelle vans: prisoner-transport vehicles with 'Russian Federal Penitentiary Service' and 'Special Forces, Russian Federal Penitentiary Service' emblazoned on their flanks. Three burly armed commandos in maroon berets, their chests studded with medals, were here to guard me – though heaven knows from whom or what. They were holding Val assault rifles fitted with silencers and wore backpacks. In addition, there were four more guards, with one of them handcuffed to me. And two drivers. I remember what it felt like, the shock, when I first set eyes on the commandos. Looking back, though, I find it amusing.

We took our places in the vans. I got into the GAZelle, where there were four partitioned iron compartments. Someone was already sitting in one of them: it was Malakhovsky. My iron compartment was cramped, uncomfortable and icy cold. The van pulled off. I couldn't see a thing, but I could hear plenty. I heard the gates of our prison-within-a-prison opening. I heard dogs barking and the guards' voices – we were driving through the gates of Matrosskaya Tishina. I heard the creaking of the gates, and we'd left the prison grounds. The hubbub of the street and the traffic sounds reached my ears. The driver turned on his siren. Our journey took twenty minutes at most. Basmanny Court was not all that far. What a lucky man I was – travelling to court in comparative comfort and with my own personal transport. All put on for us. Usually, leaving for court would turn into a long and agonising ordeal. The standard prisoner truck follows a set route, stopping at all the courthouses. The journey can take several hours. Try that in the freezing cold or sweltering heat!

We arrived at our destination: the grimy courtyard of the Basmanny District Court. I came out of the iron compartment well and truly frozen. It felt as though the metal had drawn all the warmth out of me and amplified the cold, like a thermal magnifying glass. Outside, you'd never get quite as chilled. I was let out of the van handcuffed to a guard. Malakhovsky came out next. By this time, I already knew him; we'd met in the basement of the Moscow City Court. The Special Forces shielded us. Two men were blocking the entrance to the courtyard, through which you could glimpse a street. A third walked ahead with his gun at the ready and boldly entered the building. It had been ages since I'd walked on the ground, and stepping on snow felt strange and pleasant. We went inside the building. To my own surprise, I called out loudly, 'I want to go to the toilet!' The guards convened for a moment. The toilet was near the entrance. An armed commando with a rucksack went in first. Twenty seconds or so later, he returned with the words: 'All clean.' What he was doing in there remained a complete mystery. I was released from my handcuff and allowed in. The door to the toilet was left open. At that moment, it did not bother me in the least, as I only needed to pee.

The dingy basement of the courthouse held a number of dark cells for detainees awaiting their fate. In the interests of thwarting conspiracies, Malakhovsky and I were put in separate cells. No matter that we'd be sharing a cage and calmly conversing during the court session.

One time they lost me. An escort came for me, and I was nowhere to be found in the prison! They flew into a panic. It turned out the court had issued a request for the accused to be delivered and the paperwork had gone to the wrong place – or perhaps, on the contrary, it had gone to the right place. And following standard procedure, I was delivered in a regular prisoner truck to the Basmanny Court. I sat happily in a cell, waiting to be led to the courtroom. 'Thank God for that! Finally got those Special Forces off my back!' I thought in delight. 'They must have decided to downgrade our importance; maybe they'll leave us alone, and the case will quietly die!'

Suddenly I heard a hubbub, the sound of footsteps. Somebody said my surname loudly. They were talking about me. The door opened, and I saw my trusty band of men. The chief among them asked me indignantly, 'How did you get here?'

'I took the metro!' I couldn't help but answer, choking with laughter. I found it hilarious, but for him it was no laughing matter! They were clearly worried sick. But at the end of the day, here I was! No one had attacked me along the way. I hadn't escaped, nor been kidnapped or killed. So why this whole entourage? Why the big spectacle? Couldn't they find those heroes anything better to do? Chances are they really were heroes, who had been through war zones and actually deserved their medals and awards, unlike the judges and investigators.

In the prison, there was an incident where a man charged with fraud somehow managed, with the help of his comrade-accomplices, to rent an entire prisoner truck, complete with guards. They arrived for him with the forged paperwork summoning him to court. The warden had a hunch something was up and decided to call the courthouse to be on the safe side. Suddenly the whole scam was exposed and the escape fell through.

I sat for ages in the gloomy basement cell, waiting to be taken to the courtroom, pensively studying the graffiti. Every surface had been defaced – the walls, the doors, the bench. Someone had clearly wanted to be immortalised. He'd etched deeply and strenuously into the bench: 'Igor Tagansky, Article 158 Part 3 (theft), 3 years.' 'Sasha Magadan, Article 162 Part 3 (robbery), sentence 6 years' was scratched in pen on a wall. I was to meet many more such prisoners who took pride in their 'exploits', especially in the general-regime camp, where it was the done thing to play at prison romanticism. One anonymous graffiti artist was campaigning for the criminal cause, writing on the wall: 'Long live the thieves.' I was so far removed from all this that it seemed like the paintings of some prehistoric cavemen.

Finally, the door to my dungeon opened, and they took me to the courtroom. We went up the stairs – the guards, the Special Forces in their maroon berets, the local police and me. The sheer number of my escorts merged into a blur. Malakhovsky was walking ahead, handcuffed to a guard. I was firmly shackled to my own scrawny guard. A 2-metre-tall commando headed the procession. The whole floor where the trial would be held was sealed off by armed men. In the distance, I saw the astonished faces of gawpers who had come to court on some business or other. They stared in our direction with unabashed curiosity and fear. I saw the stunned face of my wife, who later told me how one old woman, shocked at the number of armed guards, asked her, 'Who on earth have they got in here today?'

'It's the Yukos case,' said my wife with a knowing air.

'Ah, right, I get it,' answered the old woman.

I have no idea what that old woman made of it all, having come to court because her wayward grandson was on trial for some humdrum theft. But, as my lawyer later told me, after six months of court sessions, one of the guards who was present at almost all the trials could contain his curiosity no longer, and he walked up and asked, 'What is it they're on trial for, then?' I laughed for a long, long time when I heard that story. I still laugh now whenever I think of it.

They led us into a courtroom decked out in crude public-institution furniture, redolent of a schoolroom, and put us in a cage. 'Oh Lord, surely they're not going to decide my fate here in this miserable little room?' I couldn't get my head around it. Inside the cage, I shook hands with Malakhovsky for the first time. They began letting people into the courtroom. I saw the faces of my loved ones – my wife, family and friends. Some law-school trainees came in, various reporters, and also people I didn't know. They all sat down on the benches. Then a scruffy-looking unknown man came into the room; he had long hair and a beard, was on crutches and accompanied by an armed minder. Suddenly it came to me: it was Valdés-García! I could see my lawyer. Everybody took their seats. The state prosecutor Irina Shlyayeva proudly sat behind the desk directly facing the cage, where they were holding me like a wild animal. She was still relatively young, but appeared to be suffering from some kind of metabolic issue. With a height of around 1 metre 65, she must have weighed 180 kilograms, if not more, and had difficulty walking. After the trial ended, I saw her on television commenting crisply and coherently on some other high-profile criminal case. I was shaken to the core, as if I'd just seen an ape speaking in a human voice. Absolutely in earnest, I shared this with my lawyer: 'It turns out Shlyayeva is of perfectly sound mind; she knows how to talk clearly and intelligently …'

To which my lawyer wisely and quite rightly replied: 'It's one thing when there is some substance there, another thing when the case is totally phoney.'

Opposite me, around 5 metres away, sat the court clerk, a pretty girl named Katya. Despite the chilly winter weather, she wore a low-cut top that all but exposed her bosom. Neither the heat nor the cold, nor indeed our presence, perturbed her. She faithfully and unswervingly maintained that image until the end of the trial. No doubt she'd make a good judge.

Then the leading lady entered the stage: none other than Judge Yelena Yarlykova.

A few years after our trial, despite her 'stellar achievements', Judge Yarlykova would be ruthlessly banished from the bench for failing to identify during a court hearing an imposter sent there instead of another man and erroneously releasing him. Yarlykova believed the ruling against her was unfair and, suddenly remembering about the European Court of Human Rights, she decided to take her case there. Strangely enough, her case came up in the ECHR at the same time as my own against her sentencing me unlawfully to eleven years in a strict-regime colony. Truly, the Lord works in mysterious ways. Nonetheless, the gulf separating us was enormous. When Yarlykova was stripped of her status as a judge, she switched to working as a lawyer. When, through her efforts, I was stripped of my liberty, I became a powerless prisoner – with what felt at the time like an interminable sentence.

At that time, in 2006, Yarlykova made a good impression on me. Once the trial had started, during a break, the prosecutor said, 'Not all the witnesses for the prosecution have been questioned yet.' Yarlykova came back with the retort: 'What kind of witnesses are they, eh? It's a complete mystery just what they're supposed to be proving!'

The trial began. The cast introduced themselves: the lawyers, the judge, the public prosecutor. We did not challenge either the judge or the prosecutor, even though I took an instant dislike to the latter. We, the accused, were required to confirm our identities. The judge addressed me: 'Will the defendant please state his name for the record.'

'Vladimir Ivanovich Pereverzin.'

'Your year and place of birth?' The judge had to verify our identities by checking all the data in our files and examining our photos.

Having asked for my home address and satisfied herself that I was who I claimed to be, Judge Yarlykova turned to the other defendants. The same questions and answers followed.

Suddenly the prosecution filed a request for Antonio Valdés-García to be placed under witness protection. The judge began considering the petition.

'Antonio Valdés-García!' the judge addressed him. 'Do you support the request?'

Already maimed once by his 'protectors', Valdés-García furiously refused and fought back. 'I don't want any protection!' he almost yelled. 'I'm not under threat from anyone or anything! So can they just leave me alone!'

The prosecution would not budge and they stuck to their guns. At the time, it struck me as strange, but later everything would click into place. There really wasn't anything endangering Valdés-García. His truthful testimony was perfectly useless to the prosecution and neither harmed nor benefited anyone. But as they had already lured him from Spain and brought him into the trial, they needed to watch him in case he tried to flee. So the investigators came up with the clever ruse of assigning a minder for Valdés-García. From that point on, the poor man's every move was followed by the equally forlorn guardian assigned to protect him. At the end of the trial, when he heard the prosecution were seeking eleven years in a strict-regime camp for all the accused parties, Valdés-García locked his bodyguard in the shower and, hobbling on crutches, made a dash for the airport. From there, he safely flew home on his Spanish passport.

Why this Spanish national came to Russia in the first place remains a mystery to me.

The preliminary session drew quickly to an end, and I was led back to my cell somewhat disillusioned. The starting date for the trial itself was set, the date of the first sitting. And so the trial I'd spent more than a year anticipating and preparing for began at last. The trial that I'd pinned my high and sunny hopes on. The trial that would decide my fate for years to come.

11

THE TRIAL

It was the first session. We'd all assembled. The judge already knew everyone by sight and greeted us all like old friends. Malakhovsky and I were in the cage, while Valdés-García sat on a bench, leaning on his crutches and stretching out his broken legs. The guards and security escorts occupied the back row. The lawyers were seated not far from me. The public prosecutor began the long and tedious reading out of the indictment. The prosecution is required by law to announce the charges and disclose all their evidence as contained in the case materials. The whole process dragged on for days. I was ferried to court as if going to work. Each day, I'd get up, undergo a search and make the journey to court. After the session, it was all repeated in reverse order. The trip to the prison, the search and back to the cell. I'd be terribly tired and sometimes I longed to return to the cell as quickly as possible. The days flashed past my eyes like pages being torn off a calendar.

'Does the defendant understand the charges?' the judge asked me.

'I do.'

'And do you understand them?' she addressed Malakhovsky.

'No, I don't understand them,' he responded. 'Could it please be explained to me what I am accused of?'

The judge was clearly bothered by this answer, but it was the stance adopted by Malakhovsky and his lawyers. This annoyance may have been what later led the judge to give him a hard time, imposing a sentence one year longer than the prosecution had requested. He would end up getting twelve years.

My counsel advised that I testify straight away, right at the start of the trial, without waiting for all the evidence to be disclosed and the witnesses to be questioned. According to him, this would bolster our position, as only a man with utmost faith in his innocence would act this way. I had nothing to hide, no games to play. So I told them everything just the way it had happened: how I had got a job at Yukos, how I had opened their office in Cyprus. I described in detail the work I had been doing there.

'And how do you know the company you worked in paid for the oil it acquired?' the prosecution tried to catch me out.

'The evidence for the purchase and payment of oil can be found in the criminal investigation files.'

Disgruntled with my answer, the prosecutor continued reading out their 'evidence'. All one hundred and fifty volumes of it. The trial was plainly being dragged out.

Prosecutor Shlyayeva read through some documents dated 1998 and 1999. The minutes of shareholders' meetings and Yukos board meetings were read out. None of us were working for Yukos at that time, and the defence counsel objected, asking the prosecution to explain the logic behind disclosing documents that had nothing to do with us.

I looked at the judge, who was trying hard to suppress a smile and a slight snicker. Katya, the court clerk, let out a giggle. Unabashed, Shlyayeva said, 'You'll find that out later!'

Later, we would learn that, according to the prosecution, this was all part of our 'conspiracy to commit a crime'.

Suddenly Valdés-García said, 'I don't understand what's going on here!'

The judge explained, 'You are appearing as a defendant accused of a particularly grievous crime.'

The state prosecutor resumed her reading. The trial continued.

It was the next court session. Malakhovsky and I sat in the cage. The judge came out to open the proceedings. It became apparent that Valdés-García had not turned up. The prosecutor plunged into a frantic search, vanishing somewhere, coming back, making calls on her mobile. Some time passed before the source of the panic appeared: the dishevelled Valdés-García walked into the courtroom on crutches, with his bodyguard in tow. It was eleven in the morning. The judge, stunned by such insolence on the part of a defendant, who was prohibited from leaving town, asked, 'Valdés-García, where were you?'

'At work!' he answered, unfazed. 'I rushed over here the moment my shift ended.'

Somewhat startled, the judge asked, 'Where is it you work?'

'I work as a dispatcher for a company called Formula Taxi,' Valdés-García said calmly.

The judge came to her senses and snapped at Valdés-García, threatening to remand him in custody: 'Don't you realise where you are? If this ever happens again, you can be sure you'll always be brought here on time!' She nodded in our direction.

Valdés-García answered back: 'Look, I do need something to live on, a job to support myself!'

I came down with a fit of uncontrollable laughter, which I couldn't hold back. What sheer lunacy! On paper, Valdés-García, like me, was accused of stealing thirteen billion dollars and, for some inexplicable reason, laundering eight and a half billion. But here he was, working as a taxi dispatcher, escorted by his minder. Insane!

The matter was closed, and they resumed the session. Antonio Valdés-García asked yet again for clarification of the charges against him. The prosecution was required by law to disclose the significance to the case of each item of evidence, explaining precisely what it proved. For example, say you have a knife found near a corpse. We can tell from the stab wound on the body that a sharp object of a certain size was used. The blood on the knife matches the blood group of the deceased, thus proving the wound was inflicted with this very knife, assuming the sizes of knife and wound match too. The fingerprints on the blade indicate a particular man held the knife in his hand. This is how causal relationships between events are established.

Many times a day, my counsel and I would firmly request that the prosecution explain the relevance of the disclosed documents to the case. Here they had my employment-record book. Apart from the fact – which I did not deny – that I had officially worked at Yukos, there was nothing else proved by it.

The judge addressed Valdés-García.

'Do you have any comments, Valdés-García, on the documents that have just been disclosed?'

There was silence. Valdés-García had fallen asleep.

'Valdés-García!' the judge hollered.

There was no reaction. He couldn't hear her. A lawyer ran over to Valdés-García and gently shook him.

'Valdés-García!' the judge continued shouting. 'Did you hear the prosecutor?'

'No, I was asleep. I haven't slept in twenty-four hours; I was working the night shift. I don't have a clue what's going on here, and I ask you please to let me go home,' he said quietly.

The judge waved her hand in frustration, and the prosecutor carried on.

We were listening to and looking at the 'Profit and Loss Account for Yuganskneftegaz'. This document proved nothing beside the fact the company produced oil, sold it and made a profit. Neither my counsel nor I, nor indeed any rational person, could establish any logical chain in the charges brought.

Our questions went unanswered. The prosecution mumbled something about how the relevance to the case of these disclosed documents would be explained at the end of the trial, following their disclosure. Later, she drew a line under it with the hazy phrase: 'The disclosed documents prove the guilt of the defendants.' And that was that. We were guilty, end of story! With no causal relationship. Why bother racking your brains or sweating over it, when my wages, as it transpired, were in fact my share of the loot ... My share of thirteen billion dollars! 'Hey, guys! Looks like we sold ourselves short!' I wanted to jest, but things had gone beyond a joke.

Shlyayeva was lying nonstop, disgracefully and unconscionably. They announced a break. The judge and lawyers needed something to eat. In the meantime, we would be led to the basement. But I managed to catch sight of the prosecutor plunging her hand into a bottomless briefcase and fishing out a package. She pulled out one pasty after another and popped them in her mouth. The guards and Special Forces choked with laughter. I too found it funny. There is no sight sadder in this world than a state prosecutor scoffing pasties!

I had visions of Kafka running out of the courtroom, hanging his head, thoroughly outshone ...

After the lunch break, the prosecutor continued her monotone reading of documents that were irrelevant to the charges.

Everyone was tired, and the judge ended the session. We went home – to the prison. The trial took a lot out of me, and I returned to the cell feeling empty. Each evening in the jail, a doctor would do the rounds, peering through the serving hatch into each cell and asking if anything was needed. I asked him to measure my blood pressure. It was ninety over sixty. I would remember that strange, subdued state, which would come back often. The doctor recommended that I drink *chifir*, which I did. A few days of holiday were coming up, and I could catch some rest, mull over what was happening, and just take my mind off things.

There were four of us in the cell. One evening, an educated young man in glasses was brought in to us. Never did I see a man more weighed down with things than Alexei Frenkel. There were bags, holdalls, bundles and packages. The free space in the cell soon filled up with all his belongings. They were everywhere. Frenkel had reams of papers and documents. He'd been charged with masterminding the murder of deputy chairman of the Central Bank Alexei Kozlov. The prosecution theory was that Frenkel was avenging the revocation of a licence for one of the banks where he was board chairman.

My new cellmate had been a child prodigy and he had a brilliant mind. Hailing from a humble family of teachers, he swept to victory representing Saratov at the national Olympiad, completed his schooling at just fourteen, left for Moscow and won a place at Moscow University to study economics. He had a phenomenal memory – he'd remember the tiniest details, the merest minutiae, right down to the cost of a bus ticket bought ten years ago when, back in his student days, he took a trip across Russia. Alexei was horrendously pedantic and had a remarkable capacity for work. Whenever he submitted any paperwork, he'd write it out in duplicate, retaining a copy for his records. He'd draw up notes documenting everything, right down to the number of items in the fridge. He lived mostly on chocolate, and he generously bought his cellmates whatever they needed at the prison shop.

We became friends, though we didn't see much of each other, and in our leisure time we played chess. Each morning after his walk, he'd don a white shirt and suit and go off to see his lawyer and study the prosecution's case materials. 'I look upon my arrest as a journey, something of an adventure,' he once confided in me. An incurable optimist, he radiated pure *joie de vivre* and infected his cellmates with it too. One day, at around five in the evening, we heard the guard's voice. 'Surname F, get your belongings.' Frenkel, who'd made a vast number of complaints against the prison management, was not in their good books and they were moving him out of our cell. Clearly he'd been having too good a time with us. He spent a long time packing up his things, and we said our goodbyes. Once he'd gone, the cell felt empty, and I even began to grow sad. Later, I read in the papers he got eighteen years in a strict-regime camp.

It was Monday morning. Our next session in court was due to start. We were always brought along thirty minutes early, and we'd have to wait in the basement cells. The guards never put us in the same cell, no matter how much we requested it.

We went upstairs to the familiar old courtroom and took our places in the cage. Antonio Valdés-García came in with his minder carrying two big plastic buckets. Everyone stared in bewilderment at the buckets. Silence pervaded the room.

'Valdés-García, why have you brought those buckets?' the judge finally broke the stillness.

'Your Honour!' he said. 'I was in an accident and my hearing is almost gone. Can I sit closer to the prosecutor so I can hear her better? Also, I have a steel rod in my leg, and the leg goes numb. Can I put a bucket under my leg?'

The judge showed compassion and graciously allowed him to do so.

Soon after, the prosecution filed a motion to determine the competency of the defendant Antonio Valdés-García. The prosecutor said that, in her view, Antonio was suffering from a distorted perception of reality, and he displayed all the signs of mental incompetence – put simply, he'd gone cuckoo. At that moment, it occurred to me that it might be an idea to subject the prosecutors who wrote the indictment, and specifically Shlyayeva herself, to such a sanity check.

The judge considered the prosecution's request and rejected it. She had no doubts about Valdés–García's sanity. Neither did I, and I took it all as a good sign. My impression was that the judge held her own free opinion, independent of the prosecution.

Shlyayeva, meanwhile, pushed on stubbornly.

'The criminal investigation has established that Yukos Mordovia OOO and Ratibor OOO, on to whose books the stolen oil was transferred, together with Routhenhold Holdings Limited, through which the stolen oil was sold for export, were being controlled by members of an organised gang, as the leaders of the aforementioned companies were either members of an organised gang or persons dependent upon such gangs, as evidenced by: an employment contract; the Republic of Cyprus certificate of incorporation; and an excerpt from the minutes of a board meeting.'

My lawyer and I persistently filed more and more motions asking what exactly these documents proved. The employment contract proved nothing apart from the clear and undeniable fact that I worked at a subsidiary of Yukos. The certificate of incorporation confirmed that the company had been registered, and, what's more, six months before I joined Yukos. And the NK Yukos OAO board of directors' resolution to create Yukos Mordovia OOO, a company I hadn't heard of, had nothing to do with me whatsoever.

Well, indeed, the fact that all Yukos subsidiaries were controlled by their leaders was plain and obvious – hardly a matter for contention!

Shlyayeva kept churning out her lies: 'Later on, we'll explain the significance.'

From out of the blue, the words to some silly old song popped into my head: 'I shaped him out of whatever I could find. And then whatever I could find, I fell in love with.'

The prosecutor continued with her own song. 'The following items prove the guilt of the defendant: cash-flow statements for Yukos and a tax audit report.'

I could scarcely believe what I was hearing, though I knew these documents existed. We were being charged with stealing this very oil. It was odd to hear first-hand from the public prosecutor that this 'stolen' oil had been officially paid for; here we had the sales contracts, and the ownership transfer had been documented. *No theft had taken place!* The prosecution had said as much themselves. Hurray!

And the show went on. A show that was totally divorced from justice. Each day they'd disclose one, or at most two, volumes, and we still had the witness evidence to come. You'd normally get three or four court hearings per week. I tried to work out how long our case would take, and the conclusion was unnerving. My calculations suggested the trial would stretch on for around a year! 'Wow,' I thought, disappointed. Mentally, I'd been feeling as though I were already a free man.

My estimate was almost spot on. The verdict would be delivered on 1 March 2007.

As if in a trance, I heard: 'The following items prove the guilt of the defendant ...' and details were read out about transaction certificates, SWIFT messages and cash-flow currency account statements.

The realisation suddenly hit me that they should acquit me on the spot, here and now! It was plain as day that I was innocent. As if it weren't enough that I'd never signed a single payment order, and had no authority to sign them, here we had the prosecutor herself saying that all the payments for the oil sold, which had nothing to do with me, had been fully honoured. Rather than interrupt the reading of this proof of my innocence, I wrote a quick note, hoping to pass it to my lawyer. I took the sheet of paper, stood up and caught the judge's eye, conveying that I wanted to hand my lawyer the note. She nodded in assent. I offered my hand through the bars and gave him the sheet. Suddenly a commotion erupted. One of the prison guards on the back row flew forward and, destroying everything in his path, hurtled towards my lawyer.

'Yeow!' Valdés-García yelled at the top of his voice. The doughty old warrior had run over his mangled legs. The guard literally jumped on the lawyer and snatched my note from him. The judge froze in astonishment, mouth agape. There was a pause. No one said anything.

'What on earth do you think you're doing?' the judge asked the guard.

The latter kept silent and panted hard, struggling to catch his breath after the headlong tackle.

'Hand me the note,' said the judge.

The guard was clearly not keen to do so and he wavered. Perhaps he imagined it held some special secret for which he'd be decorated with a shiny medal.

'Give me the note,' the judge ordered in an imperious tone.

Without a word, he reluctantly handed the note to the judge and returned to his bench. The judge shot a quick glance at the innocuous slip of paper and passed it to my lawyer.

The judge had earned another little tick in my books.

'She's on our side!' I thought happily. 'But the guard will take it out on me tonight! I'm no doubt in for a walloping.'

The conversation took place in the basement of Basmanny Court. They didn't beat me up, but they threatened to write a report on me and throw me in solitary.

'In the courtroom, I'm the boss,' the guard told me. His shoulders bore the epaulettes of a lieutenant. I remembered a phrase Malakhovsky's lawyer had said: 'Putting on the uniform and acting like an officer are two different things.' Not wishing to enter into debate, I remained silent. Nearby, a local policeman guarding the court dungeons walked past. Musing, I eyed his epaulettes and couldn't work out his rank. His stars were embroidered in gold thread, and they seemed too small for a major general, yet too big for a warrant officer. Trying to figure it out, I rubbed my eyes in puzzlement and took a good look at the stars. They did indeed seem bigger than the regulation ones, and were clearly meant to mimic a general's stars.

'Oh yes, they're all crazy in this place,' I decided. We got into the GAZelle van and returned safely to the prison.

The summer of 2006 came, time for the recess. Judges are only human; they need time off. Their work is stressful and laden with responsibility, so their holidays are commensurately long. They announced a two-month pause in the court sessions. I mentally bade Judge Yarlykova goodbye until September.

My vacation began – a time of involuntary idleness. The daily drudge of prison life engrossed every fibre of my being.

12

SUMMER HOLIDAYS

The cell was incredibly hot and muggy. The two fans we leased from the prison management for thirty roubles a day could not save us; they merely spun the humid air around the cell. The vent-window only opened a quarter, stopping against the grille that came between cell and window. Another grille was attached from the outside. The 'deluxe unit', the block in Matrosskaya Tishina where I'd sat in an overcrowded cell, suddenly sprang to mind. 'I wonder what it must be like there now.' I tried to imagine being in that cell.

In that kind of heat, you lost your appetite. The television was permanently on. Everyone had their different likes, but we'd come to a compromise. There were four of us in the cell. Me, Volodya (a Moscow University graduate in physics and maths), Igor and Alexei. Volodya was a devout man, never without a Bible in his hands, who prayed and observed all the Orthodox fasts. Igor was a scrawny lad of modest height who'd done six years for stealing. This time he was charged with grievous bodily harm. Igor, whom I nicknamed 'Igoryan', was a reformed criminal heavy. He'd done two years of extra time while serving his previous sentence rather than being released on parole, and how he rued that decision. 'I'm such an idiot,' he moaned bitterly. 'I've lost so much time!' He had been driving with his girlfriend to a friend's birthday party. On the way they stopped at a shop to buy some presents. Igoryan left the girl in the car and went into the shop. He returned to find a gang of pugnacious young guys by the car, around five lads (later identified as minors). They broke off his mirror and started goading him. One thing led to another, and I'm not sure who struck the first blow, but Igor, who'd never done any sports, let alone martial arts, happened to land a clean hit to the temple. The bone smashed and entered the brain. End of game. The guy was dead. The indictment said, 'Motivated by thuggish intent, he assaulted a group of young people, causing severe injury with a lethal outcome.'

'Oh yeah, I decided to flex my muscles before the birthday bash,' he said caustically. 'Do I look like the kind of nutjob who'd pick a fight when it's one against five? Like something out of the Brothers Grimm, seven men with one blow of the hand?'

My other cellmate, Alexei, was a much more complex fellow. This wasn't his first time inside. He talked a lot about what life was like in the camp he'd been in. It had all gone well. His colony was a 'black' one, under the criminals' control, on the site of a disused military unit. They even had the old posters showing how to take apart a Kalashnikov. You were free to do as you liked. You could sleep to your heart's content, eat your fill, so long as you could afford it or get parcels sent. This time he was charged with running a gang that burgled high-end luxury villas. They cased the joints, did their homework – they took their job seriously. Alexei was facing ninety-five counts on his indictment. There was torture, crushed fingers and drilled knees. A loving family man who doted on his children, he said disparagingly of his victim: 'The moron decided to play at being a hero.' When they broke into the house in masks, the owner, who turned out to be not the timid type, dared to offer resistance. The upshot was he'd had to shoot the owner dead, and now, on top of the robbery, they were being done for murder! Alexei was outraged at the heinous actions of the police, as they had gone and pinned on them every similar crime committed in the Moscow region. 'I could hardly have done job after job, every three days!' he protested. 'You need to prepare meticulously, plan it all out!'

His dream was to land a fifteen-year sentence.

I banged on the door and asked for a guard to take us to the shower.

'Huh, what do you mean? I haven't had a wash myself in three days,' an unknown voice replied.

We all chortled heartily in unison. In the cell, there was plenty of everything – in fact, more than enough. Each of us was getting parcels and deliveries. The prison shop continued to brighten our lives. Cabbage, beetroot, carrots, oranges, kiwifruits, salmon – not by any means an exhaustive list of the produce on offer. There were cakes, chocolates and halva. The works. But I longed for home cooking, which was not allowed into the place. So I began mastering the art of cooking in prison. Following the already familiar process, I set out to cook some soup, using an aluminium kettle as a pot. I shredded the cabbage and grated the tomatoes and beetroot on a plastic grater bought in the shop. That was all popped into the kettle along with some water. Then I left it for half an hour to boil, constantly topping it up with more water. Towards the end, I added some salmon chopped up small. The end result was delicious. Everyone liked it. Sometimes we'd take the prison-gruel soup. We would pick out the potato chunks, rinse them in cold water and throw them in the kettle where the soup was cooking.

Later, when I was at the penal colony, I would look back on those halcyon days in prison.

'Surname Z, get your belongings.' Igor was being taken from the cell. He was a good cellmate, a peaceful fellow, and we were sad to say goodbye. If only we'd known who was coming as Igor's replacement, we'd have seen him off in a flood of tears.

It wasn't long before our new cellmate appeared. The clanking of doors broke up our tea session. The door opened, and into the cell stepped a tall, podgy guy in glasses. He had no belongings with him.

'Slava,' he introduced himself. We made our acquaintance. He had just been brought over from the police cells. Being by now an old-timer, I told him about life in prison and the rules of conduct. He simply asked, 'Have you been here long?'

'Two years,' I told him.

He could not wrap his mind around that. And he began to cry. For real – bawling and sobbing like a spoiled brat. In fact, that's just what he was. The son of wealthy parents, spoilt rotten, he used to whizz around Moscow like a lunatic in his Porsche Cayenne, which sported the sign 'Darkwing Duck' in place of a number plate. He enjoyed the high life, living it up. But pleasure wasn't enough; he also craved power over people. Someone failed to move aside for him – so he got out of the car with his friends and gave the poor fellow a beating. They used to whoop it up like there was no tomorrow. Being on the chummiest terms with an Interior Ministry official in the division for countering corruption at the highest levels of power, he tried extorting money from someone. Whether for kicks or for real …

Slava quickly settled into the cell. When everyone was asleep, he needed to watch TV. If we were already watching a programme, he'd demand we switch channels to Muz-TV. He was always chomping his way through something or other. One time, Alexei asked him, 'Would you eat twenty packets of instant noodles in one go for a dare?'

He thought for a second, and, after tallying something mentally, he set out his terms: 'Only if I can swallow them down with bread!'

Worrying dreadfully about his health and fearful of catching tuberculosis, Slava took the precaution of tirelessly devouring copious quantities of thick slabs of cured pork fat. Equipped with two bachelor's degrees acquired through the greasing of palms and a master's degree, also of shady provenance, he was convinced that the pork fat would 'absorb' all the germs.

Whenever we took turns cleaning the cell, he could be relied upon to get off the bed and walk all over the floor while it was still wet. In an attempt to assert his rights, he would allocate television time and divide up the territory in the cell. It dawned on me for the first time that I really could murder a man. All of us hated Slava, and we stopped speaking to him. The tension in the cell rose. Alexei got into a serious spat with Slava, and he picked up the kettle, threatening to douse him with boiling water. Slava grabbed hold of the plastic knife. Alexei (who was, without a doubt, experienced in such matters) said to me, 'I know his type. They're all bluff. You take guys like him to the forest, and in no time they'll be crying and crapping themselves.' We heard the voices of the guards behind the door. 'What's going on in there? Stop it right now!'

'Everything's okay, we're just talking,' Alexei told them. The row died down. But it did not pass unnoticed by the prison staff. The next day, Slava was moved to another cell. Hurray! Despite feeling like an eternity, the torment had been short-lived, and we all heaved a sigh of relief. Later I learnt that some guy's nerves had snapped and he'd given Slava a good drubbing in the cell. Slava filed a complaint against his cellmate. In prison, nothing is more despised than grassing on your fellow prisoners. Slava was your perfect candidate for the discipline and order unit. These were organisations in the camps where prisoners could enlist, and for a 'mess of pottage' from the prison management, they'd happily enforce discipline and order among the other inmates.

They helped out with the searches, 'welcomed' the newcomers to the camp, reported violations and roughed up other prisoners with impunity.

We couldn't get over our joy at being rid of our cellmate. In all my time behind bars, I never encountered anyone worse. Barely ten minutes had passed before the guard told Alexei to collect his belongings. Alexei complied with the order, fuming. 'Because of that idiot they're breaking up our whole cell!'

Volodya and I were left, just the two of us. What lay behind those numerous transfers from cell to cell? You could never tell who you might end up with. Time and again, I found myself sharing a cell with the same characters. 'What on earth is the point of all these transfers?' A question I asked myself over and over, but I never did find the answer.

Then my own turn arrived.

'Surname P, get your belongings.' I could never get used to that phrase. There were too many developments that could follow those words. No point holding your breath for something pleasant to happen. They could be transferring you to another prison or another cell. Who would you now be sharing a room with twenty-four hours a day? That one fact would decide your wellbeing and peace of mind. Feeling upset, I collected my things, packing all my food and paperwork into my bags. I folded up my mattress and blanket. And I said goodbye to Volodya, whom I liked, a lot. Later, a small miracle would happen to him. The jury would acquit him, and he'd retreat from the world to become the parish priest of one of Moscow's smaller churches.

The door opened and I hauled all my bags out into the corridor. I was taken to the cell next door. I had already seen my fair share of cells, but here I experienced not the nicest of sensations. The cell inmates were all assembled. None of the faces looked familiar. One guy was a lanky hardboiled criminal, tattooed from head to toe: Volodya Levitan. Another was Igor Losev, a nondescript rank-and-file fighter for the Medvedkovo gang. The third person's face did seem as though I'd seen it somewhere. Sergei Mavrodi – that's who it was![7] I took a free place on the top bunk. We introduced ourselves and sat down for the traditional tea ceremony. The usual conversations followed: where were you from, what were you charged with, who had you shared a cell with? Despite the secrecy, which was strictly adhered to, you got to know all the inmates in the prison through hearsay. You'd know everything about them. Of course, they'd also know about you. The cell was stuffed with food. Mavrodi had been prescribed a special diet. He had gout, or, as it's still called, the 'rich man's disease'. They hired an outside cook to deliver specially prepared food twice a week: liver, mutton, ostrich meat, sturgeon and salmon. We couldn't manage to scoff it all before the next delivery of fresh food. The prison gruel faded from memory. Levitan dined on these viands with redoubled efforts, as if trying to lay down fat stores. He'd spent much of his life in prison, and it wasn't clear what he was doing in this one, but he decided he had a sympathetic listener in me. Levitan was a pain in the neck with his endless tales of prisons and camps. At first it seemed interesting, but soon I'd had enough. I happily returned to my books, and Levitan switched his attentions to Igor.

Mavrodi and I went on the daily walk each morning. Levitan and Igor would stay behind in the stuffy cell. Although the exercise yard on the prison's roof was hardly the place for fresh air, I didn't miss a single walk. Mavrodi was an interesting person to talk to, and we talked a lot. He had a tough regime, all mapped out, and he followed it unswervingly. Not a minute was wasted. He got up, had breakfast, went for his walk. Each day he'd go off to examine his case materials, returning to the cell late in the day, by around four or five. He took his daily exercise. Lying on the bunk, he'd work his abs. His daily target was 2,000 leg raises, bringing his feet over the head. And any number of press-ups. Mavrodi was in fine physical shape. He followed his sport with a

---

7   Sergei Mavrodi is a famous fraudster who ran a Ponzi scheme in Russia in the 1990s.
     Many millions of Russians lost large sums to his company, MMM.

wash and dinner. Then he'd take a nap. He would get up a little before lights out. When the entire cell was sleeping, he'd write his book by the dim light of his own personal lamp, although goodness knows how he'd been allowed one. Such a way of life commanded my respect, but it was horribly irritating for our cellmate Levitan. While brazenly wolfing down Mavrodi's delicacies, which he clearly could not have afforded on the outside, Levitan would keep taking digs at Mavrodi and calling him to order.

'Good criminals don't do sports in the cell. There's not enough air as it is,' he said, puffing as usual on an expensive cigarette, also bought with Mavrodi's cash. Neither Mavrodi nor I were smokers. Mavrodi would take the weekends off – and I must admit, I looked forward to those days. We'd become engrossed in chess battles and conversations. The time flew as we enjoyed ourselves. I learnt that the story with MMM was not quite so simple and clear-cut. The money invested by savers had not just gone on interest payments to other savers, but had also been invested in a range of assets. For example, they'd acquired shares in Gazprom, which had seen a hundredfold rise in value. The scale of Mavrodi's operations was mind-boggling. According to him, he was ferrying money around in KamAZ trucks and storing it in apartments bought or rented for the purpose. What's more, he could not always say quite how much cash he had at any given moment. He as good as created his own political party. Twelve million depositors meant twelve million people willing to vote for your every proposal. Becoming a deputy in the State Duma posed no challenge for him. To mark the occasion, he bought his first suit and tie, up until then having preferred to go about in a track suit and trainers. He seemed not of this world, and took little interest in material possessions. What interested him were books, butterflies and fine wines.

I'd spend a whole month in that cell before once more hearing the familiar phrase from behind the iron door: 'Surname P, get your belongings.'

We had some interesting characters in our prison. There was the notorious mafia boss Vyacheslav Ivankov, known as Yaponchik, and Colonel Kvachkov, charged with the attempted murder of Anatoly Chubais.

'So, who will I end up with this time?' I wondered, hauling my things down the empty corridor of the prison. Unable to move all my bags in one go, I made two trips up the stairs to the sound of the 'cuckoo'. They were moving me to the fourth floor. A new cell, with new faces. Everyone in here was self-contained. They all had sullen, serious expressions. Sasha was my age, a native of Kingisepp. He'd been attending a boxing group when the entire collective was arrested and accused of gangsterism and contract killings for the politician Igor Izmestiev. Later, I learnt from the newspapers that the jury had acquitted him.

It was astonishing, given the negligible number of acquittals in Russia – less than one per cent, according to the official statistics – that I saw with my own eyes a fair handful of men who were found not guilty. There was the Chechen, Kazbek Dukuzov, charged with murdering the American editor of *Forbes Russia* Paul Klebnikov, who would leave the courtroom a free man. Kazbek and I shared a cell for around a month. A strong man, physically and spiritually, Kazbek was completely different from the others. I do not doubt for a second his innocence. When I'd already moved to another cell with new cellmates, we learnt from the news that the jury had acquitted him. The verdict was met in our cell with a storm of triumphant applause and yells of 'Hurray!' Complete strangers who had never met him were rejoicing for Kazbek. The NTV channel aired a programme about this momentous trial, insinuating that there had been some conflict of interest among the jury. What happened was this: after the verdict, a female juror had cheerfully waved him goodbye from the window! Under this flimsy pretext, the jury's verdict was overturned, and an international search warrant went out for Kazbek. But he was nowhere to be found. Good luck to you, Kazbek!

The prosecution, realising that trial by jury won't always go the way they want, have developed a system that allows them to manipulate and overturn unfavourable verdicts. The jury rooms are bugged; they slip in their own jurors who will lobby for the desired verdict. The Russian justice system, in collusion with the judge, who is working hand in glove with the prosecution, purposely overlooks procedural irregularities during the trial so they can later be used as grounds for overturning unwelcome verdicts.

13

THE TRIAL RESUMES

I quickly settled into the cell with my new cellmates. Along my journey, I met men from all walks of life. Some were private and uncommunicative. Others wanted to talk, to share their troubles or just take their minds off melancholy thoughts. Books and games of draughts and chess brightened up our lives. I noticed that the shorter the custodial sentence a man received, the more nervous he'd be while waiting for it. This formula, though, did not apply to me. 'Don't stew on it, man! Or else the geese will come flying!' You'd often hear this phrase from the other inmates. 'Geese flying' meant 'go crazy'. As for me, I was in a right old stew, and yet ended up with a hefty sentence.

The entire cell would go for a weekly shower, which behind bars for some reason we always referred to as the 'bathhouse'. We were given twenty minutes to wash. Twenty minutes of sheer bliss, which on the outside you take completely for granted. A shower might seem like just a shower. But once you've lost everything, once you've experienced that fine line between freedom and incarceration, you truly start to appreciate the tiny things that make up happiness.

Stepping on the scales in the shower room, I was horrified to find I now weighed 101 kilograms! For me, at my height of 1 metre 75, having kept in good shape with exercise all my life, this came as dreadful news. And freedom was not, as I dreamt at the time, close at hand. 'How can I leave the courtroom a hero, with my name fully cleared, looking such a fatty?' I thought. So I gained another enemy in my prison life: flab, which I began fighting with grim determination. The flab, in turn, began fighting me back, sometimes scoring little victories on the battlefield. Then I stopped eating altogether. I began fasting. I drank nothing but water. I went a day without food, then two. Then three. In the pauses between the fasts, the weight struck back. I desperately wanted to eat, and sometimes I would falter, but I didn't give up. After some time, I could abstain from food for eight days. The weight retreated and rapidly dropped. It did wonders for my mood and wellbeing. I felt a remarkable lightness in my body and clarity of mind. I got caught up in the fasting, and life in the cell took on new meaning. By the autumn, I was rid of my accumulated kilos and had got back my old shape. In these good spirits, feeling energised and full of hope, I waited for the trial to resume.

The summer had flown by. My lawyer came back from his holiday – spent on the Mediterranean shores of Spain. The judge returned from I don't know where, but she'd picked up a decent tan. The journeys to court began again. It was already cooling, but had not yet turned cold. I became inured to those court trips. The search, the armed guards, the van escorted by Special Forces – by now it felt ordinary, and I blanked out the lunacy of it all.

We walked into the courtroom. Nothing had changed. There was still the same miserable furniture, redolent of a schoolroom. The same old cell. Through the open window I could smell the street, and I blissfully breathed in the fresh air. After the prison cell and the court basement, that air felt so bracing, despite the Basmanny Court being so close to three railway stations. The performance continued. The prosecutor asked for the window to be shut, saying that we wouldn't be able to hear her disclosure of the evidence. Not that it was worth listening to …

'The charge against V. I. Pereverzin, namely Part 4 of Article 160 …' The 'evidence' included A. Valdés-García's employment-record book and cash-flow statements showing perfectly ordinary transfers.

I could not understand why a prosecutor ranked as lieutenant colonel was reading these documents. What did Valdés-García have to do with my case? We hadn't met, for crying out loud; we'd never even spoken! And even if we had, why would it matter? What would be odd about that? Why shouldn't employees in the same firm communicate? In our case, this detail graphically illustrates the sheer absurdity of their so-called evidence.

Armed guards sat at either side of the cage. Lulled by the inane monotone of the prosecution, they fell asleep. One of the guards slumped against the cage in such a way that the holster with his pistol jutted between the bars, ending up right next to me. The other, who was holding an assault rifle, was asleep on his chair half a metre from the first. I had merely to reach out my hand, and the gun would be mine. I wanted to shout, 'Stay alert, soldier!' At this point, the guard collapsed and his entire body accidentally pressed against the red alarm button. It took about ten seconds before two puffing and panting policemen flew into the courtroom, disrupting the calm. Seeing that everything was in order, they left again.

It's worth noting that the trial was really rather amusing; it seemed more like a comedy. I never knew what to expect at our next court session.

Day after day, the prosecutor would read out an endless number of sales contracts, bank statements and other documents that she herself found unintelligible. Some she would read for a second time. I immediately raised an oral motion. 'Your Honour,' I said, turning to the judge. 'The prosecutor doesn't understand what she's reading. The oil sales contract she's just disclosed has in fact already been disclosed. I request, for a second time, that we be told the relevance of this document to the case, as I fail to see how this contract proves anything other than the fact that an oil purchase took place.'

The judge redirected my question to the prosecutor, who, for the umpteenth time, dumbly repeated her stale old phrase, which was beginning to sound sinister: 'We will explain and reveal it all in one go, once the disclosure of all the evidence is complete.' The prosecutor stumbled over the case documents that were in English. Appended to them was a specialist translation done by an international relations expert within the Prosecutor-General's Office. I heard some kind of nonsense, an incoherent jumble of words. The prosecutor mumbled: '*Veksel!*' Meaning 'promissory note'. Without idling, I opened the relevant volume on the right page. I saw a contract for a charter vessel for the delivery of oil to the buyer. The hapless specialist from the Prosecutor-General's Office had translated the English word 'vessel', as in ship, into Russian as 'promissory note'. I immediately filed another motion about this. A strange picture was emerging: a promissory note or a ship – who gave a hoot? No matter what, we were guilty. I was guilty by dint of the fact that somebody somewhere had dollar signs in his eyes. Moreover, this 'somebody' was a ravenous shark with a lusty appetite.

Those 'translators' brought tears of laughter to my eyes. It was so funny that I could not stop laughing. The court session ended, and I went back to the cell in a good mood. With much pleasure, I drank some very strong tea, swallowing it down with a sandwich and choking as I told the story of the promissory note that was actually a ship. Everyone laughed heartily. The court hearing had turned into some kind of theatre, into a farce. Every time I took my place – alas, not in the audience – I waited with interest for new surprises to be revealed in the plot. We were each playing a character. The judge was pretending to be judging and weighing up the evidence. The prosecutor pretended to be proving something. And we, the involuntary players on the stage, were playing ourselves.

The drama was running its course. It was time for the witnesses to be questioned. The farce continued to unfold.

'The participation of V. I. Pereverzin, A. Valdés-García and V. G. Malakhovsky, operating as members of an organised criminal group for the theft of oil between 2001–2003 [no matter that I left the company in 2002!], is confirmed by the testimony of: V. G. Malakhovsky; A. Valdés-García.'

The investigators who cooked up our case were a match for the English-to-Russian translator.

'What on earth is all this? What kind of utter tosh is this?' I said impotently, as if addressing the air. 'How can these people testify about my guilt if we didn't even know each other, if we'd never even spoken to each other?!'

The other witnesses began to appear. Some of their faces I'd seen in the Yukos dining room. I'd come across some of the surnames. But, as luck would have it, there were plenty that I did not know.

The judge questioned Witness N. The woman was feeling awful; she was in tears, on the verge of breaking down.

'Witness N., do you know the accused?' the judge asked.

She didn't know me, but she recognised Malakhovsky and Valdés-García, she told the judge in a trembling voice.

'Can you tell us about the circumstances in which you first met the defendants?' the judge persisted.

'Why, it's obvious! We worked together, sat in the same office, at the same desk, and we signed the same documents …' She was sobbing, aware of how easily she could have taken our place. They could just as easily have thrown any other random Yukos staff behind bars. In her case, they wouldn't even have had to change anything in the indictment – just the surnames. Their pseudo-evidence would have remained the same and led to the same end result.

Malakhovsky's lawyer filed a motion, asking the state prosecutor to explain how his client's role differed from that of this witness. We were not to get an intelligible answer, and, in any case, it had been abundantly clear for some time: there wasn't a jot of difference! The witness was the same type of hired employee as we all were. They just so happened to have picked us to play the role of the accused.

Witness K., a pretty girl, announced to the court that she was going to speak from her conscience. Prosecutor Shlyayeva pounced on this phrase and asked sneeringly, 'And what does this conscience of yours tell you?'

The girl calmly replied, 'It tells me that taking this approach, you could lock up the entire staff of Yukos, and I feel desperately sorry for these men here today.'

All the participants in any trial, including the defendants, have the right to question the witnesses. The judge, seeking to observe all the formalities, courteously inquired whether the defendants wished to question the witnesses. I had no questions. Valdés-García demanded they stop this outrageous nonsense and quit their buffoonery. He managed to speak about how he'd been abused by the staff of the prosecution, and he'd had his crutches thrown from the thirteenth floor. And, for the umpteenth time, he said he didn't understand what was going on here, and that he hadn't read the whole document, which was written in gibberish. In despair, he quietly said, 'They've crippled me, and I don't know how to carry on with my life, what to do with myself ...'

'You should have thought of that earlier!' sniped the prosecutor. 'Well, there's always the Olympics for the disabled!'

'Now, that would be the perfect place for you to perform!' I wanted to say for all to hear. I was already imagining her wobbling and panting in the 100-metre race. The judge restored calm and announced a break. My heart was pounding in indignation, and I was gasping for air. I felt ready to strangle the prosecutor. It was clear to me that a prosecutor with a conscience was a contradiction in terms.

I often had to restrain myself. I wanted to yell at the top of my voice, 'Wake up! What the hell are you doing, you bastards!'

There would have been no point. They knew perfectly well what they were up to.

My lawyer regularly held instructional talks with me to keep me from taking such action. I just couldn't calm down and accept things. Here is what it looked like to me. On the table you have an ordinary white teacup with tea in it. The prosecutor points to it and says it's an iron. Everyone can see the idiocy of this, but each person plays their role. The lawyers call out, 'Look, there's tea inside! It is a teacup!'

'Of course it is a teacup, that's obvious!' I say in support of the arguments for the defence.

At this, the prosecutor fanatically, foaming at the mouth, keeps insisting, 'No, it's an iron.'

But the moment we're gone from the room, the prosecutor will pick up the teacup-iron and happily, smacking her lips with pleasure, sip the tea.

The examination of the witnesses continued. One or two people showed up per day. Each new witness barely differed from the previous ones. We heard pretty much the same questions, the same answers. None of them knew me. Those witnesses upon whose testimony – according to the indictment – my guilt was allegedly proved did not even know me … Ordinary employees of the company appeared for questioning, and they spoke about their official duties.

Autumn stole up on us; it started turning cold. The judge wanted the trial wrapped up before the New Year of 2007, and she began pressing the prosecution to hurry things along.

During a break in the court session, from the cage I caught the prosecutor saying, 'We still haven't questioned all the prosecution witnesses!'

The judge pondered for a moment, and said to herself, 'Hmm ... How are they witnesses for the prosecution? It's a complete mystery to me what they are meant to be proving!' These words were heard by the entire courtroom. Excited by this, I gave the judge another big, bold tick in my books. 'Now I'll surely be acquitted,' I thought.

People I knew were now appearing for questioning – colleagues I'd worked with. Memories came flooding back.

Witness R., who'd grown thin and drawn, had worked with me in Cyprus and been director of the same company as me. He'd done precisely the same job as me. Visibly nervous (and looking somewhat awkward in front of me), he told the court honestly all about our collaborative work.

Witness G., an employee at the Moscow representative office of the Cyprus company, also gave truthful testimony. He told the court about the moment (which had slipped from my memory), after I'd left Yukos and shortly before my arrest, when I'd asked him about the thefts in Yukos and about Malakhovsky, which I'd learnt of from the newspapers.

I was on friendly terms with this man, and after my arrest he began to help me and my family, continuing to do so during my time behind bars.

Witness P., the head of the Moscow office for the Cyprus company, fully confirmed the testimony of Witness G. He gave a thorough and detailed account of all the nuances of his work and the company's activity.

Everything was clear and obvious. We didn't even have witnesses for the defence, as all the witnesses called by the prosecution had clearly shown my innocence and that I wasn't implicated in the occurrences being absurdly depicted as theft. My mind even threw up the idea I might see in the New Year on the outside.

'So, could they acquit me and let me out in time for New Year's Eve at home? No, there wouldn't be time,' I reasoned.

The trial was coming to an end. A mountain of documents had been re-read, dozens of witnesses interviewed. Malakhovsky and Valdés-García had been questioned. The examination ended, and we moved on to the next phase of the trial: the arguments. It was not long now. After the arguments came the summing up and the verdict ...

The prosecutor offered her closing arguments and declared, 'The evidence heard in the course of the trial has fully proven the guilt of the defendants.'

She told a shameless lie: 'The defendants knew each other and consorted with each other; they co-ordinated their activities.'

The sheer gall – no, not even gall, it was barefaced fabrication – rendered me speechless. My lawyer and I exchanged glances. He had, in the past, worked in the prosecution himself, yet he was staggered by what was happening.

The state prosecutor asked for us each to be given eleven years in a strict-regime penal colony. Such a generous New Year's gift from the Prosecutor-General's Office! I saw Valdés-García's face contorting in horror. He had come from Spain voluntarily, to defend his good name, and the prospect of spending the next eleven years in Russia clearly didn't appeal. Malakhovsky also looked bewildered. I myself was stunned by what I'd heard. It's one thing when abstract sentences for abstract people are being discussed, but it's another when we're talking about years of *your* life. To shield my wife from worry before New Year's Eve, I asked my lawyer not to breathe a word to her about this monstrous sentence.

'The fact is the judge will have the last word,' I calmed myself. 'And, in any case, they can't convict me if I'm innocent.' I still hoped to be acquitted, but in my mind I'd already accepted the idea of a guilty verdict with a small sentence.

'This whole thing is some kind of hideous mistake. What do they mean, eleven years! Have they all gone mad?' I could not calm down. 'Why ask for me to get eleven years?'

And here ended the latest court session. We would reconvene after the New Year holidays, on 11 January. I was taken back to the remand prison. I was all stirred up and for a long time couldn't sleep. I was stewing on it, worried sick, and was turning over the different possibilities.

'The worst the judge could do is to hand me nine years,' I reasoned. 'She simply can't give the requested eleven years if it hasn't been established that a crime took place and there's not one shred of evidence.'

I quickly dismissed that idea as highly inadmissible and unlikely.

'No, they're bound to acquit me! In the worst-case scenario, I'll get sentenced to time served, so no matter what, I'll soon be free!' I convinced myself.

14

NEW YEAR'S GIFT

New Year's Eve was a few days away. It would be my third New Year spent behind bars. Everyone received parcels, and the cell was groaning with food. There was more than you could wish for. In the prison shop, we bought lemonade, Coke and Fanta. The preparations for our festive table were moving along nicely. We were making a dressed-herring salad and something as close as possible to a Russian salad. Going on past experience, I knew we were allowed to watch television after lights out until around 3.00 a.m. On 31 December, the prison staff brought some branches of spruce into each cell, immediately filling the room with their scent. We used foil chocolate wrappers and paper to make Christmas decorations to adorn our New Year's tree. Despite everything, a holiday atmosphere was building. 'Good Lord, could this really be my last New Year behind bars?' I thought gladly. Every now and then my mind turned to the court, where I still had to make my closing statement and await the judge's decision, before quickly falling back into the festive swing of the cell.

The television was on, with Putin's seasonal greetings playing in the background. We were waiting for the bell chimes so as not to miss the moment the New Year came in. 'Hurray! Happy New Year!' we called, clinking mugs of Fanta. The year was now 2007. Each man sat lost in his own thoughts. Vadik, far from the pleasantest of cellmates, charged with racketeering and robbery, said dreamily, 'What do you think, guys? Wouldn't it be great to get together like this on the outside to see in the New Year?'

'Yeah, that would be fantastic!' said Nikolai, charged with murder.

'God forbid!' I thought, and smiled enigmatically ... The entire cell was engrossed in the television, where they were airing the *Little Blue Light* show.

The singing and dancing did nothing to cheer me up, and all the jokes seemed stupid. After watching a bit of the show, I climbed on my bed and fell asleep. Through my broken sleep I heard the muffled sounds of the television and my cellmates chattering.

'Everybody up, make your beds,' a guard said. It was six in the morning. From behind the door came the sound of the trolley carrying our gruel.

'Boys, it's breakfast.' A female cook offered us our meal through the food hatch. Sometimes we'd take the bread and the sugar. We didn't eat the gruel, though it would be the envy of any prisoner in the camps. In the model detention centre 99/1 of the Russian Federal Penitentiary Service, the rules and regulations were stringently adhered to, and the ingredients that went into the gruel were used in the prescribed quantities. This was perhaps the only place in Russia where the prisoners were served by a civilian cook.

'No thanks, I don't need any,' I said, politely refusing their gruel. 'You can treat yourself to it!'

The prison staff were categorically forbidden from taking anything from the inmates. And in this tightly and meticulously controlled place, unlike the other Moscow remand prisons, the rule was strictly observed. There was no slipping of bribes, no prohibited items, which I must say suited me fine. I was very pleased with the cleanliness, the order and the chance to work through the documents and prepare for the trial.

The men got up, made their beds on autopilot, and lay down to sleep some more. Their slumber was cut short. We heard the clang of doors opening in the neighbouring cells. An inspection. Everyone rose to their feet. The head of the detention centre came into the cell himself. He was a colonel – an intriguing character. He was not yet forty. Well-mannered and courteous, he wished us a happy New Year, and inquired whether we had any complaints, suggestions or queries. We had just one wish: to show him the door and quickly lie back down to sleep. Our wish was granted and he made himself scarce.

The guys had watched television into the early hours and lay sprawled on their beds. I blissfully drank some instant coffee while waiting for the walk. Today I'd go for my walk alone. For me, here in the remand prison, spending some moments in relative solitude was a huge pleasure. It was cold outside, and I put on all the clothes I had. The exercise yards were on the roof of the prison building and cut off from the outside world by walls tangled in barbed wire, an overhead grille and a roof made of galvanised iron, fixed high above the grille. You couldn't see the sky straight above you, but it was visible if you looked to the side and into the distance. I trod with delight on the newly fallen snow. Loud music was blaring away. They played it not for the gratification of the strolling prisoners, but to stop the prisoners in different yards from shouting to each other. A guard was walking along the wall, watching over the inmates from a height.

'White roses, O white roses, You poor helpless thorns,' rang out from the speaker. I walked my laps briskly.

'See what the frost and the snow have done to you, the glacial window display?' I quickened my pace and broke into a run.

'You'll be used for a few days to dress up the party, Then left to expire on the icy white sill.' I began dancing to this ridiculous song.

I got back to the cell flushed, breathless and happy. My cellmates were already awake; they'd tidied the cell and sat drinking tea, passionately discussing last night's concert. In the days following New Year, time practically stood still. It was the first day of January, the second, the third ... And then 9 January arrived. At last, the holidays were over and the working days began.

I was brought to the courthouse. As usual, they led me to the cage, where Malakhovsky was already waiting. I could feel there was something wrong. Something had happened. A tension hung in the air; the judge was in a heated discussion with the public prosecutor. The lawyers kept whispering. I couldn't see Valdés-García. The prosecutor hemmed and hawed, before officially announcing that on the night of 2 to 3 January, Antonio Valdés-García had fled Russia and absconded. It turned out he'd locked his minder in the shower, caught a taxi and rushed to the airport. On his Spanish passport, he was not Valdés-García, but Antonio, say, Pereira, and he safely passed through passport control and returned to his native Spain. His adventures in Russia had come to a lucky end. The Kingdom of Spain deemed the case politically motivated and would not extradite their subject at the request of the Russian Prosecutor-General. The Russian authorities didn't scruple to try him disgracefully in absentia, sentencing him to eight and a half years.

'Good for you, Antonio! Bravo!' I was sincerely happy for him. But it meant the trial was delayed again. At the prosecution's request, the judge severed the criminal case against the fugitive Valdés-García from our trial, and we returned to our arguments in the court. Prosecutor Shlyayeva repeated her earlier lie word for word: 'They knew each other, consorted with each other and they co-ordinated their activities.' And she asked for the same sentence of eleven years each.

In my closing statement, I said that the evidence read in the trial attested to the lawful and official business activity of Yukos, that I had never engaged in any illegal activity and I was just a plain, ordinary employee of the firm, carrying out my duties. I asked to be acquitted.

Malakhovsky's closing statement differed little from mine. He also spoke about the absurdness of the charges and asked to be acquitted.

And the curtain came down. With that, the trial ended. The judge withdrew to write the verdict. Its delivery was scheduled for 1 March 2007. Now all I needed to do was to wait. This period of waiting was for me the most difficult part. My fate was being decided. I could not read any books. After mechanically scanning some page, I'd realise that I hadn't absorbed the meaning. I tried keeping myself busy with exercise. Squats and push-ups helped take my mind off my thoughts. I was counting the days until the final judgement.

In the cell, I gave away my things. My tracksuit went to Alexei, who had no family in Moscow. My mattress, the object of my pride and the envy of my cellmates, which I'd personally fashioned out of two mattresses, was bequeathed to Kostya. He was an important businessman from St Petersburg who said he'd known Putin personally when the latter was working in the St Petersburg city administration as a nondescript clerk. Kostya faced charges of masterminding the murder of Igor Klimov, head of the defence firm Almaz-Antey. The jury would acquit him, and he'd leave for the exotic shores of Ecuador, only to be abducted from there by the GRU and brought back to Russia for a second trial. He was acquitted for a second time.

Kostya gave me some wise advice: 'Vladimir, first get yourself freed, and then we'll sort out who gets what.'

'Giving your stuff away before the court ruling is a really bad omen,' some old-timers later told me – and how right that proved.

The night before the announcement of the verdict, I couldn't sleep and was trapped in a carousel of thoughts. 'I'll be acquitted; no, I won't. They'll let me go free; no, they won't.' Unable to stick with any one of the thoughts spinning endlessly in my mind, I arrived under escort at the courthouse. Everything was ready: the television crews, reporters, family members. I saw the faces of people dear to me. My best friend, Leonid Belenky, was there. He would stick with me and help me throughout the years. When you know there are people ready to do anything for you, you can endure so very much.

The judge began her announcement of the verdict. She read out her text: 'I find Vladimir Ivanovich Pereverzin and Vladimir Georgievich Malakhovsky guilty of crimes falling under Article 160 Part 4 and Article 174.1 Part 4 of the Penal Code of the Russian Federation.'

From the very first words it was clear the verdict was guilty. So, my miracle hadn't happened. I looked at the judge in disappointment.

'How could this verdict have taken her a whole month?' I couldn't make sense of it. 'She hasn't even written it herself, she's just taken the diskette sent to her from the Prosecutor-General's Office and copied and pasted the entire thing into her verdict. It's word-for-word identical – the same typos, the same errors.

'Hey, come on! What about the evidence? What about the glaring facts?' I couldn't believe what was happening. You tell someone white is white, and they answer brazenly, 'No, it's black.'

Now all that remained was the announcement of the sentence. I still hoped to be released, having already done two years and eight months. The sentence filled 180 typed pages, and the judge did not have time to read it in one day. I returned to the cell.

'My liberation has been postponed till tomorrow!' I said in an effort at humour, once back in the cell.

But it was delayed for another day as the judge read out and cited all the evidence of guilt referred to in the verdict. She was now coming to the summing-up section. The most interesting part was left for day three.

I said goodbye to my cellmates, finalising my instructions on what to do with my things, of which I only needed one bag of papers. As I left, they said, 'Fingers crossed!'

'Fingers crossed!' I said, and walked out of the cell. I was visibly nervous. I was hoping everything would finally be sorted out, it would now go the right way.

The courtroom was packed. Everyone was waiting for the final judgement. In a monotone voice, the judge resumed her reading.

'In deciding the sentence, the court has taken into account the dependence of Pereverzin's child, a minor born in 1995, on the defendant. Given the circumstances of the acts committed, and the role and degree of involvement of each of the defendants, the court finds that the reformation of the defendants V. G. Malakhovsky and V. I. Pereverzin will be possible only if they are isolated from society. With regard to the aforementioned, pursuant to Articles 307, 308, 309 Code of Criminal Procedure, it is the judgement of this court:

'To find Vladimir Ivanovich Pereverzin guilty of committing crimes under Part 4 of Article 160 of the Penal Code and Part 4 of Article 174.1 and impose on him a custodial sentence as follows:

'For Part 4 of Article 160 of the Penal Code, six years' imprisonment.

'For Part 4 of Article 174.1 of the Penal Code, ten years and six months' imprisonment.

'The sentence for the totality of crimes committed by V. I. Pereverzin will hereby be eleven years' imprisonment in a strict-regime penal colony.'

Everything went dark before my eyes.

A soft murmur ran through the room.

For me, the world turned upside down. The sky fell to earth. My entire life flashed before my eyes.

I saw my childhood … school days … student years … my mouth went dry, my tongue stuck to the roof of it.

'Does the defendant understand the verdict?' the judge asked me.

'Yes,' I said, in a trembling voice. 'I do.'

We were led from the courtroom, and with an aching sadness I caught the astonished glances of my loved ones, full of tenderness and pity.

'What for? What for?' This answerless question was pounding in my head.

Some reporter in the corridor of the court managed to slip me a silly question: 'How would you like to comment on today's ruling? Do you agree with the decision of the court?'

'It is utter rubbish … lunacy!' I answered him as I was led away. 'We will appeal to the European Court of Human Rights'

The curtain had fallen! The show was over. I returned to the cell with an eleven-year sentence.

'The bastards gave me eleven years!' I informed my cellmates the moment I stepped through the door. One or two of them might have been delighted to land such a sentence. But for me it was out of the question. My mind refused to accept what was happening. I was reminded of a story about some guy who came back from the court, and his cellmates asked, 'What did you get?'

'Three years,' he tells them. And he gives them the verdict.

The men read it and see he's been given twelve years. They ask him, 'Are you quite sure about that? It says here, in black and white, twelve years!'

'No, that wasn't me,' he answers. 'My sentence was three years …'

You would simply refuse to trust your own ears; you were unable to take in what you'd seen. Only later did it sink in, when I felt the full weight of those years in the strict-regime penal colony. By that time, though, I'd been locked up for three years, which already felt like an eternity. Suddenly I sensed what a tiny portion of eleven years those three amounted to, and it dawned on me that eight whole years of imprisonment lay ahead of me! It seemed like a timeless sentence that would never end. The very thought was enough to oppress me. It would take me a very long time to come to terms with what was happening.

15

LAST HOPE

My cellmates thoughtfully offered me something to eat and a glass of tea. Realising I'd worked up a hunger, I dug in. I ate a couple of sandwiches, unable to taste them. My mind was in turmoil. I have often wondered whether the judge might have acted differently, if she could have found us not guilty or handed us shorter sentences. Had she acquitted us, it is clear she would have lost her job, and within her set of values, that would have been tantamount to death. But she could easily enough have given me, say, nine years, not eleven. And how could she have handed Malakhovsky twelve years – a year more than the prosecution had asked for! If she'd had a shred of conscience or human decency, we would have got lighter sentences. It is obvious the system washes every last drop of humanity out of people, or else it appoints people who were devoid of honour and conscience to start with.

I still had a slender hope through appealing to the Moscow City Court, which in popular parlance was justifiably known as the Moscow City Rubberstamp. The next morning, my lawyer arrived. He too was upset. Although he hadn't shared my illusions about an acquittal, he'd been expecting a shorter sentence. To buy time for preparing the full appeal, the day after the verdict he lodged a brief appeal against the sentence: 'We disagree with the verdict. We consider it legally invalid and unsound. We shall be lodging a full-scale appeal as soon as it is ready.'

We agreed on a clear plan of action, and my lawyer set to work on the appeal. As for me, I couldn't just stand idly by, so I pitched in by writing my own case for it. The verdict was replete with contradictions and inaccuracies; the court's findings did not match up with the evidence used in the trial. I performed a gargantuan task: I set out my arguments clearly and in detail, asking for the verdict to be overturned and for my acquittal. Then I sent my appeal to the Moscow City Court. Soon after, I received a copy of the appeal sent by my lawyer to the Moscow City Court. It was as clear as could be, perfectly simple and coherent; by law, the verdict simply had to be overturned. Unfortunately, though, the Yukos case was operating, as one prominent lawyer put it, outside 'the bounds of the law'. I'd reword this idea more simply: when facing the Yukos case, the law stood down.

Now I was waiting for the hearing at the Moscow City Court.

'What if they really did overturn the verdict? It's total hogwash!' These thoughts flashed through my mind. There was still hope, but the chances were slim. I knew that within ten days of the judgement coming into force, I'd be sent to the prison camp. The judgement would take effect once the Moscow City Court had heard the appeal.

The Moscow City Court was clearly in no hurry to consider our case, and they scheduled the hearing for mid-July. I began getting ready for the journey to the camp. According to the old hands, the prisoner transport was the most unpleasant and dangerous phase in the life of an inmate. I'd heard a lot about how the prisoners would be maltreated in all sorts of ways, how they'd be roughed up. 'What are they beaten for?' I asked my naive question. 'Just for the hell of it!' came the reply. One experienced guy advised me to take the minimum of things and not to eat or drink for twenty-four hours in advance.

'Why's that?' I asked, not following the reasoning behind this.

'It's so you won't need the bog!' my adviser said. 'They won't let you out to the toilet. Just in case, bring an empty plastic bottle and some plastic bags. And take ciggies, tea and dry food: biscuits, rusks, gingerbreads and sweets.'

I drank in every word. Later, I would remember this educator with gratitude.

Mentally, I'd already left the remand prison and was now at the camp. I was sick of the sight of the prison, where I'd been cooped up for around three years. There was no telling where I'd be taken, but I painted a pretty picture of some place under a cloudless sky. 'I'll get to the colony,' my reasoning went. 'The police will read my file, and, realising I'm innocent, they'll treat me differently. They'll offer me a nice job in the library or the school. And I will serve my sentence and live happily ever after.'

The prisoner transport scared me, while the prospect of moving somewhere new, swapping the prison for the camp, was actually rather exciting. I drew up an entire list of food and items needed for the journey and for my first spell in the camp. 'Nobody knows how we'll be travelling or how long it will take, so I'll need to stock up on food,' I thought. In the prison shop, I bought packs of cereal and cigarettes. The bag I'd set aside for supplies quickly filled up.

My summer flew by in a flurry of preparations, and finally I was taken to the Moscow City Court. The monumental building, the light-filled basements and spacious dungeons did not create the impression of a place that administered justice. It all felt routine and prosaic. Technological advances had made their mark here. They put us not in a cage but an aquarium. The thick bulletproof glass divided us from the courtroom. Malakhovsky cryptically told me that our verdict was going to be overturned. He'd been informed of this by the lawyers.

I wasn't so sure I believed it. Through the glass, some distance away, I saw people dear to me who were rooting for me and offering their support. It meant so much. Without them, I couldn't have survived.

The judges entered the room – two women and a man. From beneath the robes, their everyday plain grey clothes peeped out, garments that attracted no attention whatsoever. There was this unexceptional man walking along; were you to see him, he'd barely catch your eye, and you certainly wouldn't think this was someone who decided people's fates. One of the judges was carrying a shopping bag. It gave the impression these judges had popped in to the room between shopping trips or some other such business. Everything moved quickly and fleetingly. They had already examined our appeals and prepared their responses. 'White is not white, it's black. And black isn't even white, it's red,' the judges said in their three voices.

'Good Lord, this is utterly bonkers, it's a madhouse!' I made a desperate plea to God Almighty: 'Please, Lord, take me away from here, save me!'

'The arguments made by the defendants are without merit; the verdict is upheld,' they said.

I looked at the judges, experiencing no malice or hatred towards them. All I felt was a wave of disgust for those creatures. We returned to the prison, where I would spend my final ten days.

My lawyer arrived, and we compared notes. We now faced the challenge of scaling an entire pyramid of higher courts before we could vainly reach its summit – the chairman of the Supreme Court. Given the way colleagues cover up for each other in Russia, we realised that justice could not be achieved in my case. Our only hope was the European Court of Human Rights.

Rather than saying a final farewell, we parted for a time. Our fight would continue.

I went back to the cell, and a little later I heard, 'Surname P, get your belongings.'

'Can they really be sending me away so soon?' I thought. I gathered my things and said goodbye to my cellmates, embracing them. I was moved to an empty cell. My belongings had already been brought there from storage. There were warm winter clothes, my jacket and shoes. Several bags had accumulated. I began going through all my stuff, sorting the essentials from the nonessentials. I assembled the bags that I was taking on the journey. After countless rearrangements and difficult decisions, I was down to two holdalls and a large sports bag. 'The sports bag can go over my shoulder and I'll carry a holdall in each hand,' I imagined. I spent another two days alone in this cell, before being told on the third that this was the day I'd be leaving.

'Let me sit for a moment before the road.' I smiled wryly to myself. 'Let me sit for a quick eleven years behind bars!'

'Surname P, you ready?' I heard from behind the door.

'I'm ready,' I called back.

16

PRISONER TRANSPORT

The bolts clanked, the door flew open with a bang and I saw the unfamiliar faces of normal guards. No more Special Forces or other theatrics. 'So they've no further interest in me; I've outlived my usefulness,' I thought, much to my relief, and gladly quit the prison. It was only later, upon arrival at my destination – a strict-regime penal colony in the village of Melekhovo, Vladimir Region – that I'd appreciate how good things had been in there. After signing the paperwork, they handed me over to some armed escorts and we left the prison building. Out in the courtyard, a prisoner truck stood waiting.

I tossed my bag into the truck, then climbed in myself. I found a free cubicle. Behind the partition, there were women. Hearty laughter was trickling from their cells. I struck up a conversation with them. When they heard how long my sentence was, they gasped in sympathy. Perched on my cell bench, I tried in vain to catch a glimpse of the Moscow streets, which had already faded from memory. Barely a thing could be seen in the dim light, and the journey was soon over. I detected the smells of a railway station and could hear the sound of trains. I tried to guess which station we'd come to. Childhood memories came flooding back: journeying as a schoolboy by train each summer with my parents to the Crimea. I remember sitting glued to the window for hours on end, entranced by the scenery whirring past. Who could have thought back then that one day I'd face a trip like this?

We drove on to a far-away deserted platform, almost right up to the railway coach. I heard the guards discussing which prisoners to unload first. 'Let's start with the strict-regime one, then we'll do the others.' The 'strict-regime one' meant me. I grabbed my things and jumped down from the truck. They handed me over to my new escorts. The senior guard took my massive police file with a look of surprise and verified my details. I correctly reeled off my convictions and sentence. It was hardly as though some imposter would set out for eleven years in the colony in my place! I struggled to haul my luggage up onto the train. The bag got caught in the doors, making it hard to move, while the holdalls weighed me down. Squeezing my way through the narrow corridor, I reached the compartment. It was empty – a normal, standard-sized compartment without windows. Instead of a door, there was a grille. In the corridor was a small window, which, when open, offered a glimpse of freedom. Below were two sets of seating, with two pairs of bunks above them. Three levels in all. The prisoners called this type of coach a 'Stolypin'. Following Pyotr Stolypin's agrarian reforms, they used to transport peasants in cattle cars. And not much has changed since those days; we Russians have made scant progress.

A guard entered our coach.

'Where are we heading?' I asked.

'Hand in your prohibited items,' he said, meaning an inspection was coming.

'I don't have any,' I told him truthfully. 'I'm straight out of Special Detention Unit 99/1. You couldn't sneak a needle into one of those cells.'

The guard wouldn't take my word for it and began his search. He unfolded each paper wrap, opened each little box that I'd packed up so carefully in the prison cell. All my belongings were checked, every last scrap. It was all messed up and mixed about. I had a hard time stuffing it back into the bags. The compartment was filling up with passengers. I could hear a search being conducted in the neighbouring coach. Fellow travellers were joining me – first one, then another. I moved my things over. A third came in, and a fourth. The compartment would soon be crammed with bags and people. A fifth man came in, a sixth, a seventh. People climbed up and settled on the upper berths. On the lower seats, five men sat squashed tight. The empty spaces between and below the berths were wedged with holdalls. Finally, eighteen of us were packed into the compartment; it was extraordinarily cramped and stuffy. The rules were that the guards could not open the windows until the train was moving. And they could only let us out to the toilet once we were on the move. It was late July, and the heat outside was merciless.

The usual conversation filled the compartment: who we were, where we came from, what we were in for, the sentences we'd got. I heard their different stories, discovered acquaintances we had in common – people I'd already shared cells with. We boarded the train around 9 p.m. The train began moving at seven the next morning. The guard gave in to the prisoners' relentless demands and broke the rules: he opened the window a little. I saw the far-away platform, some passengers waiting for a commuter train, people heading for their dachas, weighed down with young plants. 'Hey, chief,' someone yelled in the next compartment. 'Take me to the lav, I'm dying!'

'It's against regulations,' said the warrant officer. 'Once we get moving, you can go.'

'Wouldn't mind giving the bastard who wrote the regulations a taste of his own medicine,' I thought angrily, but then, once again, I gratefully remembered my mentor consultant. For twenty-four hours, I hadn't eaten a thing and had drunk barely a sip. While I couldn't claim to feel well or comfortable, at least I had no urge to answer the call of nature. My excess fluids were sweating out copiously, and most of the time I sat silent, just listening and toughing it out. Of the eighteen men, I was the only one who didn't smoke.

Our coach crept tardily along, making plenty of stops. It was tracing its route, coupled to one train after another. We were travelling to Vladimir, an almost twenty-four-hour journey. I was all clammy with sweat, steeped in cigarette smoke, driven crazy from the stench and the small talk. My body had gone numb from the hours of sitting in one position. It was utter torture, which I would look back on in horror. In the coach, I met Andrei K., sentenced to nineteen years for racketeering and murder. I had already shared a cell with his accomplice, Dima. Both of them were Masters of Sports in boxing who had worked in a private security firm for a certain businessman, handling his problems. By confessing to their crimes and giving testimony against their boss, they'd got off with the lightest possible sentences.

We were approaching the city of Vladimir. At one point, before Yukos, I'd worked for a company with a branch there. The branch director had invited me to visit, but I'd never got around to going. 'Well, I'm on my way at last,' I thought grimly.

We arrived. Our coach was uncoupled from the train and shunted out to the far platform.

The guard bawled his instructions to the prisoners: 'Come out one by one, in a duck walk; only move when given the command. No lifting your heads, eyes down. It's shoot on sight.' Things were serious. These were real assault rifles, with live rounds, safety catches off. To the sound of barking dogs, I jumped from the train with my bags and squatted down. We had to negotiate half a kilometre along the railway tracks before we got to the prisoner truck. Out of the corner of my eye, I saw people in the distance blithely scuttling along the platform.

'On the command, go! Start moving,' the guard hollered. I could barely haul my load and cursed myself for bringing so many provisions.

Bang! My heart felt as though it would stop. It was the strap on my holdall snapping under the load, with a sound like a gunshot. It fell from my shoulder and got left behind. I carried on moving. 'To hell with the bag. The thing is to stay alive!' I thought with a tremble.

'Stop!' the officer ordered. 'Go back and get the bag.' It didn't immediately sink in that he was talking to me.

'Help him,' he said to another prisoner who was carrying a small bag.

We grabbed hold of my things and headed for the prisoner vehicle.

With difficulty, sweating all over, I made it to the truck, where I thanked my saviour for lugging my holdall. The realisation dawned on me: 'I have to dump some of this stuff urgently! The second time round will kill me. I'll die of a heart attack!'

My saviour, Valera, turned out to be a hard-boiled recidivist. At the age of thirty-five, this was his ninth conviction. He had done a good many stints behind bars, but none of them long. He was a thief – a pickpocket – and drug addict who suffered from epilepsy. A crafty rascal if ever there was one. We ended up in the same camp. I had to repay him for the bag many times over, until my patience finally snapped and I told him where to go.

The truck took us to Vladimir transit prison No. 1, known to the prisoners as Copeck. This old brick building with its beautiful giant arches, built 180 years ago, had absorbed all the human vices over the period of its existence, as well as pain, grief and suffering. I could sense the sinister breath of the prison.

We were taken to the basement for processing – to a cell with some benches, a slop-pail toilet and a dirty basin. It smelt of mould and damp. Dog-tired, we sat down and waited for further developments. Availing myself of the lull, I set to work lightening my bags. I pulled out a bottle of water and a packet of biscuits, which I shared out with my fellow unfortunates.

'Cell Number One, answer me,' came a sudden voice from inside the toilet. I shook my head, wondering whether I'd lost my mind. The water closet makes an excellent communication device. The ingenious prisoners managed to lay down 'wiring' – stretching out cords made from woven threads – and they delivered the prison post from cell to cell along the waste pipes.

Then we had another inspection, the third in twenty-four hours. They turned our things inside out, muddled up the contents of the bags. One by one, we were searched and taken to another processing point. Soon we were all back together in the same cell. We were ready for whatever came next. They did not leave us waiting for long. We were issued mattresses and sheets, and suddenly they led us all down some serpentine corridors. Along the way, in the corridor, we ran into some guards with a huge Alsatian, who seemed to look at me with his kind eyes and wink. We reached the second floor and walked towards cell No. 39. The door was opened; together we entered the cell, and I saw a ghastly picture that had almost slipped from memory. The overcrowded space, the hazy smoke, the revolting stench, the lines of laundry. The floor was covered in tarmac and littered with countless cigarette butts. To the right of the entrance hung a sad little curtain made from a grubby sheet, notionally closing off the toilet from the cell. In front of the curtain, several prisoners were moping as they waited their turn. Nearby, right at their feet, a man was sleeping on a mattress laid on the filthy floor. 'He's the corner guy,' I realised.[8] Otherwise known as a shunned prisoner,

---

8   The inmates treated as untouchables are made to sleep by the toilets in Russian prisons.

an untouchable. It's an entire caste of prisoners, further divided into sub-castes, condemned to perform the most undignified tasks. Cleaning the toilets, for example. You mustn't shake their hands, eat from the same plate, sit at the same table; it's as though they had the plague. The prisoners follow these rules implicitly, because there is no worse punishment than joining the ranks of the untouchables. No wonder the prison community itself punishes inmates harshly for certain transgressions, boxing them into the corner. That is the fate awaiting nearly all the paedophiles who land behind bars.

My attention was caught by the ceiling of the cell, towering almost 5 metres tall and dotted with iron patches. That was how the prison management fixed the holes in the ceiling that the inmates bored for their telegraph system.

I quickly picked out the criminal heavyweights. They were in a corner carpeted with an old blanket and curtained off with sheets. Shirtless guys adorned with tattoos and engrossed in a card game.

We went over and sat at the table, introduced ourselves to the man running the cell. Some *chifir* was brewed. A letter of enquiry went out, detailing the names of the new arrivals, the offences they were convicted for and the remand prisons they'd come from. The letter would pass through all the prison cells, and if someone had unfinished business with you, then you could be fined, beaten up or kicked out of the cell.

To accompany the *chifir*, I took some chocolate and cigarettes from my bag and treated my new cellmates handsomely. I put a carton of Marlborough into the communal box that stood on the table. These guys hadn't smoked a filtered cigarette in a long time, and they drew closer to the table and quickly helped themselves. I was happy to be rid of those unwanted cigarettes and their excess weight. The men took delight in each cigarette smoked. Despite the horrendous amount of *chifir* I'd drunk, I was overcome with tiredness and felt myself falling asleep. The head inmate picked a bunk for me to have to myself, where I could rest to my heart's content. I reached it, and the moment I closed my eyes, I was out like a light. Neither the sound of the television nor the chatter of my cellmates could disturb me.

My sleep was deep and pleasurable. I was woken by a tickling sensation. I could feel something tickling my face. It all came flooding back: the events of the last few days, where I was now. A cockroach was crawling across my face, and I woke up properly. I felt hungry. I got up, had a wash, boiled some water and made myself porridge. My wits and strength came back to me and my mood lifted. Valera showed up, as he always did whenever I took something out of my bag. I treated him to porridge and sweets and gave him a cigarette. Satisfied, he cleared off for a while. I tried in vain to find a packet of green tea among my belongings that had been all mixed and muddled during the search, hoping to share it with Misha, a cultured-looking Muscovite. Seeing my fruitless attempts, he smiled and said, 'It's okay, don't worry! You'll find it when they carry out the next search!'

I began finding my feet and settling in. I found out that twice a week they took prisoners from this cell to the camps. On Mondays they sent them to Vyazniki, on Wednesdays to Melekhovo. The prisoners here knew everything. The strict regime in Vyazniki was more relaxed than the one in Melekhovo, where the prisoners were in for a nasty time. I acquired a friend, Hare, who was one of the cell leader's circle. He was from Vladimir, and he thoughtfully offered to sort matters out to ensure I'd be sent to the Vyazniki camp. All I needed to do was pay $5,000 to his friend at the Vladimir Regional Federal Penitentiary Service. I could see it was a scam, and told him I wasn't bothered where I ended up. He had a mobile phone in his hand, and I couldn't resist asking if I could make a call.

Hare told me of their kitty and asked me to contribute as much as I could afford so they could put credit on the phone. I agreed to. He handed me the mobile. My donation to the kitty would buy the men no tea or cigarettes, just a plain old drugs orgy for the heavies with a habit. For the first time in my life, I saw junkies zoning out – actually falling asleep while on their feet.

It was a long time since I'd last held a phone, and I made several calls to people whose voices I hadn't heard in ages. After talking, I wiped their numbers from the phone. Then I called my wife and forgot to remove the number. This would all end in a whole heap of frazzled nerves and money paid to the lawyer. Before I had even had time to leave the four walls of the cell on transit to the camp, my wife would get a call from some unknown man. I expect it was Hare. In an agitated voice, he told her that the pigs had locked up Vladimir – meaning me – in solitary, and were beating and torturing him.

'We need money urgently to buy him out of there!' he told her.

He asked for the relatively small sum of 10,000 roubles.[9] I can imagine my wife's state as she heard the story! The lawyer had to go to enormous lengths to find me – safe and sound – in the strict-regime penal colony at Melekhovo village and allay my family's fears.

Monday came. They were sending prisoners to Vyazniki. The guard reeled off a list of names. Mine was not among them. 'So, I'll be going to Melekhovo on Wednesday.' I took in this news with a feeling of doom. The strict-regime colony in the village of Melekhovo was notorious among the prisoners. It was a 'red' camp, controlled by the prison management, where they broke prisoners and forced them to sign all kinds of papers. But at the time, I had no idea what all the fuss was about, and meekly awaited my fate.

Wednesday came. I heard my name called out among some others. There were a dozen of us. Valera was in our group, as was Kostya, who had been hanging around the heavyweight criminals. We took our bags and left the cell. There was a search again. I opened my bags, which were now noticeably lighter, and laid out my things for inspection. The guard grudgingly went through my belongings, squeezing a few plastic bags between his fingers, before letting me put them back.

---

9   Around £200 at the time.

In the prison courtyard, a prisoner truck was waiting; it took us to the railway station. The vehicle drove right up to the train coach and we somehow scrambled aboard. Inside the Stolypin-style cattle car, another search awaited us. We handed in our shaving equipment, which we'd get back once we arrived. The train began moving, and we headed to the city of Kovrov. Strictly one at a time, the guard led us to separate compartments, where they checked the contents of our bags. Kovrov is 100 kilometres from Vladimir, and the guards didn't have time to search all the prisoners before we reached the station, where a prisoner truck stood waiting.

They handed out our personal files. I recognised mine straight away. The three-volume dossier was stuffed in a huge paper envelope marked with my details and photo. What it contained remains a mystery to this day. I called out my name, sentence and convictions and climbed into the truck. The journey lasted what felt like forty minutes or so. I heard the gates creaking open and some dogs barking. We drove through. The prison camp welcomed us in its tight embrace. My new reality now sank in. To the barking of dogs and the yelling of guards, we jumped out of the truck. 'At the double,' I heard the guards shouting shrilly. 'Faster, faster.' There was no dragging your feet. I heard the whack of a rubber baton landing with a whistle on someone behind me; I heard the shriek of the poor fellow, who'd dawdled for just a second. We were made to squat down and embrace our bags. We had to keep our eyes down. If you raised your head just a little, you'd be struck with a baton.

17

WELCOME TO MELEKHOVO

I was in luck. We were received gently. The party that had arrived before us had been given a good drubbing. The prisoners who came after us the following Wednesday got a pasting too. While washing in the showers, I personally saw the smashed heads, bruises and marks on the bodies of the convicts. Each group would get a different reception. Some were beaten less, some more. Some weren't beaten at all. It all depended on the mood of the guards. They could overdo it and maim a prisoner, which happened regularly. It would be written up as an accident: 'The prisoner tripped over and hit his head.' Not a single complaint could leave the colony unless you were visited by relatives or a lawyer.

'When you get the command, take your things, on your feet and double march!' the officer yelled.

Out of the corner of my eye, I saw a beautiful wooden church, just a few metres away from us. A naive fellow might easily think it was all happening with God's blessing.

We grabbed our bags and ran into some courtyard. Then we piled all our bags into a heap and formed a line. I was third in the row. A burly man in fatigues, wearing the single star of a major on his shoulders and holding a broom, said curtly, 'Now each of you must pick up the broom and make a few sweeping movements.' Nearby, his colleagues stood wielding their batons menacingly along with several prisoners, who, as I later learnt, enjoyed the special confidence of the camp management and helped with the reception for newcomers. The last thing I wanted was to pick up a broom. But it was some kind of ritual. Kostya was the first to come forward from the line, and he began sweeping with vigour. Next was Valera, who made a few limp movements. The blow of a baton across his back made him more lively. Then it was my turn. Unwillingly, gritting my teeth, I picked up the broom and began sweeping. 'That's enough,' came a voice from behind me. I stopped and handed the broom to the next man.

Nobody from our group refused to sweep. The prisoners were well schooled in these high-pressure methods. If you refused, they'd beat you there and then in the courtyard, without compunction, right in front of the other prisoners. And if, after that, you still wouldn't sweep, you'd be taken to the office and roughed up some more. If that didn't break you, they'd bring you an untouchable prisoner and tell you to choose: either become an untouchable like this man, right now, following a certain penetrative procedure, and join the untouchables' corner, or go ahead and pick up the broom. Everybody chooses the broom. As far as the prison management were concerned, the convicts were not human beings. So they viewed any attempts by the prisoners to assert their rights with extreme negativity and irritation.

Until a few years ago, prisoners following the thieves' code would refuse to let any convicts joining the transit prison from Melekhovo into their cells. They would say, 'You have no place among us,' throwing the poor prisoners out of the cells and forcing them to use the cells for the 'red' convicts – the prisoner-orderlies, caretakers and other suspect types.

Downhearted, we took our bags and went into the building. This was the main office. We were led into a large room, where a massive search began that seemed more like a robbery. I saw two hefty prisoners swaggering about the office with some sheets of paper. They were walking up to each new arrival and 'asking' him to sign a form. Everyone signed it blind, without even checking what they were signing. While some warrant officer was rummaging through my things, the same couple came up to me and put a sheet and a pen in my hands. They were inmate-orderlies working in the quarantine area. The lowest of the low, out-and-out bastards and swine. Thugs willing to do anything at all in return for the right inducement from the authorities. The right cheek of one of them was adorned with a scar – from ear to chin. 'Now, that's a son-of-a-bitch scar,' an old-hand prisoner would tell me later. 'It marks him out for all to see, so everyone will know he's a son of a bitch.'

I studied the writing on the paper, trying to catch the drift.

'Come on, just print your name and sign it; he reckons he needs to read the damn thing!' the orderlies grumbled in unison, trying to hurry me along. I saw the words: 'Pledge: I, so-and-so, do voluntarily renounce the thieves' code and the traditions of the thieves' world, undertaking to adhere to the prison rules and to comply with the demands of the prison authorities.'

'What the hell is this lunacy?' I signed the paper in amazement. The two men walked off satisfied.

I stared in pity at my belongings all strewn about. Anything not on the permitted list was to be confiscated. The guard stumbled upon a small bag of medicines and wanted to take it away. I desperately protested and managed to save some of the pills. Each little packet was pored over and meticulously checked, each notebook was leafed through. My luggage shrank by one holdall. All the confiscated items were sent to a storeroom for personal belongings. My head was shaved in a buzz cut, and I got a new uniform. I put on a frightful cap with a white stripe, a cotton suit, or some kind of outfit, decorated with the same white stripes, and I tried on the black shoes with cardboard insoles. Looking in the mirror, I scarcely recognised myself in my new guise. Now I was a proper convict in my own right – that is to say, without any rights.

A new stage of my life was beginning, and I needed to survive it.

Sheared and re-clothed, we walked in single file into the quarantine block. We were led in by prisoners unlawfully authorised by the prison management – whatever it takes to lighten the workload! – to oversee us. How exactly the head of the unit – a captain by rank – filled his time was a complete mystery. I often caught sight of him going into his office, which was in the adaptation block. He never deigned to talk with any of us. That honour was reserved only for the inmate-orderlies, who doubled up as his flunkies. One of the strategic objectives of the orderlies was providing the unabashed captain with a continuous supply of tea, sweets, chocolate and other confections, with which he entertained the heads of the other units at his morning tea gatherings. 'What do I do? I have to come up with the goods!' one of the orderlies shared his troubles, racking his brains over where to get comestibles for the head of the unit. As it happens, this is a common practice in Russia's penal colonies. I came across it many a time, and was surprised to find that the officers in some colonies are not averse to scoffing food stolen more or less straight off the inmates' tables.

We went into the small quarantine block, which was enclosed by a solid concrete wall. There was a small courtyard and a sleeping block, where a number of orderlies lived. I soon understood why Muscovites were so out of favour, and I too began hating certain representatives of that city where I myself was born and raised. All the inmate-orderlies, as if specially chosen, hailed from Moscow.

Sasha Utyugov, nicknamed 'Iron', was a former aerospace-defence officer in the strategic rocket forces now doing time for peddling drugs. He'd found himself a haven here and was serving the last few months of his short sentence.

The inmate-orderlies, as a general rule, were made up of people riddled with insecurities or burning with ambition, ready to do anything for an extra crust. In normal life, on the outside, they would more often than not be complete nobodies. But in this place, given a taste of power over people with the help of the prison authorities, they revealed themselves in all their hideous glory.

On the outside, Nazar – or Sasha Nazarov – lived very close to my own home, near Kakhovskaya metro. Looking at his pint-sized clothes, I dubbed him the 'little fellow from the toy shop'. Less than 1 metre 60 tall, with a great big colourful dragon that didn't quite fit across his back and had crept around the front of his skinny little body, he was a seasoned prisoner, doing time for grievous bodily harm and theft. Having got the post of orderly in the camp, and the chance to maintain order into the bargain, he himself became a dragon and 'found his wings' by plotting all sorts of intrigues and nasty tricks against the other convicts.

The senior inmate-orderly, or caretaker, for the quarantine block was given a room of his own. By law, people could only be kept in the quarantine block for up to two weeks. To bypass this limit, the prison management came up with the ploy of creating the 'adaptation block'. In reality, it was no different from the quarantine block. Among themselves, the inmates even called them upper and lower quarantine.

We were taken to upper quarantine. Nazar told us about the customs and mores in this camp. He filled us in on the daily routine and the correctional sessions. The inmates rose at half past five in the morning, followed by exercise, then breakfast. They had to do three correctional sessions per day. This re-education took the form of drill practice. The marching lasted sixty to ninety minutes, and was marked by a special attention to detail. I always wondered at the zeal shown by that inmate – who was essentially still a convict just like us. He would tirelessly monitor how we lifted our legs, watching that we all marched in sync, staying in step. You'd think it was a matter of marching back and forth a bit, passing the main office for appearance's sake – and then back to the barracks. But no! We rehearsed for hours, marching to his drill commands, freezing on the spot, our legs poised in the air. Vitaly, as our marching-specialist orderly was called, seemed to derive untold pleasure from the process. Whatever was he experiencing, what feelings flowed through him as he led this throng of prisoners, twirling his chain?

'Ri-ight turn. Le-eft turn. Halt! Left, right. Ab-out turn!'

A native of the Moscow satellite town of Lyubertsy, Vitaly was around twenty years old. He was a diehard skinhead, and was doing time for grievous bodily harm. Empty-headed and uneducated, Vitaly was incredibly full of himself. 'For-ward, march!' he ordered, and the flock obeyed. Confident in his own superiority, he loved to make fun of certain inmates, lobbing long streams of cuss words. It was from him I first heard the expression 'tree climber', which had a wholly negative sense, denoting someone mentally retarded in the extreme.

135

'Once I'm out of this place, I swear I'll hunt down and kill the fucker!' I often heard such threats muttered not only at Vitaly and Nazar, but also at other orderlies. They were issued by men who were not there merely for theft or armed robbery …

An avenue stretched out from the main gates, sloping gently down through the entire camp. The tall birches were a joy to behold. After being locked in a closed space for nearly three years, what a thrill to look at each tree, to see the sky and the sun. Just stepping on the ground was a whole new experience. Flanking the avenue was a church, the main office, the barracks, the social club and the various zones of the camp. As we walked the length of the path, we came up against the checkpoint and the iron gates of the industrial zone. The grounds of the accommodation zone also had a small industrial area made up of a few sewing workshops.

'Rea-dy, halt. Left, right!' Vitaly shouted. 'Ab-out turn. For-ward march!'

A terrible 'Boom!' rang out, the earth trembling under our feet. The rumbling echo of the blast lingered in our ears. Not far from the camp was a dolomite quarry. The colony itself was built in the fifties by German prisoners of war and lay in a hollow formed by long years of ore mining.

We turned around and walked back, climbing a hill until we ran up against the barrier before the first set of gates, which bared its huge toothy spikes at us. If it entered anyone's head to ram the gate, he'd impale himself on this barrier. We covered this distance hundreds of times a day. Back and forth we'd march, up and down the hill. I managed to force myself to enjoy this strange activity, which was not only pointless, but also plainly bad for you. I imagined it as some kind of fitness routine, and began performing the task in earnest. Deprived of an active lifestyle, I had piled on the flab. I soon began shedding the pounds.

It was August 2007. We were sweating like pigs and reached the quarantine grounds drenched from head to toe. Washing was forbidden, as there was no provision for it in the daily routine approved by the head of the camp. Ablutions were strictly timetabled, with a ten-minute slot each morning and evening. But even in the evenings, it wasn't enough time. Two washbasins for twenty inmates meant barely a minute each at the sink. The orderlies had the unimaginable luxury of entering the barracks whenever they wanted, and they strictly enforced the daily routine. As for us rank-and-file convicts, in our time off from marching, cleaning, loading and unloading, we just had to stand about or walk to the little courtyard enclosed by the concrete wall. There was no place to sit and nothing to sit on. 'You're already sitting – behind bars!' quipped one orderly. We could squat, though. In another camp where I'd find myself in similar conditions, squatting was strictly forbidden, as it was deemed a custom of the criminal underworld, a cultural habit of the thieves.

Under the scorching sun, our sweat dried quickly, leaving salty white patches on our black outfits. Grubby and stinky, but fully compliant with the daily routine, we were taken once a week to the showers. I remember what was stated in the Penitentiary Code, which they had evidently not studied themselves: 'The convicts must observe the sanitary norms and rules followed in society.'

'It could be they haven't read it, or maybe they just move in circles with somewhat different norms,' I figured, taking it philosophically.

Once in the shower, we got thirty minutes. There was one shower head per five or six men. You had to wash yourself and launder your things in that time. Many men would go into the shower in their clothes and soap themselves over, getting two jobs done at once. Then your 'laundry' was left in a special drying room to be collected by the orderly and put in a sack. The jumble of poorly cleaned, sometimes merely wettened things would be tipped out on the desks in the re-educational-work room. We spent a long time picking our items from the pile, sifting through other men's underwear. I began to adapt to the local conditions. The next time we washed our things, I tied my socks and pants together, attaching my T-shirt to them, and soon found my 'snake' in the pile.

At night, sleep was impossible, and a terrible stench hung in the barracks. We waited for the heat to die down. You'd always feel uncomfortable. It was never pleasant; it would either be too hot or too cold. We were deprived of sleep, food, rest and comfort.

Each morning began with exercise. We barely had time to open our eyes before we rushed outdoors. The whole camp took part in the workout. The convicts poured out of their barracks in the various zones and exercised to music. 'Wave your arms,' we'd hear from the speaker. 'One, two, three, four. That's enough. Now let's do some squats.' The workout was accompanied by classical music. We did the exercises several times until we achieved perfect synchronicity. They replayed the recording specially for the quarantine block. After the workout, we made our beds and performed our ablutions. We didn't have long to brush our teeth and splash our faces. Then we went out into the courtyard and waited. We heard the simultaneous stomp of hundreds of feet, and a voice calling: 'Halt. Left, right.' They had come for us. The convicts from lower quarantine waited as we joined their ranks. We lined up and began marching on the spot. I slipped a quick question to the man next to me: 'What's it like in lower quarantine?'

'A bit easier,' he said.

'Forward, march!' Vitaly bellowed, and the formation began moving. We were taught how to address the colony's staff. When greeted by any officer in the camp, we had to give a loud and lively response.

'Hello, Citizen Convicts!' Vitaly bawled at us.

'Good morning, Citizen Chief!' we yelled back at full force.

Our teacher shared the finer points with us. 'You've got to take a deep breath, then roar out your greeting with all your puff.'

While rehearsing, we had to shout this phrase over and over. To make it worse, almost every guard we passed would relish the opportunity to say hello.

The first marching session was followed by breakfast. Still in lines, we trooped into the dining room. I had my spoon ready and waiting in my pocket. I wouldn't need to make a dash for the cupboard where we kept the bare essentials: a mug, spoon, toiletries and, for those who had it, tea. Not every inmate had a spoon, and some had to take turns eating with a shared spoon.

I had no appetite, but I swallowed down a breakfast of cooked cereal, a slice of bread and a glass of some sweetened liquid that dimly resembled tea. Our time for breakfast was severely restricted. We barely had time to sit down before the orderly gave the command: 'Stand up, the meal's over.' If you got up early, before receiving the order, that was a blunder – a violation. You'd be deprived of tea or 'rewarded' with extra marching. We were flatly forbidden to talk with the convicts from other units, who were eyeing us curiously, seeking out familiar faces. Eighty per cent of the camp was made up of men from Vladimir Region, who were looking for locals, neighbours or former classmates – and not without success. One of our group dared take a pack of cigarettes from another convict. News of this 'misdemeanour' reached the orderly, and the inevitable penalty followed swiftly. That day we marched ourselves silly and lost the tea that we were sometimes allowed to drink after drill.

We walked back to the quarantine block. You had ninety minutes or a couple of hours to wait before the next drill, during which time you had to stand in the courtyard – if no other tasks were found for you. The convicts were a free labour force – put simply, slaves. We were often led off to do a range of jobs. Loading things and hauling them from place to place was our holy cause! Unloading cement, planks and boxes from the sewing workshop became second nature to us.

'Under Article 106 of the Penitentiary Code, each convict is obliged to work on penal-colony estate maintenance for a minimum of several hours per week.' This article from the Penitentiary Code setting down the prisoners' obligations was read out to us. It slipped the minds of the inmate-orderlies and the camp staff that we convicts were also granted rights in that same code.

'Food is to be consumed in the designated areas, at the prescribed time! See, being allowed to drink tea outside the dining room is a great privilege bestowed on you by the leaders of the colony,' an orderly told us, bringing out a kettle of boiling water. The hot water quickly disappeared into the mugs. There was not enough to go round, and not everyone was in possession of tea. Most of the prisoners were hooked on *chifir*. This ultra-strong tea brings the body back to a normal state. I watched the prisoners who'd missed out on hot water chewing their black tea leaves and swallowing them down with water from the tap. Tobacco was running low. The guys finished their last cigarettes, dragging one out among several men. Things were so much easier for me. I didn't smoke and I could go without tea. Seeing the guys suffering, I told them I was willing to offer all the cigarettes in my bag and share out my tea. What might seem a simple task, though, was not easy to pull off. Our bags were held in the storeroom in a separate block, beyond the confines of the quarantine area. We were allowed access twice a week at set times, on Tuesdays and Thursdays. It was Wednesday. The orderly promised to take me there the next day.

A short, stocky Chechen was walking in the courtyard. He was an aloof guy who barely spoke with anyone, and he'd been in quarantine for several months. I could see from his broken ears that he was a fighter, meaning we'd have something to talk about. We made our introductions. Aslan was a member of the Russian national freestyle wrestling team, an international-level

Master of Sports, a European champion and a silver medallist in the world championship, who had been convicted of terrorism under Article 205 of the Penal Code. He was sentenced to twenty-three years. One of his numerous relatives from Chechnya had stayed overnight at his flat in Moscow and played some kind of role in blowing up a car outside a McDonald's. Aslan was arrested too. Later, the police officers who'd detained Aslan were themselves taken into custody. It turned out they were bent cops. Now the entire cast were behind bars. 'Why on earth did I bother representing Russia?' he once rued.

Misha K. was walking near us. He was a towering figure, heavy-set, and put away for the same article as Aslan: terrorism. He'd landed a nineteen-year sentence. Misha was convicted for attacking a Grozny–Moscow passenger train. The train had been derailed by explosives on the line. The site chosen for the attack was distinctly odd. The way it had been carried out suggested the terrorists had been keen to minimise the damage. The trains always slowed down as they were approaching that spot. The perpetrators had been thoughtful enough to place the bomb under the right-hand rail, meaning rather than being thrown off the rails, the train would remain on the embankment. Misha's friend had a dacha not far from there. According to the investigation, these adult men decided to have some fun and games. Misha allegedly rode to the scene of the crime on his friend's daughter's little bike to detonate the device. Misha and his lawyers requested a crime reconstruction to see how he could have squeezed onto the bicycle given his size, but the judge turned their petition down. The jury acquitted Misha, but their verdict was overturned and a retrial ordered. By the time of the second trial, the cycle, which had been produced as evidence in the original case, had gone missing. The moment it became clear that the child's bike was proof of innocence, the exhibit mysteriously vanished.

With his history of combat, Misha made the ideal scapegoat. A smart and educated alumnus of the Moscow Institute of Steel and Alloys, he had tried his hand at many professions. He'd been a journalist and a photographer. He'd written a book, *Russian Volunteers in Serbia*. He had fought there himself and been wounded. Misha was interesting company, well-versed in history, with a lively mind and a phenomenal memory. He lived in his own world. I found him a kindred spirit, and took refuge from reality with him. Being a forthright guy and not in the habit of fitting in with others, he was having a particularly tough time inside. We became friends.

Soon, the first week was over. A new party of convicts brought two fresh faces to our quarantine block. We already knew that a large party was arriving the following Wednesday, and we would all be transferred to lower quarantine, known on paper as the adaptation unit. And how we longed for that moment, while continuing to hone our skills in drill. Whenever anyone in the line started falling out of step, the entire column would falter. There was a young guy called Sasha, convicted of murder, who picked up the nickname 'Troyar'. We called him that in honour of the drink he'd guzzled on the outside: a bathtub cleanser branded Troyar with an alcohol content of up to seventy per cent. The systematic consumption of this cocktail has irreversible consequences. Aside from the obvious impact on the drinker's mental faculties, it causes impaired motor co-ordination. Sasha just could not learn to walk in step, and because of him, the whole column would mess up. After much anguish and discussion with the orderly, usually ending in an act of petty violence, he'd be sent to the last rank. Unable to hold back, I went up to Vitaly and asked him to leave the sickly lad alone. My request went unheeded. Clearly, Vitaly was fully focused on realising the dream embedded deep in his skinhead brain: to mock the weak with impunity.

The orderly broke into my conversation with Misha K. and called me into the quarantine building. A local star wanted to have a chat with me – Kirill Sayenkov, the caretaker of the quarantine block. He had his own luxury suite. I went into his little room with a television and DVD player. I saw a table and a small cabinet with a photo of his son. By local standards, Kirill was quite a bigwig. He was the only prisoner in the colony allowed to walk around the camp in trainers. According to the orderlies, he'd won that right as a reward for some deed or other – and from none other than the camp's deputy head of security. Kirill was a specially entrusted face (or rather, as I thought to myself, some other body part) for the prison management. He would always personally get involved in the reception of new arrivals and join in the beatings.

Oh, the yarns he spun about himself! I sat and bit my lip to keep myself from laughing in his face. He lied like a dog. 'I'm a captain in military intelligence! I graduated from the Main Intelligence Directorate Special-Forces Institute! I'm a Master of Sports in boxing! I'm a this, I'm a that …' He broke off and nobly offered me a glass of tea and some chocolate. Unable to say no, I accepted his offer and barely managed to nod my head and sip on my tea before he was at it again. He had never heard of the Yukos case, but offered to set me up with a good role, promising me a quiet life in the camp. I didn't believe a word he said and turned him down. The audience was over. The orderlies were frightened to death of Kirill and they bent over backwards to please him, while counting the days to his release. Nazar once took me to fetch some cigarettes and, studying the contents of my bag, he began trying to scrounge my tracksuit and trainers for Kirill. My refusal drove him to thinly disguised anger, which he later took out on me many times.

When the new convicts arrived, the eagle-eyed orderlies would spot who was wearing what, and they'd beg, barter and wheedle to get their hands on the civilian clothing held in storage outside the camp. Many would go along with this. My own confiscated clothes did not catch anyone's eye, and they were returned to me when I left the colony. The orderlies were collecting things for Kirill's release. Kirill thought it was the height of cool to walk to freedom in civilian clothes. He had a few months to go before his release.

Tuesday came, and I was transferred to lower quarantine. Aslan and Misha were staying behind. We did not say our goodbyes. We knew we'd still see each other on our daily marches. For more than a year, we would stay in the same unit.

Happily, we dragged our bags to our new residence. I knew for a fact that things could not get any worse. My expectations proved correct. The two-storey building of the adaptation unit held a number of prisoner dormitories, an office for the head of the unit, a toilet with a basin, a dining area with a fridge, and a re-educational-work room, which had a television. In some small ways, life became easier. You had a bedside table where you could keep a minimum of things, and the rest could be stored in your bags. Those bags were kept right here in the building, in a special room that could be accessed without too much trouble.

Each bag had a tag with the owner's details and an inventory of the contents. Each bed had a tag with a photo, surname, criminal conviction and sentence. Each convict had a tag with a photo and surname. There were a huge number of us crammed into the barracks. The beds were packed tight, with the spaces between them so narrow that I could not even squeeze through sideways and had to climb on to the bed from its end. At wake-up call, a genuine crush would begin. We had limited time to make our beds; everyone would jostle and rush. I did not even bother trying to get to the sink in the mornings. But I did manage to reach it almost every night. We were banned from entering the dormitory during the day. In the morning, I'd shove some soap, toothbrush, toothpaste and loo paper in my pockets, as well as a couple of tea bags. All day long, I'd carry my precious load, and come evening, at the bedtime command, as all the prisoners ran to the sleeping area for their toiletries, I'd make a dash for the sink. Sometimes I managed to wash my feet and launder my socks. What saved me were the wet wipes I'd had the foresight to bring from the prison. Lying in bed before going to sleep, I swabbed myself down with the utmost pleasure, scrimping on each wipe.

I'd barely been two days in the adaptation unit when I was called to see my lawyer. The orderly asked in amazement, 'Why's there a lawyer visiting you? How much does that cost? What salary were you on?' We weren't able to move around the camp alone, and so Nazar and I headed for the main office. Before being led to the room for the visit, I was searched. I emptied out the entire contents of my pockets. Toilet paper, soap, tea, a toothbrush, a spoon, toothpaste, some tissues and a handkerchief appeared on the table. The orderly's jaw dropped open, and he asked in bewilderment, 'Why have you got all this stuff?'

'What do you mean, "Why"?' I repeated his question, and imagined how it must look to an outsider. Stifling my laughter, I answered in earnest: 'I use it all.' The sheer idiocy of it all was beginning to give me the giggles.

The lawyer had come to visit just to be safe, so he could see for himself I was alive and well and all was in order. Glad to be missing the marching session, I chatted pleasantly with him on irrelevant matters and played for time. Our meeting ended. I carefully put my things back in my pockets and returned to the unit, accompanied by Nazar.

Tired from their marching, the men ambled about the local zone. In the barracks, you could go to relieve yourself only with the permission of the orderly and strictly one by one. Thus artificially creating a queue. Someone told me that in one of the camps, they gave out numbered tickets to visit the toilet! After all I've seen, I don't for a moment doubt it happened. Nobody could have made that story up; the convicts simply didn't have the imagination for it.

Another nauseatingly dreary day drew to an end. It had consisted of marching, loading and unloading, hauling sand, cement and other objects pointlessly from place to place – as well as the interminable cleaning bouts and other moronic chores that had been dreamt up by prison psychologists doing their postgrad research somewhere in the bowels of the antiquated system. The fundamental principles of how to crush men's minds en masse were successfully trialled during Stalin's political repressions of the 1930s, and now they've been updated and given a slick of sophisticated cynicism and hypocrisy. The penal servitude of the 1930s has been replaced with a modern form of slave labour.

Those days of backbreaking re-educational toil drained me of emotional and physical energy; the harsh reality of my fate and the realisation of my own helplessness tormented me. Powerless to change a thing, I was reduced to a speck in the dark mass of prisoners who had turned into meek zombies. The shoddy black uniforms dehumanising the prisoners were the crowning touch in the prison psychologists' plan. The constant lack of sleep, the state of being half asleep and half awake zapped me of the strength to resist. But I carried on existing and persevering ...

Bedtime preparations began at 9.05 p.m. The weary prisoners would be let into the barracks. Groaning and coughing, they filed into the building. After taking off their misshapen boots, half made from cardboard (they were issued to last for two years and you wore them all year round, come snow or shine), they entered the sleeping area. Many did not even try to wash themselves or clean their feet. Three sinks for sixty people left you with a slender chance of cleanliness ... Lights out was strictly enforced. At 9.30 p.m. everyone had to be asleep – no walking around was allowed. Specially trained prisoners kept a strict watch over us. The dormitory was 9 metres by 4, packed tight with two tiers of bunks. Reaching your bed – or, indeed, leaving it – was not the easiest of tasks. Plus, you had to get dressed and undressed, which only complicated things.

I lay pensively on my creaky iron bed, observing all the convicts close by. It felt as if I were in a railway station, and long-distance train passengers were scurrying around me. I couldn't shake off the sensation that it was all just a very long dream.

Peeling off his black uniform and exuding the odour of unwashed clothes and an unclean body, Krugly slipped past me, painted from tip to toe with prison symbols. He had stars tattooed on his knees, epaulettes decorating his shoulders, church domes were engraved upon his back and chest, while his arm featured a tiger's head and his fingers were painted with rings and inscribed with the letters 'BARS', meaning '*Bey Aktivistov, Rezh Suk*' – 'Smash the Collaborators, Knife the Traitors.' Krugly was serving his latest eight-year sentence for armed robbery. Having been transferred for unknown reasons from a camp in Sverdlovsk Region, he had set himself up here as an orderly, and, wearing an armband reading 'SDIP' – Section for Order and Discipline – he stood guard at the entrance to the barracks.

Vasily was creaking around near me with door hinges tattooed on his knees. There was old Khromov, limping towards his bed more dead than alive – he was already past sixty. He'd got three years under Article 119 (making threats to kill). Khromov had been caught by a neighbourhood cop. I'd like to lay eyes on that 'heroic' police officer. Karmanov, an alcoholic of around fifty-five, sauntered past. He walked with a limp and was no taller than former president Dmitry Medvedev. Karmanov had chopped up his drinking buddy. With a whopping eighteen swings of the axe! 'I did it so my sister wouldn't get mad,' he explained to me. He used to get drunk on the streets. One time, he invited his drinking buddy to the home he shared with his sister. The two of them got drunk, and his buddy decided to take a rest on the sofa. Karmanov warned him: 'Beat it, my sister will be back any moment; she'll get mad.' But, apparently, to no effect. So Karmanov grabbed hold of the axe and … To keep his sister from getting upset …

A towering young hulk went past who entirely befitted his surname – Merzayev, meaning 'disgusting'. He had raped and killed two girls as coolly as enjoying a picnic with his friends, and for his crimes he landed twenty-three years. He had a wife and a six-year-old daughter on the outside. 'Cucumber' flashed past, his skinny neck decorated with a spider crawling up a web. He was a twenty-five-year-old junkie and drunkard who'd got two years in a strict-regime camp for stealing a few jars of cucumbers, tomatoes and stewed fruit, which he'd snacked on at the scene of the crime. I saw proof of his sentence with my own eyes.

Drozdov hobbled by. He was fifty, but he looked at least seventy, with his nightly coughing and spluttering. He was in for Article 158 (theft). Later, he was diagnosed with tuberculosis. Nearby, forty-two-year-old Povarnitsyn, who'd already been cured of tuberculosis, was getting ready for bed. Tattooed on his closed eyelids were the messages 'Do not wake' and 'I'm sleeping'. His neighbour Sergei had eyes inked upon his eyelids, creating a very strange impression. And there was my Moscow neighbour Nikolai, who had marked International Women's Day with a memorable party for his common-law wife. After an almighty drinking spree, he had woken up in a pool of blood and found her with her throat sliced open. He couldn't even remember if he'd killed her or not. He was still puzzling over it. He would tell me candidly: 'I'm curious to know if it was me who murdered her.' He regretted calling for an ambulance and the police. 'I should have taken the corpse out to the forest and buried it.' He used to talk about it quite calmly, chewing his bread and sipping his tea.

Abbasov was rooted to the spot in reverie, repeating to himself: 'How do I get to my bed?' He slept on the second tier, on a hard-to-reach bunk squeezed between two others.

'My God, how did I find myself in this place? Why did it happen? What am I doing here?' Asking myself this unanswerable question for the umpteenth time, I mentally wished myself good night and went to sleep.

Each prisoner has a story to tell. Some are interesting, others not particularly. Some are true, others false. Some of the stories evoke sympathy, others bring up conflicting feelings. But these were the guys I had to spend my time with. By that point, I no longer had any thoughts of release; I had ceased imagining the day I'd walk free. Years and years of prison life lay ahead of me ...

My stay in quarantine was evidently being prolonged. Each Tuesday, between ten and a dozen men were led from our unit to the main office for allocation. The convicts were sent out to various units. I was utterly fed up with the situation, and each Tuesday I hoped to hear my name among the lucky ones leaving the unit.

It seemed the camp management weren't sure what to do with me, so they kept me in quarantine for ages. Their reasoning must have gone: 'This unknown fruit has been sent, and we have no idea how to store it. Nor how it should be eaten. Nor whether it's even edible. Maybe it needs to be kept in the cold? Or somewhere warm? Should it be fried or boiled?' No one would normally remain in quarantine for more than three weeks, but they needed a lot longer to study my case.

I was constantly seeing new faces. Somebody would be brought in, somebody else taken away. Before you knew it, the next batch of prisoners had arrived. I was there for a few months, during which time the composition of the quarantine changed several times. A young man with one leg arrived in the unit. Alexander Umantsev, born near Grozny, spoke Chechen without an accent. He was convicted of involvement in an illegal armed group and of murdering a local policeman. He said after witnessing first-hand how the Russian Army had killed civilians and ripped open the bellies of pregnant women, he'd embraced Islam and left to fight on the side of the Chechens.

Misha K. and Aslan were transferred from lower quarantine. I began cheering up; I was in good company now. Time flew by. Marching, inspection, doing shifts, and breakfast, lunch and dinner swallowed up the days. We had morning and evening roll calls. We'd line up on the drill ground and wait for an official from the camp management. He turned up with a stack of cards. There was one registration card per convict. They kept a record with personal data for every prisoner. The official yelled out your surname, and you had to shout back your forename and patronymic, your criminal offence and the start and end dates of your sentence.

Each day, the orderly would appoint the inmate-on-duty. You had to clean up the barracks, sweeping and washing the floors. And then lay the table in time for the unit's arrival. The job was stressful and a heavy responsibility. We would assign all the roles in advance. One man would fetch the bread, another would help the first carry the vats along, the third would ladle out the slops. If you didn't get everything done on time, you went hungry yourself. I was doing shifts with an old timer. We got into conversation. Andrei Zuyev was a year older than me and he had spent twenty-eight years inside. He first did time as a kid at fifteen, and then there was no holding him back. He had spent just six months on the outside. His latest sentence was twenty-three years, ten of which he'd served in a special-regime closed prison. None of his relatives were alive. His brother had died, as had his parents. He had no one and nothing. I gave him the rest of my cigarettes and offered him tea. We continued to find ourselves on the same shift; many a time, I washed the floors of the quarantine block with him. We worked well together, quickly completing our tasks and managing to steal a few minutes to relax.

Our marching continued no matter the weather. On Saturdays and Sundays, films were shown in the re-educational-work room. The orderlies selected the programme. They made themselves comfy in the front row, sipping their tea. The room was packed to the rafters with prisoners, all sitting on top of each other. It was stuffy. I found it genuine torture, and I would have gladly chosen marching over it. But we had no alternative. I watched from start to finish *A Nightmare on Elm Street*, *Chainsaw Massacre 1* and *Chainsaw Massacre 2*. Action movies and horror flicks went down a treat. The more maniacs, murderers and hold-up artists, the better. Whenever I caught wind that one of the orderlies had found an awesome movie, I immediately knew what was in store.

I was utterly worn out. Sometimes the entire day would pass without a single chance to sit down. By the evening, I was dead on my feet and would sink onto my bed. From the moment we rose, my first thought was of bedtime. Dog-tired, I would be out like a light. But I slept badly. At night, I often woke up and trudged to the toilet. There would be a queue again. The night orderly kept a special notebook in which he recorded the exact time of your visit. We were allowed to go strictly one at a time. 'It's all a bad dream,' I told myself yet again. Sipping the fresh air in the toilet, I returned to the dormitory, but I couldn't go in. A revolting stench hung thick as a wall. I steeled myself, held my breath and stepped inside. Finally back in bed, I tried falling asleep. I remembered some sci-fi film in which they built a gigantic sphere with hardly any oxygen in order to protect the Earth from cosmic radiation. Selling the air, which was in plentiful supply beyond the sphere, became a lucrative business. I am convinced that our jailers would have leapt at the chance to create something similar in order to control every breath the convicts took.

Gasping for breath in the – literally and figuratively – suffocating atmosphere of the quarantine block, I made an appointment with the head of the camp. He was away on holiday, so I was seen by his deputy in charge of re-educational work. A raging alcoholic, the colonel occupied an office larger even than our dormitory, which housed around forty prisoners. After listening to my grievances, he did absolutely nothing to solve the problems. A man with no clear function, he was a complete waste of space. Neither harmful nor helpful. If he didn't go in to work, no one would notice his absence. The number of these chairwarmers clogging up the system with their fictitious functions and powers! In my view, men in military fatigues should not be allowed near convicts. They should only be entrusted with guarding the camp perimeter of the colony so the prisoners

151

do not escape, and protecting the civilians who work with the inmates – the teachers, psychologists and instructors.

The deputy chief political officer informed me that the question of my transfer to another unit could only be solved by the head of the camp himself. Disheartened, I returned to the quarantine block. I found Misha K. looking agitated; he was on duty that day. 'Ivanovich,' he addressed me. 'I'm afraid I can't take any more of this – I'm going to kill that punk!' He was talking about Vitaly, the marching orderly. Vitaly had been openly provoking Misha, picking a quarrel with him. 'You haven't washed that bit properly, you didn't sweep over there. The mirror wasn't wiped enough, the beds weren't done right.' He got a kick out of goading Misha. Imagine how Misha felt, a grown man, father of two, a graduate and a veteran to boot, having to put up with all this from a grotty kid! 'That's it, I've had it,' Misha said, and he took off. 'Right, I'm going to smash this bedside table over his head,' he said as he walked. Convinced he was deadly serious, I rushed to stop him and managed to hold him back. Misha would have had no trouble carrying out his plan. The thought that I'd saved the life (or at least the health) of that nasty little skinhead was depressing. But I was glad to rescue Misha from landing in trouble and earning himself an extension to his sentence.

At morning drill, Kirill solemnly informed us: 'Today our marching is called off! We have a visit from a human rights commission! If anyone suddenly asks about marching, you say: "We don't know the meaning of the word!"'

A group of civilians accompanied by men in uniform slowly headed down the path towards our barracks. Everything around us was spick and span. Birches were growing; the kerbs stood out, marked in chalk. There were lovely green lawns. The church delighted the eye. All was calm and orderly. At first glance, you might think you'd stepped into a summer camp. But the truth was that the lovelier it seemed from the outside, the harsher life was for the convicts inside. Dirt, mess and havoc are the faithful companions of relative peace of mind for the prisoners. The commission approached the site of our barracks. They had a TV cameraman from the city of Vladimir. A prepared story awaited him: the script had been written, and the actors chosen. The toilets, the sinks and the dining room were filmed. Specially chosen prisoners, stripped to the waist, splashed themselves happily at the white basins. This heart-warming narrative was to be shown on Vladimir's main TV channel. Hundreds of thousands of viewers would find out what happy lives we prisoners were leading behind bars.

As fate would have it, the very next day we were visited by another commission. A seminar was being run at the camp for jailers to share their experience. Penal-colony officers from all over Russia convened in Melekhovo. They were holding the all-Russia gathering of prison-camp deputy heads for security and operational work.

At morning drill, Kirill said, 'Guys! Can you give it your best today! If you do a good job, we'll call off this evening's marching!'

Everyone filed into line, leaving the barracks empty.

'For-r-ward march!' Vitaly bawled.

We yielded to the caretaker's request and, stomping our feet with all our might, moved towards the main office.

On the path was a crowd of men in uniform, everyone from majors to colonels. Some had cameras and were taking photos of the local scenery. Our own deputy head of security and operational work, who had the rank of lieutenant colonel, was saying something to the guests. Hammering out our steps, we approached the crowd.

'Hello, Citizen Convicts!' our lieutenant colonel addressed us loudly.

'Good morning, Citizen Chief!' we yelled. The column came to a halt. At the command 'Right', we turned to face the participants of the gathering. They filmed and photographed us. One of the guests addressed us with a rather sticky question: 'Any former members of the underworld among you?'

'Well, of course!' our lieutenant colonel replied.

Two men stepped out of the line. 'Convict So-and-So, former criminal leader of a prison,' the first one introduced himself.

'Former criminal leader of a penal colony,' said the second.

'So how are your relations with the management here?' the guest persevered.

'We have a good relationship with them,' one of them responded. 'We always manage to see eye to eye.'

For today, the performance was over. Everyone was happy. The officers had not been disgraced. We went back to the unit for our well-earned reward. In place of the marching, we were shown yet another horror film. When I suggested watching the news on TV, everyone looked at me as if I were a madman.

The criminal underworld really did get along fine with the orderlies. They ate together, watched television and happily played football with each other.

18

HUMILIATED AND INSULTED

Artyom lived in our unit like a leper, hounded into the corner. He was a twenty-three-year-old from Moscow. Life was tough for him. He was gay. This was his second stint behind bars, this time for theft. He'd been working in a nightclub when he stole from a customer and was sent to prison. Artyom was HIV-positive. At first, he was sent to the special Unit 6 for men infected with HIV. His relations with the others weren't exactly great. He was responsible for cleaning the toilet, and, on top of that, he became the sexual plaything of the frustrated prisoners and was regularly subjected to violence. When he tried to hang himself, Artyom was moved to the quarantine block.

His life in quarantine could hardly be described as a great improvement. From morning to night, Artyom washed the toilet and took the used loo paper out to the refuse. In the breaks from these activities, he did the laundry for the orderlies, washing their towels, T-shirts, underpants and socks. And when he wasn't busy doing that, he was regularly beaten by the orderlies. The bruises and grazes never faded from his face. And, at night, the local grandees of the quarantine block would make Artyom recount memories of his life on the outside, using him for their own carnal delights. Artyom found it all too much; he slit his veins and … back he went to Unit 6 for the HIV-infected.

Later, while in another unit, I heard the following story about Artyom. A semi-underworld character, a Gypsy nicknamed Budulai, began to pester Artyom. The Gypsy asked him to do something that went against his nature. He insisted that Artyom take the active role in the unmentionable deed. 'No, I can't!' Artyom resisted fiercely. 'If you want to do it to me, be my guest! But I myself just can't do that.' The Gypsy would not back off. Artyom complained about the Lothario to the local criminals who followed the thieves' code. 'Hey, you bastard, trying to smear an honest con!' They didn't believe Artyom. But they gave in to his insistence and agreed to check the Gypsy out just in case.

'Make a date with him!' they said. 'We'll be lying in wait nearby. If anything happens, we'll step in.'

When night fell, trying to evade detection, our couple made their way to the site of the rendezvous: the re-education room. Budulai did not suspect that a trap had been laid for him. At the crucial moment, the light came on, and in front of the wide-eyed prisoners, the naked Budulai was caught in an unambiguous pose. Keeping his wits about him, he jumped out of the first-floor window, smashing through the glass. Miraculously, in a few seconds he managed to scale the high fence of the local sector, fitted with special coils of barbed wire. If you tried to climb over, you'd be caught on the rail; if you pulled yourself up, the barbed coil would come twisting down. And you'd be unable to move, like a hamster in a wheel.

With screams of 'Help, they'll kill me!' the naked Gypsy flew into an observation booth along the avenue – a place from where the prisoners' movements were monitored. No one could exit the local zone without the security staff on duty noticing. That night, the Gypsy burst in on their sleep. The Gypsy was rescued, and they gave him sanctuary in the quarantine block.

19

SHOPPING

With each day, it was growing colder and colder; autumn was on its way. We were issued thin padded jackets, all in the same old white stripe. The jackets did not rescue me from the cold, and I waited for a lifesaving parcel of warm things from home. Suddenly my stay in quarantine showed a bright side. The opportunity arose to make calls from a phone box. You had to write an application addressed to the head of the colony: 'I request that you allow me telephone conversations with so-and-so who lives at such-and-such an address. The number is such-and-such. The conversation will not last more than fifteen minutes.' The quarantine caretaker then signed the application at the unit commander's office, the latter did so at the head of the camp's office, and then an orderly accompanied you to a pay phone. Everything would have been fine, but these calls required a phone card with a pin code. You could only buy the cards once a month at the shop.

The shop held an important place in the life of each prisoner. You could spend no more than 2,000 roubles a month. Not all prisoners went to the shop, as not everyone had money. The caretaker would check who from quarantine was able to go to the shop. The orderlies could go, because they were all getting paid. Not much, it's true, but by prison standards it was enough. The guys in the industrial zone had to slog their guts out for the same money.

I too was among the lucky ones. While I was in remand prison, many of my friends had transferred money, and I had amassed a handsome sum: 70,000 roubles. For the city of Vladimir, and for the prisoners in particular, this was a huge amount of money. The head of the unit knew – meaning the caretaker did too; and if the caretaker knew, that meant the orderlies did. The news that I had this amount in my account became headline news and aroused heated discussion. Whispered conversations and comments reached me: 'And the man claims he didn't steal anything!' I was to hear this story about me many a time. It took on a life of its own, mutating and distorting. 'They say you've got a million in your prison-camp account,' the convicts would tell me in hushed tones.

Nazar circled me like a piranha, not for the first time prying into my business: 'So what was your salary?' I was bombarded with requests to buy things for people. Many did not have soap, toothpaste or other essentials. We headed over to the shop. We entered a small room with a counter and shelves stacked with goods. There were cans of food, tea, cigarettes, candies, *zefir* marshmallows, toothpaste – to name but a few of the goodies on offer. The store had two saleswomen and a manager known to the convicts affectionately (and ingratiatingly) as Pavlovich. He was a retired prison officer who had decided to carry on working with the convicts, so he'd got a job in the shop. His son, a lieutenant colonel, also worked in the camp – as deputy head of security and operational work.

Despite the inflated prices, a good fifty per cent higher than on the outside, all the goods were in great demand and flew off the shelves. We had no choice: it was take it or leave it. Pavlovich enjoyed considerable power. He could put aside a particularly scarce product; he could let you buy things for a large sum. Waiting in turn, first you had to speak to Pavlovich. He checked how much money was in your personal account and asked what you would be spending. I took an instant dislike to this Pavlovich. And the feeling was mutual. Seeing I had 70,000 roubles on my card, he asked sternly, 'How much are you spending?'

Remembering all the many requests, I casually answered: '10,000.'

'Whoa-a-a.' His jaw dropped. He began wheezing, trying to say something, and his eyes were bulging. I thought he was having a stroke or some kind of fit. 'Wha-a-t? No way!' he yelled.

'So how much can I spend?' I asked.

'You can have 2,000,' said Pavlovich, charging my account and issuing a ticket.

I moved to the saleswomen further down the counter and bought some phone cards, spending the rest of the money on all sorts: cigarettes, tea, sweets and biscuits.

We went back to the unit. I gave two blocks of cigarettes and several packs of tea to Zuyev, my floor-washing partner. I was in the mood for something sweet. The biscuits and sweets were demolished in an instant. There would be no other chance. I treated all my friends: Aslan, Misha and Andrei Zuyev.

'Now all that's left is to arrange with the orderly to be taken to the phone box,' I thought, dreaming of talking with my loved ones as I tenderly twiddled the phone cards in my hands.

Feeling content and at peace, we stood in the local quarantine zone. We had marching in another forty minutes, and we whiled away the wait in conversation. Nearby was the smoking room. Only three men could smoke at a time, and we heard the men dividing up the queue. A few metres away from us, in an improvised sports complex, some of the orderlies were working out. They had a pull-up bar, some parallel bars and a barbell. Orderlies needed to look intimidating, so they worked out intensively and frequently. A flunky was dashing back and forth. He was an ordinary prisoner who, in exchange for tea and cigarettes, volunteered to wait on the caretaker – making him tea, washing his dishes. I was always taken aback by the manic desire of convicts who had risen to some role or other to have servants of their own – or 'helpers', as they sometimes called them. From the storeroom where our bags were stored and the quarantine caretaker lived with his assistant, we heard constant cries of 'Yuri, some tea'. And poor Yuri would rush around with cups at the ready, all to please the caretaker, the orderlies, the former underworld criminals and a colony officer who regularly dropped in.

'Pereverzin!'

Krugly, who worked in the Section for Order and Discipline, stood at his post shouting my name. 'Upstairs, to the caretaker!'

I was being called to see Sasha, the new quarantine caretaker. The cash in my personal account was giving him no peace. The conversation began from afar.

'See, we do all the repairs here with our own money,' he grumbled. 'The pigs demand we fix one thing after the other. We had the door break; the tap for the sink needs fixing.'

I caught his drift. 'If you pay just once, you'll show your weak side, and they'll start bleeding you dry,' I reasoned. 'I've got eight more years ahead of me to get through. And, more's the pity, I don't have any embezzled billions to dip into.'

'Why should I repair what I don't actually use?' I asked. And then I gave vent to all my pent-up frustration: 'We can't use the toilet, we can't get to the washbasin, we can't sit on the beds, we can't drink tea! Oh, it can all go to hell, your wonderful quarantine along with your orderlies! I can't wait to be out of here, I'm counting the days!'

As a result of our long and surly conversation, I fired off the following statement addressed to the head of the colony: 'I'd like you to take out 5,000 roubles from my personal account for the maintenance of the unit.' In return, I was given unimaginable perks and privileges: I could go into the barracks whenever I liked, rummage through my things to my heart's content, drink tea, have a wash, go to the toilet when the need arose. Unlike me, Sasha was none too pleased with the outcome of our little chat, but nevertheless apparently decided that even a bad sheep gives a bit of wool. The bad sheep, in this case, being me. The way was open for me to make full use of the pay phone, which I immediately did.

I heard my wife's and my friend's voices on the other end.

'Volodya, my dear Volodya, how are you coping there?' These voices came from another world, another dimension. My loved ones would not be able to understand or grasp what was going on in the camp.

'All's well, everything is going okay, no need to worry about me,' I reassured my loved ones. I asked them to send me a parcel and dictated a list of things I needed: woollen socks, insoles, a scarf, warm underwear, black gloves. You could send up to twenty kilos. Working up to this threshold, I continued my list: tea, chocolate, cheese … My mouth started watering and my stomach rumbled.

'We've been given dates for a meeting,' I told them happily. 'Will you come? Can you bring Denis?'

I missed my son enormously; it was three years since I'd last hugged him!

'Yes, of course we'll come! When will it be?'

I told them the dates and began looking forward to the meeting with my wife.

When you are behind bars, you find yourself forever looking forward to something. You look forward not only to freedom, but also to something more real and close, something you could reach out and touch. You look forward to a parcel or a transfer, you look forward to the next meeting with your loved ones. Your life is smashed into little fragments that together form one monstrous sentence. But each fragment brings you closer to freedom and helps you survive your time inside, which is gradually dwindling, one crumb at a time.

20

A TASTE OF PRISON MEDICINE

It was getting chilly. Black ice was already forming. To save us from slipping and sliding, we switched to a special winter marching step. By now, the jackets they'd issued us were not much help. People began falling sick. Given the overcrowding, our lack of vitamins and poor nutrition, the slightest infection would spread in an instant. One man would sneeze or cough – and the whole barracks fell ill. It was vitally important to avoid falling ill. As one of the orderlies put it, 'You're not allowed to visit the infirmary! You can only be carried there on a stretcher!'

'Not that they'd be likely to help there anyway!' I told myself, remembering my first – and so far only – visit to the medical unit.

The day after we arrived in the camp, Nazar had led us to the infirmary for a medical. Queuing in the corridor, we waited our turn. Behind the open door, a man in a white coat sat at a desk. Nazar was sitting next to him on a chair. We had to go in and introduce ourselves, giving our surname, our conviction and the start and end dates of our sentence. Valera, who had travelled with me in the train and helped me carry my bags, went in and out of the room five times. 'Get the hell out!' I heard this 'doctor' shriek, and Valera leapt from the office.

'Next!' Nazar called.

'Yikes, what a set-up!' I thought, shocked by what was going on. It was my turn. I went into the office and introduced myself. I didn't have to go in and out several times. I introduced myself correctly, without missing anything out. Valera, it turned out, had forgotten to declare his conviction, then his sentence, and that's what had angered the doctor. The man had a very important job. To turn a blind eye to the bruises and grazes on the prisoners who'd been beaten up upon arrival and to declare each patient healthy – this was a core part of his difficult duties. I nicknamed him Doctor Evil.

He glanced casually at me and skimmed over my medical card before releasing me: 'You may go.'

It was a relief to leave his office. I had not been keen on discussing my health in front of the orderly. Now I realised that had I done so, it would have been pointless anyway.

I resolved never to set foot in the infirmary again.

One day, I felt myself coming down with something. A cold or flu. I had a nasty cough, felt shivery and woozy. I wanted to rest in bed and sleep it off, but fat chance in that place. Instead of recuperation, I faced three marching sessions a day. I was counting the hours to the extended visit, hoping to get some rest when it came. On the phone to my wife, I asked her to bring me some medicines.

21

AN EXTENDED VISIT

The day of the long-awaited meeting arrived. After the morning's marching and roll call, the ever-present Nazar led me to the room for extended visits, where I was handed over to a guard. After a search, I changed into a tracksuit and went up to the room. A long corridor with a communal shower and toilet opened on to the kitchen, where you could cook. In the corridor was a shared refrigerator, packed with food brought by people's relatives. There were eleven double and triple rooms to serve the entire zone, which housed around two thousand people! There weren't enough days or rooms for all, and so the convicts first patiently waited for their right to an extended visit in compliance with Russia's Penal Code, and then waited their turn to exercise that right. The orderlies, those working for Order and Discipline and the other collaborators could jump the queue.

I went into the small room and saw my loved ones. I felt light-headed. It was all like a dream. I saw my wife and son, who had grown bigger and become unaccustomed to me over the past three years. The boy acted shy and unsure of how to behave; he embraced me awkwardly. I struggled to hold back

162

the tears. I didn't want them to know how bad things were for me in that place; I didn't want to upset them, and I tried to smile and joke. There were iron beds in the room, with wooden boards thoughtfully placed on them for the comfort of the relatives. Plus mattresses, blankets and pillows. We made up the beds with the bed linen that my wife had brought and went through the bags. I saw foods that I had not even dreamt of, which I'd completely forgotten the taste of. You could bring whatever you wanted for the visit – with the exception of alcohol and drugs. As much raw meat and potatoes as you liked. I had lost my appetite, so I took the medicines, drank some tea, lay on the bed and sank into sleep. When I woke up, I quickly came to. We sat drinking tea and talking. I went into the grimy shower, where I washed myself thoroughly and laundered all my things. These few days outside the quarantine block offered a precious chance to catch my breath and get my strength back. My son would not leave my side for a moment; with a boyish sincerity and spontaneity, he kept kissing and hugging me. He mustered all his strength, trying to fight back the tears that came spilling down …

Those two days passed in an instant. The time for parting drew near. It was terrifically painful. The thought occurred that I should give up extended visits entirely, just to avoid going through that pain time and time again. In those few days of being with your relatives, you forgot all about where you were and what awaited you in that place. The moment you said goodbye, you remembered it all. I hated to part from them, but I had to leave.

Denis broke down and started crying. He didn't want to go home and, trying to find the words for his feelings, he hugged me and said, 'Daddy, I feel miserable without you.' Those words made my heart stop. It was time to leave. We said goodbye. I had to go to marching, Denis had school, my wife had her job. I walked away. There was another search. After checking me thoroughly, they let me head back to the unit.

What life was like in each camp was determined not by the law, but by the degree of despotism shown by the head man and his entourage. The legal framework not only allowed but obliged the administration to make the prisoner's life tolerable. But the closed nature of the system, the lack of genuine (rather than sham) public scrutiny, the conspiracy of silence had bred a culture of lawlessness and impunity. The upshot was that everything came down to personality. In all my years of imprisonment, I got to see some fairly decent visitation rooms. But they would not allow medications nor let you make calls. At the strict-regime colony in Melekhovo, you could freely subscribe to magazines or receive them in parcels and packages. Yet at the general-regime camp in the town of Pokrov, in that same Vladimir Region, the woman working in the visitation room, deeply loathed by all the convicts, writhed in hysterics and ripped the pictures out of a copy of Men's Health *I'd received in a parcel. In that Pokrov camp, we were strictly forbidden from receiving honey, which I dearly loved, while in Melekhovo you were free to receive as much honey as you liked.*

22

BACK TO THE FUTURE

Having regained a little strength, feeling uplifted and yet downhearted, I went back to the unit, where endless marching, cleaning and other such delights awaited me. It was already the fourth month of my life – of my existence, rather – in that place. I learnt that the head of the camp, Colonel A. V. Novikov, had returned from his vacation. Having sent him several requests for a meeting to discuss personal matters, I was biding my time. Finally, after a few weeks of waiting, they took me to see him. He kept a special office for such meetings, rather nicely done up (evidently with the prisoners' money). He also had two more offices. One was in the main office on the camp grounds, the other outside the compound. The colonel felt he was king of the roost, and with good reason. His lordly manner showed in everything he did – in his swagger and his contemptuous gaze. He twiddled my letter in his hands and eyed me with curiosity. I introduced myself: 'Convict Vladimir Ivanovich Pereverzin, born 1966, convicted under Article 160, Section 4, and Article 174.1, Section 4 …'

Rather than letting me finish, he cut me short and motioned for me to take a chair.

'Citizen Chief!' I said to him. 'I've been in quarantine for coming up to four months now! Couldn't I be transferred to another unit?'

The colonel knew about my case. Somewhat perplexed, he asked me an odd question: 'How on earth did you land up here?'

And he continued pensively: 'We haven't had a call about you …'

It was then I realised why I'd been held in quarantine for so long. They were waiting for orders from Moscow.

'Well, no one is going to call you!' I told him confidently. 'As far as the Prosecutor-General's Office is concerned, we've outlived our usefulness. There's nothing more to take from us. The prosecution have got what they were after: the trumped-up conviction.'

They would forget all about me for a number of years – until I agreed to appear as a witness for the defence in Khodorkovsky's second trial. Up to that point, we were dumped in the lap of the camp authorities, who decided how to perform their tacit missions in different ways.

'What if Moscow suddenly calls wanting to know what's going on with Pereverzin?' Clearly this was the thought running through the minds of the camp authorities.

'No cushy job for him! No way can he work in the school or library! Lifting and hauling loads, sewing in the workshop – now that's another matter entirely. Nothing but manual work, with zero leniency!' And that's what I would endure for the full three years in that camp. I became a genuine galley slave. Readers, if anyone ever tells you he's working like a galley slave, don't believe a word of it! The guy's a fraud! But I was the real deal.

Through my hard labour, I was to earn several commendations and a good reference. As I'd later learn, my 'accomplice' Malakhovsky, who was serving his sentence in another region, was living in more tolerable conditions, but he didn't win a single commendation. In each region, the local despot would kowtow to his superiors in his own style.

After the talk with the head of the camp, I returned to quarantine with raised hopes of soon being moved to another unit. I waited impatiently for the next set of transfers. Then, on Tuesday, Zuyev and Misha K. were moved from quarantine – to Unit 3, the unit with the strictest regime, where they kept convicts with long sentences, men who posed a risk of escape and disorderly types transferred there in punishment for their misdemeanours. A feeling of sad loneliness stole over me.

My sadness lifted when I visited the library, where prisoners could take out annual subscriptions to periodicals. I promised to buy Nazar a subscription to his hallowed *Football* magazine, and in return, I was led to the library. It gave me huge pleasure to leaf through the Russian Post Office and Rospechat catalogues, and I eagerly subscribed to a vast number of newspapers and magazines. *Kommersant, Vedomosti, Rossiyskaya Gazeta, Profil, Ekspert, Kompania, Sekret Firmy, Moskovsky Komsomolets, Forbes, Maxim, Men's Health*, crossword magazines – to name a few of the publications I chose. The amount charged to my account for the subscriptions boggled the minds of the other men and merely bolstered their confidence that I'd 'pilfered billions'.

As I came out of the library block, I saw a huge poster offering guidance on coping with stress. It commended: 'Hot baths and massage are especially beneficial.'

'Yeah right, having your back pounded with rubber batons does you the world of good! And sharing one shower head among five men – what a dependable cure for stress!' I began wondering what kind of idiot came up with this guff. The whole avenue was decked out in similar slogans. During marching, I had managed to read only the headlines on the billboards. One particularly stands out in my memory: 'What is the meaning of life?'

Another day was coming to an end. It was after supper and I was walking around in the quarantine yard. This was the most pleasant time of day. As I waited for the bedtime command, I mused over the events of the last few days. A prisoner of around fifty was walking near me. He ruefully told me this was his third time inside for one and the same thing.

'How is that even possible?' I asked in surprise.

'It just is!' he answered, and told me his sad story. In their village, they had just the one shop, and Nikolai raided it fair and square for the very first time. The local policeman had no trouble tracking the culprit down in the little village. Nikolai got his first jail sentence. He was released, got drunk and … went straight back to that unlucky store. And again he got jail time. Three years went by. Nikolai returned to his home village. The owner of the store gave Nikolai a friendly welcome and treated him lavishly. 'I'll hand everything over, Kolya, just don't raid the shop,' he said, and he stocked him up with vodka, sausage and other goodies. Kolya was happy and left to enjoy his feast. After a while, as he was dining, it suddenly struck him: 'My whole life was chewed up and spat out because of that bloody shop.' He impetuously grabbed a knife and ran inside the store …

Nearby stood a young guy. Lost in reverie, he was looking at the sky, then suddenly he turned to me and said, 'What are stars exactly? They're stones, like, or sort of bonfires?'

I stood stock-still, not even finding it funny, overcome with sadness. 'My God, where have I ended up?' I thought, and stared into the starry sky. That was my last evening in the adaptation unit.

23

VALIANT UNIT 3

The next day, after marching, I had the joy of hearing my name among the lucky few being called to the main office for relocation. In the vast office of the deputy chief political officer, some men in uniform sat behind the desks – they were members of the commission. The local elite were gathered here: the head of the colony, the operational officers, the security officers, the production manager. We convicts sat on the benches opposite. We had to stand up, introduce ourselves and name our line of work. Sergei K. went first, convicted of murder. He cheerfully introduced himself and called out his occupation: 'Beast battler.' He was not kidding; it really was true. Sergei worked at a slaughterhouse. One day he got drunk and killed a man. Well, he flipped and in his drunken haze slayed the wrong species … He could not practise his usual job in here, and so they sent him to Unit 1 to work as an unskilled labourer.

My turn came. On the desk, I saw my own tatty personal file in three volumes. It immediately caught the eye due to its size. The head of the colony leafed musingly through the pages and looked at me. I introduced myself and named my profession, which sounded rather exotic in these parts: economist. 'Well …' he muttered. 'We can offer you clothing production, Unit 3.'

Not having much of a choice – it was marching or clothing production – I gladly agreed to the latter and headed back to quarantine for my things. I quickly packed, rolled up my mattress and left. It wasn't far, just a 150-metre walk up the avenue. I went along the road so minutely familiar from the months of marching – I knew every last pit and groove of it. Nazar escorted me for the last time.

We reached the local zone of Unit 3, where the prisoners were walking about. The courtyard looked like it had been hit by a bomb, with pitting and potholes everywhere. Jutting from the ground were chunks of asphalt and concrete once laid by German captives. In the distance, I saw a pull-up bar, parallel bars and a bench. A warrant officer emerged from his booth and opened the gates. I found myself inside Unit 3. I was met by Zuyev. He helped me carry my things to the barracks. It was a huge place, holding over a hundred men and densely packed with two tiers of bunk beds. The caretaker was Kolya Fomin, or 'Foma', a former member of the underworld. Inked from head to toe, his hands plumped up with vaseline (some prisoners would inject petroleum jelly into their fists, making them swell up massively and lowering the pain when landing a punch), Foma ruled the roost. A good bunk could be had by earning it or by coughing up the cash. I was put on the second tier, near the front door, right where the draught was. Below me was a fat and amiable Tajik, doing time for drug dealing. I would often be woken in the night by his tossing and turning. Whenever he moved in his sleep or rolled over, my bunk would rock and sway from side to side, like a ship's deck in a storm. Sometimes I barely managed to grab hold of the rails so as not to fall overboard in the face of these rolling waves. The gusts of wind stalking the barracks put the finishing touch to this impression of the elements.

After quarantine, one bedside table per two men seemed like a vast amount of space and could hold so many bits and bobs. You could store a kettle element, a mug, a spoon, some books, tea, snacks. In the communal cloakroom, I hung my tracksuit and jacket up on a hanger and put the sneakers saved from the quarantine orderlies on a shelf. Our bags were kept in the storage room, where Foma, the caretaker, liked to hang out with his assistant Fatuy. We could access our bags strictly according to the schedule, three times a day. Each bag had its own place. You needed to queue in advance. The bags enjoyed perks too, just like the men. It was one thing for your bag to be kept on the bottom shelf in the front row, another thing entirely if it had to live right at the top, where it could only be reached by ladder once you'd yanked out several other people's things. My bags had better luck than I did.

Having unpacked, I sat down to drink tea with Zuyev. We could sit on the bunks. A stool served as an improvised table for our simple spread: sweets, biscuits and tea. I felt the curious gazes of the prisoners on me. For them, I was a legend – Yukos's financial head honcho, a billionaire, Khodorkovsky's partner. Suddenly looking up, I caught dozens of eyes fixed on me. I carried on drinking my tea and getting to know the unit.

It was a strict-regime unit, with guards constantly scurrying around. It held thirty-odd men identified as 'posing a risk of escape'. The camp authorities would put some prisoners on a pre-emptive register and keep a close eye on them. Their bedside nametags and the badges on their chests were marked with a diagonal red stripe. They faced inspections every two hours. At night, each one would be approached by an officer shining a torch in his face, making sure he was still there. The guys in this place were hard as nails and devil-may-care. I wandered up and down the aisles and checked out the bedside nametags. They read: '24 years; 19 years; 23 years ...' These were not the convicts' ages, but the lengths of their sentences. Nothing but murders, armed robberies and muggings.

Zuyev lavished care and attention on me. He made my life so much easier. Having got twenty-three years inside for murder and armed robbery, and on top of that a previous breakout, he was automatically deemed to pose a risk of escape. Aged 45, after twenty-eight years behind bars with the last ten spent in a special-regime, he commanded the respect of the others. He would tell me himself how some excited prisoners came up to him and said, 'Nice work, stripey! Got your hooks into Yukos!'

Nor did our friendship escape the notice of the caretaker, Foma, who called Zuyev in for a friendly chat and suggested he set out to fleece me. Time and again, we would find homemade knives and other prohibited items planted among my things. An old hand, Zuyev never relaxed his vigilance, and he monitored his surroundings beadily. He would place a dead fly on the bedside table or stick a hair to its door – he always knew what was going on around him. The caretaker and his helpers had long ago divvied up my money, and when I refused to sponsor them, they took it as a personal slight. I lived in constant fear of set-ups and dirty tricks.

24

THE SEWING WORKSHOP

It was my first working day. We got up, exercised, had breakfast and were led to the industrial zone. We came to the small site where the sewing workshops were based within the residential zone of the camp. You were searched upon entering, and again when you exited. The head of the workshop, who was a major, taking into account my education, immediately offered me a number of options. I could clean the grounds; trim loose threads off the finished items; join the Section for Order and Discipline where I would wear an SDIP band on my sleeve and police the men's smoking for strict adherence to the timetable and the designated areas; or sit at a sewing machine. Without a second thought, I chose the last option. 'Why not try my hand at sewing?' I said to myself. 'Might as well at least learn a skill while cooped up in this colony.'

Eager to get cracking, I began my apprenticeship with a prisoner from another unit. I knew many of them from quarantine, and many of them knew me through the grapevine. My instructor asked me, 'Do you really have a million in your personal account? Is it true the head of the camp called you in and told you to send the money back?' I smiled and told him it was nonsense. Sasha looked at me in disappointment and mistrust. He was inside for murder. A Moscow man, he had at one time played football and was a sub in a reserve team for Spartak. In this place, he was a star. This was the first time in my life I had laid eyes on a sewing machine, and I watched every move of Sasha's like a hawk. He shared the tricks of the trade with me. Sasha made one part of the cap, sewing the bands to the body. He had a production plan and output quota, and I only got to sit at his machine during smoking breaks. Quick on the uptake, I asked another prisoner to give me a chance to learn sewing on his machine. He agreed to this. So, running from one sewing machine to the other, I penetrated the mysteries of sewing.

At 12 p.m. it was lunch; at 3 p.m. work stopped. The gates opened, we were searched, then we walked in file to our respective units. At four o'clock, we had inspection, after which came our free time. You could sit down, read, drink tea. You could go out into the local zone and get some exercise. And that was just what I began doing. One thought filled my mind: 'Don't let your time go to waste; spend every spare second, every minute productively.' Unfortunately, I had little free time, and it was largely taken up with pointless tasks.

After a gentle warm-up on the sports ground, I elbowed my way to a broken sink with six taps, where I washed my top half with relish. Then came dinner, another hour of free time, lights out. The day flew by in a flash.

I was sleeping badly and kept on waking. Each morning I rose, still drowsy, and like a zombie went through the same motions as the previous day. The day after and the day before were as indistinguishable as pebbles on a beach. I could no longer remember what was happening and when. The exception was Saturdays and Sundays, when the industrial zone was closed. I began longing for the weekends. Time was passing more quickly.

To avoid the scrum for the sinks, I got up half an hour early and went off to wash with icy water. There was no hot water in the unit. When all the other prisoners went for their wash, I made my bed.

I began adapting to life in the unit. I was enjoying learning to sew, which did not escape the notice of the administration keeping an eye on me. Someone was unhappy that things were going relatively well for me. So I was transferred to another area. Now I was a packer of caps. The caps were sewn in the adjacent workshop – in vast quantities and catering to every taste. We were swamped with prisoner caps and deluged with military ones. I barely had time to trim off the threads, brush the caps with a wire brush and fold them away into the boxes I made. The conveyor belt worked non-stop. Clouds of dust and synthetic wadding hung in the air, leaving us nothing to breathe. The caps began to take on a life of their own, crawling towards me from all sides. I had only to dash to the toilet for a few minutes to find a horrifying mountain of hats on the worktop when I returned. I could not get a moment's peace, let alone a proper break.

There was one advantage to this new job: the shifts would whizz by in a blur. For my first month of zealous labour, I earned 700 roubles. Finding out from the foreman what the production norms and quotas were, I quickly deduced that the camp administrators were skimming off money from the prisoners' earnings, while registering the payments as bonuses. Something clicked in my mind: the Penal Code articles on fraud and the use of slave labour. 'Good Lord, they're the ones who should be locked up, not us!' I thought. But those men compensated the prisoners fairly and freely with 'air'. Instead of money, the convicts received commendations, and on the whole, they were happy with that.

25

HUMDRUM DAYS

16 December 2007. Exactly three years had passed since my arrest. I wanted to be alone. After finishing my shift in the industrial zone, I wandered about the local zone. The men from quarantine came marching eerily down the avenue, familiar prisoners glancing enviously in my direction. It was a ghastly

sight, gave me the shivers. I caught myself thinking about how not even a week had passed, and I had already begun to dislike the unit. I'd survived three whole years behind bars, and it felt like an eternity, a lifetime of pain and suffering. 'I've done a mere three years, and have eight more to do until my sentence ends,' it suddenly hit me. 'That's double what I've done plus two years on top!' I began to feel physically oppressed by the weight of the years that lay ahead – a veritable aeon. I headed back to the unit to drink some rather strong *chifir* with Zuyev ...

So began the fourth year of my imprisonment. After meeting our target, the team was not taken to work for some days, and I stayed in the unit. It was calm and unusually quiet in the barracks. Most of the prisoners were at work. I very much wanted to sleep, but it was strictly forbidden. You couldn't lie down, either – you'd immediately get an infringement, which would be remembered when you came up for parole. Despite these pointless and stupid restrictions, I enjoyed being in the unit. I worked out and read some books. The weekend lay ahead, with the bathhouse awaiting us, where you could give your things a wash. I asked Zuyev to bring me the clothes I'd left in the industrial zone: some warm socks and long johns. We all walked in a line to lunch, where Zuyev handed me my things. After lunch, we stopped at the local zone for our unit. 'Convict Pereverzin, step forward!' said the warrant officer, and he asked me to go inside a booth.

'What's in your pockets?'

'My personal belongings,' I said and pulled out the socks and long johns from my pockets.

'And that's all? Nothing else?' he said in a disappointed drawl.

'Nothing else.'

'A report will be made about you. You'll get your things back from the head of the unit,' he solemnly informed me. Surprised at the speed with which we'd been snitched on, I went to see the head of the unit, whom I hadn't yet met. Major Kuzmichov was a strange man. I'd read about people like him in Dostoyevsky's

The House of the Dead. Kuzmichov couldn't walk past a prisoner without taking something away, punishing him or picking out some fault.

Armed with a letter of explanation, I knocked and entered his office. I introduced myself and asked him to return my things. After giving me a long lecture, he opened up the safe and gave me my dirty socks and long johns with a regal gesture. 'We had to look into it, investigate the incident,' he told me. 'What if these clothes had been stolen from another prisoner?' Trying to work out whether he was saying this nonsense in jest or for real, I realised he was being deadly serious. Flabbergasted, I left the office.

The next morning, as I was washing, out of the corner of my eye I saw the head of our unit slinking off to the toilets. A second later, I heard the triumphant cry: 'Hah, caught you!'

In fairness, it should be noted that our toilet was an utterly abject and miserable sight. It bore no resemblance to a facility for attending to a call of nature; rather, it looked like a ravaged stage for the theatre where this comedy was playing out. Eight holes had been made in the tall pedestal, and these were fitted with Genoa squat pans, as I learnt from the listing at the entrance to the toilet. Such was the official term for our latrines.

I rushed over and was met by the most astonishing scene. Then and there, I became truly convinced that the staff working in the colony were incurably sick. Before my eyes, a prisoner was squatting over the Genoa pan, a cigarette between his teeth, peaceably relieving himself. Major Kuzmichov was hovering over him like a vulture.

'Smoking in an undesignated area! And not for the first time!' the head of the unit called out gleefully. 'You'll be doing a stretch in solitary now!'

And, sure enough, that day Vitaly was locked up in the isolation unit.

In the camp, each unit had a designated day and hour for washing. Our allotted time was on Sunday. At the set time, after the morning roll call, the men clustered around the exit from the local zone. We waited for the warrant officer to open the door and let us out of the cage. In the neighbouring local zone for Unit 16, the prisoners were also crowding and fretting. They shared the same wash time and would be washing alongside us. The door from the zone opened, and in an orderly throng mimicking a column, we ran towards the bathhouse. The men from Unit 16 lagged far behind. Another obstacle lay ahead: the top-security facility known as the 'bathhouse-laundry complex', inviolably protected by a towering grille with gates reminiscent of those at the St Petersburg Winter Palace. The orderly at the complex opened up the gates and leapt aside to avoid being trampled by the crowd. With screams and jeers, the crowd took off like a shot. Shoving and overtaking each other, the prisoners ran towards the showers. The first there would nab the best spots in the cramped changing room, they'd snap up the plastic tubs for washing clothes and be first to take a long-desired shower. Three or four men would collect under a single shower head. While one soaped himself, another would rinse himself and a third would slosh his laundry about in the tub. Lean, emaciated bodies decorated with prison symbols swarmed in the clouds of steam. All their domes and stars would dance before your eyes.

The fun lasted for hours. I managed to have a wash and give my clothes a quick clean in the warm water, whereupon I went back to the unit.

A large order for caps came through in the industrial zone, so we returned to work. Our humdrum days started up again.

Yura S., quite the comedian and a jolly fellow, was working side by side with me. The wisecracks flowed in a turbulent torrent, to the constant sound of lively laughter. He was charged with the important task of imprinting each cap with the letters 'QC', stamping on the size and passing it on to me. Our hands were busy, but our tongues were free and loose. The only entertainment we prisoners had was chit-chat.

Yura was HIV-positive, and he was working in the industrial zone to earn his parole. An inveterate drug abuser and serious gangster, Yura had gone on a business trip from the city of Volgograd to Vladimir Region. They'd decided to raid the glass-fibre factory and steal a furnace – one made from eighty kilos of pure platinum. They prepared long and hard, planning for every possible scenario – they even knew what time the lady night porter would be asleep. It was the porter who messed up their plans. They disarmed the guards, then made their way to the factory entrance, but, as luck would have it, rather than sleeping soundly, the old woman was engrossed in a television programme. The moment she spotted the uninvited guests, she pressed the panic button, alerting the police. A genuine battle ensued. Yura was wounded, one of his accomplices killed. A policeman died in the shoot-out. They were all caught. Yura got thirteen years – though he would win parole. His brother, convicted in another case, is doing time in Volgograd. Their father, meanwhile, is serving his sentence in a nearby camp in Vladimir Region. When the investigating officer reproachfully asked his mother what kind of children she'd raised, she proudly answered, 'I have the best children in the world, and I'm the world's happiest mum!'

Every three months, the 'happiest mum' takes time off work and selflessly tours all three prison camps.

Passing the time in chatter, our shift soon ended, and we returned to the unit. There, I met a couple of new guys.

Roma K. from Murmansk had been convicted of robbery and double murder. The gang broke into an apartment and tied up the occupants. Then they took their haul and cleared out. The occupants were later found dead. Roma said he didn't do it, claiming someone else must have popped into the apartment later on and killed them.

Valera was nicknamed Winnie. A gentle-looking oaf, he'd been sentenced to twenty-three years for robbery and double murder.

He had stopped a car in which drug dealers were transporting their collected takings. It was a short conversation, ending in two dead and one wounded. Fortunately for Winnie, the driver survived, otherwise he would have landed a life sentence.

Roma Y. had a twenty-three-year sentence for double murder. A graduate from an institute in Kovrov and Candidate Master of Sports in chess, Roma had been working as a croupier in a casino. He and a friend had travelled on some business to a hotel in Nizhny Novgorod and gone to the room where their acquaintances were staying. Nipping off to the toilet for a moment, he emerged to find two corpses in the room. And his friend wielding a hammer, dealing the final blow to the maid, who'd unwisely come running at the noise. Roma protested his innocence, claiming he'd been framed so the casino-winnings scheme he'd invented could be snatched. Roma had quite plainly been assigned the task of spying on me; he made no secret of his friendship with the colony's operational officers.

Every prisoner dreams of a love life in the camp. And for some, romance behind bars would fizz with a frisson undreamt of by those on the outside. Thousands of letters flew out from the camps in all directions – each man hoping to find his perfect match. And, sure enough, they found them. They got to know one another by letter, then met and began a relationship. Sasha S. corresponded with a number of women at the same time, and they sent him parcels. Nikolai K. was sentenced to twenty-three years for robbery and double murder. He had fourteen more years to go! He managed to find his Miss Right, tying the knot inside the prison camp. Curious to know who this selfless woman was, I went along to see her. An attractive and well-spoken Russian woman, she was a school teacher for junior classes. She knowingly took up this cross and bore it through her life. She came for visits with Nikolai, bringing him packages. It made her so happy that she shared her blessings with a girlfriend, whom she introduced to one of Nikolai's friends. Now they both set out on visits together. Her friend's new husband was doing a long sentence for murder. I don't know what connects these couples or what motivates these amazing women, and I merely wish to bow in admiration, for their heroism is incalculable.

The atmosphere in the unit was oppressive. I recalled the words of the clinical worker in Matrosskaya Tishina prison about bad vibes. The vibe in this place was abysmal. Over a cup of *chifir*, Zuyev shared his pain with me and told me how he landed his last sentence. After his release, he turned up uninvited at an old classmate's place to demand her husband repay a debt. The husband refused and grabbed a knife. Zuyev wrested the knife from him and pounced on his debtor. One blow and he was a corpse.

'I had no choice,' he explained. 'It was either I kill him or he kills me.'

He then tied up his classmate and went on the run. Andrei does not regret the fact he didn't kill her – it was she who gave him up to the police. Had he acted differently, he might never have been caught. Compared to the other convicts, he got too long a sentence for just one corpse. He was very considerate and polite, and he became my good companion. Roma Y. later told me how baffled the operational workers were at our friendship. Apparently they asked him, 'What could Pereverzin have in common with that uneducated recidivist?' That uneducated recidivist was a hundred times more honest and decent than the police investigators and judges who sent me to that place, and I treasured my friendship with him. Throughout our time together, he helped me survive.

I never forgot Andrei, and to this day, I still treasure his friendship. He is serving out his sentence in a strict-regime colony in the village of Pakino in Vladimir Region, where I sometimes visit him. He has another ten years behind bars. I hope that my parcels and packages brighten his existence in the camp …

I often talked with Misha K., whom I knew from quarantine. Misha K. was having a tough and lonely time. He was struggling to adapt to the situation and relate to the others, finding little common ground with them. Whenever he got a parcel or package, the number of guys wishing to hang out with him rose sharply, but fell again as the goodies disappeared. Having lived through a war, he was ready to share his last shirt with his neighbour. He was a generous and magnanimous man. Once, Misha ran up to me in quite a state and confided his troubles: 'Can you believe it, Ivanovich! They've tagged me as a prisoner on the escape list!' And he continued, 'I got called to the operational main office and they asked me: "What's all this, hoping to escape, are you?"'

Misha was seething at the injustice and could not understand what the whole thing was about. It turned out a story he'd told someone over a cup of tea while they were plundering his parcel had reached the ears of the operational officers. Being a history buff, he enjoyed having an audience. Without any hidden agenda, Misha had told the prisoners, who listened with mouths agape, the story of Devyatayev, the legendary pilot and Soviet hero. Captured by the Germans, the pilot managed to seize an enemy aircraft and escape from a concentration camp.

The story made the intended impression on everyone – including the operational officers. They began round-the-clock checks, once every two hours, on Misha's presence in the unit.

He was seriously ill, highly on edge and sometimes his nerves would snap. The doctors were plainly abusing him, prescribing him Clozapine, which could make him doze off while standing up. The ban on daytime snoozing and resting on the beds was sheer torture for him.

Meanwhile, I was asleep on my feet even without any Clozapine. I wanted to sleep all the time and everywhere. But when I finally got to bed, I couldn't doze off for ages. Relocating to a new spot changed nothing. Quite plainly in concert with the operational department, they moved me to a lower bunk closer to Roma Y. To make it easier for him to keep an eye on me. I still woke up often in the night and heard all the mumbling and shrieks, sobbing and moans of the others. Many of the prisoners' sleep was far from serene and, judging by the shouting in their dreams, it was punctuated by nightmares. But some slept sweetly and calmly. My neighbour Roma was among them.

Every morning, when they woke up, the prisoners shook hands and said good morning. Unable to make sense of this tradition, I firmly asked those near me not to bid me good morning. I failed to see how anyone's morning could be good while confined in these walls. At any rate, mine couldn't be. In desperate moments, as I drifted off to sleep, I sometimes asked fate not to wake me up …

I began to settle in and find my feet. A trip to the shop in the run-up to New Year brought yet more disappointment. You had to be cunning about how to spend the money you had in your account. After making some purchases at inflated prices, the allotted 2,000 roubles disappeared in a flash. I bought the all-important cigarettes for Zuyev, tea, sweet things, a wafer cake to be saved for New Year's Eve. The money left over was enough for several cans of food: fish, sprats, sweetcorn, green peas. The choice in this place was meagre compared to what you'd get in a Moscow prison, but you could still live it up. A month later, Zuyev would have money in his account sent by my friends and relatives, and we'd walk out of that miserable shop with bags crammed full of sundry items.

26

NEW YEAR

The industrial zone was closed over the New Year holidays, and I had several days off, which I endeavoured, as ever, to put to good use. Sport and books were my faithful companions.

This laid-back life was overshadowed by a series of searches as New Year's Eve approached. Mass inspections were taking place across the entire camp, and there was no escape for our unit. One fine morning, we were amiably led away to the social club, while a horde of men in military uniform swooped on the barracks. After the raid, we returned to survey the damage. Overturned beds, bags open with their contents ransacked, things cast from bedside tables … Not cataclysmic, but unpleasant nevertheless. Zuyev and I spent a long time sorting through the mess. Today was New Year's Eve! We were allowed to watch television until five in the morning, we could skip breakfast at the dining room, and most important of all, we could sleep in till nine! I mapped out my holiday. 'We'll sit around, have some food, see in the New Year – and sleep! At least one night a year, I can get a decent night's sleep!' I mused.

Between the repositioned two-tier bunk beds was a small passage – an aisle where the prisoners' bedside tables stood. This was the prisoners' personal space, where a good part of their lives was spent. In our aisle, we rustled up an improvised festive spread. On the rearranged chairs, we had hors d'oeuvres and salads, lovingly prepared by Zuyev from the goodies I'd received in a package. Our cake and sweets were waiting in the wings. Within my brief time in the unit, I'd made a good few friends, and we got many invitations to visit others in their aisles and chat about life. I also invited people over, and they took me up on the offer. Misha K. visited us, as did Kolya M., a new friend of Zuyev's from the sewing workshop.

Kolya was a complete psycho. He'd lopped off his neighbour and drinking buddy's head with an axe. They'd had a quarrel once, and Kolya went to make peace. The neighbour refused. So Kolya felt the need to pick up an axe. But, notwithstanding this misdeed, he was as open-hearted, sincere and guileless as a child. And so I saw in the New Year of 2008 in this vibrant company. At midnight, after hearing the cheers of 'Hurray' from the re-educational-work room, we stood up, amicably clinked mugs of tea and wished each other a speedy release. I shut my eyes and, already for the fourth time – softly, so that no one would hear – I recited my chant: 'Dear Lord, please make this the last New Year I spend behind bars.' At that point, I had no idea that my spell would only work when cast for the seventh time …

We went on celebrating the evening, wandering around the barracks. After paying our respects to various prisoners and wishing our generous hosts a happy new year, I used the washbasin, got undressed and went to bed. The din seeped into my dreams – the conversations of the prisoners, hyped up by the holiday, who sat long into the night watching television in the re-educational-work room.

The New Year passed without incident.

'How strange, no one did any killing or stabbing!' I liked to jest. 'This can't be a strict-regime penal colony, it has to be some kind of summer camp.'

27

FREEDOM OF THE PRESS

The holidays slipped by pleasantly, offering me a little time to rest and recover my strength. Then the working days began again. I had to return to the job that I'd quickly grown to hate. Those damned caps were killing me and sapping my energy, and I'd get back to the unit fit to drop.

A pleasant surprise awaited me in the unit. A stack of newspapers and magazines lay on the bunk. Almost every day, the librarian brought over the periodicals I had subscribed to. A queue would form for some of the publications. Hardly anyone wished to read *Kommersant*, *Vedomosti* or *Ekspert*, but *Maxim* and *Men's Health* magazines and the newspaper *Moskovsky Komsomolets* were snapped up eagerly. Having the chance to hold in my hands magazines and newspapers from the outside, to be able to leaf through them, I felt a huge wave of joy. For me, the press meant a bridge to freedom, a whiff of fresh air. I received the *European Court of Human Rights Bulletin* regularly, and studied each issue closely.

Over time, as they observed me, the prisoners began turning to me with requests for consultations, asking me to write appeals against sentences they disputed. I did not help everybody, but agreed in some cases, and I wrote all manner of petitions and appeals.

My 'human rights' activity quickly drew the attention of the operational officers.

One evening, twenty minutes before lights out, the operational officer Captain Mishanov came flying into the barracks. Bursting with a sense of his own importance, he demanded I hand over the forbidden literature. I did not understand what he meant.

'Oh, so it's like that! You don't want to play nice!' he said, and he opened up my bedside table.

Between the porridge oats and the buckwheat flakes, next to a can of stew and a packet of tea, sat the *Constitution of the Russian Federation* and the *Penal Enforcement Code*. The sight of these works inflamed the captain, and he took me to the storeroom to search my bags. The captain's joy knew no bounds when he discovered at the bottom of a bag several issues of the *European Court of Human Rights Bulletin*.

'Get dressed, we're going to the main office to write a letter of explanation,' he ordered me.

I was led to the office of the head of the operational unit for an interrogation. They wanted to know how I'd managed to get forbidden literature into the camp.

On the operational officer's desk was a cardboard box with my things. They had taken the trouble of going to the industrial zone to bring the box over. It contained gloves, tea, a spoon, a mug, some hand cream and an ordinary notebook.

'Are you preparing an escape?' the officer bawled.

The idea had not occurred to me, and I squarely informed him of the fact. I also let him know that I had a subscription for this journal through their own library.

'You bring me these magazines yourselves from the main office,' I said, trying to persuade him of my innocence.

The operational officers did not believe me and called the library manager, who reeled off the steps involved.

'First, the newspapers and magazines arrive at the camp from the post office. The head of the re-educational department or the deputy head then summons me to the main office,' said the librarian, giving his straightforward testimony without a clue as to what was going on. 'And they hand me the publications. Then I distribute the newspapers and magazines to the units on the lists.'

I wrote a 'confession' in which I came clean about how I'd got hold of the unfortunate journals. The operational officers confiscated them and released me back to the unit. That evening I felt rotten; mentally and physically, I hit rock bottom. I brooded all night long.

I am certain the officers had no idea they were committing a criminal offence punishable by law: using their rank to rob me and deprive me of property worth a hefty sum, sufficient to justify criminal proceedings. Each magazine cost around 900 roubles.

The story reached the chief of the colony and had a happy ending. The head of the unit solemnly returned the magazines stolen from me and asked for a receipt slip.

At one point, there was a bulk theft of newspapers in the colony. The prisoners did not receive their copies of the newspaper *Kovrovskie Vedomosti*, which they had paid for out of their own pockets, when an article appeared in it about the head of the operational department in our camp. Mr Pashchenko had been caught red-handed using slave labour on his own hacienda. Several convicts were peaceably working at his dacha. There was talk of instituting criminal proceedings against the valiant major.

Destroying a portion of the edition, our jailers preserved the honour of an officer …

Throughout my whole sentence, I hankered after a job in the library, but it was an impossible dream. Just as in the olden days of the Soviet Union, persons of Jewish ethnicity were denied jobs in the top-secret military sector, so too I, tarred by association with Yukos, couldn't work in the library.

28

THE PATH TO PAROLE!

Setting my sights on parole and accepting the rules of the game, I decided to do everything in my power to secure my release.

For their work in the industrial zone, the prisoners could earn commendations in the form of written acknowledgements, extra visits from loved ones or additional packages from visitors. If the prisoner had no black marks, then once a quarter he would be given the sought-after commendation.

By that time, I had already heard stories about how the court treated parole applications. A judge could simply ask a prisoner who'd been slaving away for many years: 'So why didn't you take part in any amateur performances? Don't you sing? Can't you dance? No, you can carry on serving your sentence.'

The guys toiling at two shifts and returning to the barracks dog-tired resented such a set-up, and, quite rightly, torrents of invective were unleashed against those judges.

'Correctional facility'. Those words convey the meaning and core purpose of the institution: the reform of convicts. And yet that name is not only at odds with the reality, but is diametrically opposed to it. Whatever they might do in those institutions, the last thing on their

minds is reform. Anyone who has done time in such a place will lose all faith in justice. The penal colonies 'reform' the prisoners with slave labour, drilling the idea into their skulls that their hard work won't earn them money, before releasing hordes of embittered, disheartened men, maladapted to normal life, most of whom will end up back inside. The system churns out its product with an eighty per cent chance of recidivism. Is that not reason enough to think seriously about the health of a system that racks up a budget of astronomical proportions? The Federal Penitentiary Service burns through cash at a similar rate to the entire Russian public-health service.

Deep in the bowels of the system, they think up so-called re-educational activities. They devise, develop and put into practice all sorts of pastimes and amusements for the convicts. And I too had no escape from the songs, dances, theatre productions, comedy contests and sports days running rampant in the Melekhovo prison camp.

One day, the orderly in our unit issued the call: 'The camp will be holding a choral singing contest. Those who'd like to take part can register with me. All the contestants will get a prize!' By prize, he meant a commendation.

I had no singing ability and little interest in taking part. The other convicts apparently felt the same way. Slowly, a handful of men signed up for it. The officers' honour was at stake! What was this, the convicts not willing to sing? The head of the unit summoned the refuseniks, one by one, to his office. I was among their numbers, along with over half the unit. After standing in line, I entered his office.

'Now, why do you, Pereverzin, refuse to take part in our re-educational activities?' the chief asked me.

'I'm no good at singing,' I answered truthfully.

'Look, it's in your own best interests. If you don't do it, I'll write a report for your file saying you refused to comply with the management's requests. You'll get a poor character reference, and you won't be released on parole,' he tried to convince me.

Knowing who I was dealing with, I caved in. 'All right,' I said. 'I'll sing.'

The choir leader was Anton K., who had a conviction for grievous bodily harm and who, in my opinion, sang rather well. We were given the chorus. After several rehearsals, our entire unit took to the club stage, before the gaze of a horde of officers.

Anton began singing:

And may our childhood never end,

Though we've all grown up,

Because our parents yearn for us

To be forever young.

Our choir, made up of maniacs, murderers, rapists, robbers, thieves and terrorists, stumbling over their words, started up:

The home of our parents, where it all began,

You're the steadfast harbour in our life.

The home of our parents, may the sweetest light

Glow in your windows for an aeon to come.

The song was sung in turn by the entire camp. We took second place. The colony's leadership were delighted to report on the re-education of the convicts. The only one of us to receive a commendation was our choir leader, Anton, while I managed to escape chalking up an infringement ...

When I told my wife I was singing in the choir, at first she wouldn't believe me. Then she remembered how tuneless my singing was and had a good, long laugh. I too laughed when I saw the serious faces of the colony's staff, listening intently to us and assessing our performance.

'My God, where am I?' I thought in those minutes. 'This place is a genuine madhouse!'

How could I fail to be reminded of a scene from Alexei Tolstoy's book *The Adventures of Nevzorov, or Ibikus*. Forced to abandon Russia after the October Revolution, the main characters open a brothel in Istanbul. At the opening, Colonel Rtishchev asks Nevzorov to sing.

'But I've never sung before!' answers the count.

'I command you to!' the colonel insists.

So Nevzorov sings. At the very first notes, Rtishchev clasps his head in his hands in despair, and a drunken officer in Denikin's army sitting nearby says, 'Shoot him!'

I also wanted to say, 'Gentlemen officers, please read the Russian classics.'

After performing in the choir, I wasn't afraid of anything, and I willingly enrolled for the Spartakiad to mark Defender of the Fatherland Day. I applied for several events: weight-lifting, tug of war and the biathlon. We had to ski down the avenue that I knew so well from all the marching and fling snowballs to knock down the targets – some empty bottles lined up on the tables.

The chairman of the sports club, Andrei, doing time for rape and murder, sized me up at a glance. My figure, fleshed out from the years in prison, did not fill him with confidence. But, yielding to my pressure and scratching his head, the back of which was tattooed with a target, he reluctantly included me in the list of participants.

The camp authorities treated such events with the utmost seriousness. In the interests of media coverage (and for the aggrandisement of the authorities), the local press was invited along. The curious journalists marvelled at the troupe of performing convicts, all running and jumping and instantly forgetting their tricks the moment they were released from their cage. The spectacle drew crowds of gawkers from among the camp staff and the prisoners, fiercely rooting for their units' teams. On that day, shouting, noise and fun took over the camp.

Kitted out with some shabby old skis and poles, I put them on – miraculously, they fitted – and went to the starting line. The track began in the adaptation unit's local zone and ran uphill along the avenue. We had to run up the slope, turn around, go back down and hit the targets with the prepared snowballs. Everything was ready for the race, but we were let down by the weather. The snow began melting, and the avenue became perilously slippery. Several participants immediately took their positions on the starting line, but on the commands 'On your marks, get set, go!' they could not move. Skidding about on the spot, they fell on top of each other. Helped back up by their caring comrades, they got to their feet and fell down again. Watching this pile-up of people, I laughed so hard I almost fell down myself. This comical scene had the whole camp in stitches. Somehow getting back up on their skis, the prisoners, tumbling down and rising over and again, managed to navigate the avenue, then, tumbling down and rising some more, made their way back. A judge picked from among the convicts was holding a stopwatch and impartially recording the results. My turn came, and I took my place on the starting line.

'The trick is to dodge your tumbling rivals and push a few steps ahead of them,' I thought, working out a war plan. 'And the rest comes down to technique!'

My father was a cross-country ski coach, and from a young age, I used to hang out in the nearby Bitsevsky Park, where I looped around the ski trails. I kept the habit up even as an adult and haven't abandoned it since my release. To this day, you can find me in the same old park, skiing the same old routes.

Despite the pounds I'd piled on, with a cry of 'Now I'll show you all how it's done', I clenched my teeth and with all my might tore up the avenue in a skating stride. Having sailed along the avenue in one burst, in the wink of an eye I came back and smashed several targets with the snowballs, establishing a local 'world' record. It was my hour of glory!

The spectators were speechless; no one had expected such verve from me. My spectacular speed march was not lost on the invited journalists. They covered the event in the local newspaper, publishing an article with a photo of me captioned: 'Melekhovo takes the place of Courchevel.' From reliable sources, I found out this article caused quite a stir in local circles and became a hot topic at the board meeting for the Vladimir Region Federal Penitentiary Service. For me, the article ended in a slap on the wrist from the staff in the colony's operational department, after which I always steered clear of the many journalists who loved to visit our showcase prison camp. The head of the operational department, to his great displeasure, was carpeted and scolded for allowing Pereverzin to live it up in the camp! After this dressing down, the number of my ill-wishers increased by one, and a very dangerous and influential one at that.

My record inspired respect among the prisoners and boosted my status in the camp. Andrei was to tell me, a man who had spent half a lifetime in wrestling: 'And we thought you were just an office worker. Thought you'd never handled anything heavier than a ballpoint pen ...'

For a long time, the prisoners kept saying to me, 'Hey, Ivanovich, wow! Good on you!' and they'd shake my hands. Each day would bring me new acquaintances, sometimes very interesting ones. I acquired connections in the criminal world. The staff of the camp, in contrast, all blurred into one, and for a long time I could not remember who was who. I'd get muddled between a security officer and an operational officer, or the head of the re-education department and the fireman, and for a long time I would pester Roma Y. I'd poke my finger through the grille of the local zone at the passing men in uniform, tirelessly asking him, 'Who is that one? And what about that one?'

My sporting record was honoured with a commendation in the form of an additional parcel or visitor's package. After earning my just reward, I went back to the production line in the caps workshop. There, records of another kind awaited me ...

29

CAPS

We were expecting a visit from representatives of the buyer of the caps. They were coming to look around and inspect the quality of the product. Outwardly, the caps may have seemed identical, but in fact each one was unique. There were a lot of rejects. If the fur was inferior, bald spots would form at the seams or the folds. And no matter how much I rubbed the spot with a wire brush, it wouldn't make it better. The foreman gave me an important task. I was instructed to fill several boxes with perfect caps, carefully picked out. Flattered at the trust shown in me, I spent an entire shift working on the selection process. Soon, I had several boxes around me with ready-to-show merchandise. The crucial moment arrived; my time had come. The women entered the workshop and walked in my direction. With the sleight of hand of a conjuror, I slipped the caps I'd just made far under the table, then pulled out and began lovingly combing the ones I'd prepared earlier. The women looked on, took the products from my hands and nodded in satisfaction. They opened the box next to me, also prepared in advance, and saw the same marvellous caps. But I might as well have shouted, 'Hey, watch out! You're being scammed!' I should have pulled out the box full of bald hats! I was not destined for a career in that workshop; rank ingratitude awaited me ...

A haze of dust hung in the air. Entirely coated in the dust, outside and in, I packed up the caps unstintingly. The workshop was running at full pelt, churning out its products. Finishing off the latest order, the prisoners were working flat out and eagerly produced an extra batch of hats, which I physically could not keep up with. At lunchtime, with the foreman's permission, I stayed behind and quietly carried on trimming the threads, gently brushing and folding the caps in the unusually empty workshop. Some men in uniform dropped in, among them Major Morozov, the head of the security department for the camp. He gravely informed me I had violated the daily routine by failing to attend a security event.

'What do you mean?' I said, attempting to absolve myself. 'But what about the production plan, the quota?'

'The production plan is none of my concern,' he said firmly. And he wrote a report on me.

'You toil like a slave, and all you get for it is a sanction!' I thought, and headed back to the unit. I was overwhelmed with outrage, seething inside. In Misha K. I found a sympathetic ear; he was ready to listen to my outburst. In return, I had to listen to him too.

'What a preposterous sentence those creatures gave me!' he said, with thunderous indignation in his voice. 'What gives them the right? Why do they do it?'

We were speaking the same language; I understood him perfectly.

A few days later, the head of the unit called me in and handed over a copy, signed upon receipt, of the decision to impose a sanction. I wrote down: 'I do not agree with this decision and will challenge it in court.'

'You're off to a bad start, Pereverzin,' he told me ominously. 'I wouldn't advise you to sue the colony – you'll only pick up new sanctions. And in fact, we still need to check out what you were up to there – maybe you were digging a tunnel or sewing your own line of clothing.'

I was waiting for my lawyer and needed an appointment with the head of the camp. He was new in the job. His predecessor, after a meteoric rise, had become the head of the Vladimir Region Federal Penitentiary Service. We now had Lieutenant Colonel Okunev, a former chief of production and the loveliest person. A man of rare sophistication for this office, he was not to work in the system for long. After stumbling by chance into prison production and carving a successful career there, he would later choose to resign. In his case, the resignation genuinely was voluntary, unlike all the men who adopted the wording of voluntary dismissal when they fell from their high-profile posts for serious misconduct verging on the criminal.

To my surprise, I was given an appointment quickly. After standing for a while in a short queue, I went into the head of the camp's office and saw an aquarium in which piranhas were peacefully sploshing about. He'd heard about the Yukos affair and grasped the key points. Showing something resembling sympathy, he listened to my story about the sanction. The issue was solved on the spot. He made a call in my presence to the head of the workshop and ordered him to write me out an emergency commendation, thus instantly cancelling out the new sanction. Delighted that I no longer needed to pursue the case in court, I happily made my way back to the unit.

A constant hubbub reigned in the unit, with music playing loudly and the place all astir. Prisoners scurried to and fro, and the barracks was heaving. Some played backgammon, others sat and drank tea. On rare occasions, you'd see someone reading a book. The re-educational-work room would be packed with men watching the latest action movie. From time to time, the head of the unit wandered into the barracks. He'd survey his domain and nose out transgressors. One of his favourite activities was pulling out from under the mattresses underpants and socks that had been buried by the prisoners. Every two hours, a warrant officer entered the barracks to count the prisoners on the escape list. It was one hell of a situation: we weren't allowed to lie down on the bed, so you couldn't relax at the end of a working day. Every now and then I caught the glance of Sasha Serebryakov, the unit's orderly. He kept an eagle eye on me and relayed everything seen and heard to the caretaker and the head of the unit. The network of informers encompassed the entire barracks. Roma Y. repeated our conversations straight to his boss – operational officer Major Vlasov, whom he called 'Papa'. Evidently, Papa was a prolific breeder, fathering many such 'sons'. Another operational officer, Captain Mishanov, had agents of his own and regularly called on the caretaker in the storeroom, where, over a cup of tea, they discussed what was happening in the unit. After he had gone, the orderly would hurry into the storeroom and rush off to the sinks to wash the dirty teacups.

One day Foma the caretaker asked me, 'Do you know why the pigs dislike you so much?'

I didn't know the answer to this question, just as I had not realised they disliked me.

'They think you robbed the state!' he said. It was clear they imagined I was the source and origin of all their woes: the disorder in their lives, their low wages, poor education, problem drinking and many other troubles besides.

The situation weighed on me, and I wanted to escape it. Gradually, I formed a clear and highly detailed picture of life in the colony. I learnt about the existence of a sanatorium on the camp grounds that had a small gym. The sanatorium was a holiday retreat where the prisoners could find sanctuary from their daily routine. The employees with the highest productivity, the collaborators and others useful to the camp authorities won places there. Getting into that sanctuary became my dream for the next six months.

After the incident in the cap-sewing workshop and the heated exchange with its foreman, I was transferred to a different workshop where they produced peaked caps. There was the same dirt and din. Blaring music drowned out the noise of the sewing machines and the hiss of the irons. I met the foreman. Vladislav B. (or Blin, as he was known) carried considerable clout among the prisoners. It was not his first time behind bars. He was doing fifteen years for multiple murders. He had been sentenced to death, but when they brought in the moratorium on the death penalty, his sentence was commuted to fifteen years' imprisonment. We found some common ground, and on many occasions he would help me. Just what is it that makes him a worse person than Judge Yarlykova, who convicted at the bare minimum two innocent men? At least Blin freely admitted his guilt, saying bluntly, 'Oh yes, they really got me mad! So I had to get out the old blade!'

To my surprise, he once came out with the following: 'Ivanovich, there's something I've wanted to ask for a long time. How could you have robbed Yukos if everything there belonged to Khodorkovsky?'

This uneducated guy who'd spent half his life behind bars could see the holes in the case against us!

I learnt a new prison trade: trimmer-of-threads from the finished items. I was now swamped in completed caps with threads protruding in all directions. My task was to snip them off neatly and make the product look fit for purchase. Then I passed the finished caps through a window in the wall to quality control, where my old partner from the cap workshop, Yura the platinum-furnace stealer, had already settled in. My new job was much easier than the previous one. But I grew ever more tired of the empty chatter, of the need to hang out with men whom I found unappealing. It was deeply galling that I had to waste precious time, whole years of my life, on these pointless, inane activities. Yura was constantly joking away. 'Nobody will believe me that I was working side by side with Khodorkovsky's accomplice!' he said, and he doubled up in merry laughter. I smiled sadly and waited for the shift to end, so I could get back to the unit.

Preparations were underway for the arrival of another commission. The leadership decided to dazzle by bringing springtime to the camp. All the snow was swiftly shovelled away. It was scraped back to reveal the ground below. The snow-removal team spent a long time – with the help of some sacks – dumping the snow into a melter. A group of prisoners was hurriedly painting all the kerbs. Panic and commotion reigned in the unit, whipped up by the unit leader. He ordered the men standing in lines: 'Everyone is to clear out their bedside cabinets! No repeat of last time, when they opened up Pereverzin's and found a total mess!'

Well, indeed, if you're going to pick one cabinet out of a hundred for a good old rummage, whose will it be? Mine, of course! The generals and colonels could not resist the pleasure of having a nose through my things!

The bedside tables were hastily cleansed of anything 'superfluous'. The tea, canned food and sweets were all hidden away in bags. There remained only a mug, a spoon and some toiletries.

Each unit's local zone had a specially fenced-off spot for drying clothes. All laundry was always removed from the drying area in time for the commission's arrival. Too bad if you hadn't finished drying your clothes. The orderly for the unit would take all the damp things from the clothes lines. Underpants, socks, towels and sheets would be bunged into a sack. It was the way things were done, always and everywhere – certainly at all the camps I stayed in. Even after seven years, I still couldn't fathom why. The mystery remained unsolved.

During the commission's arrival, the sleeping areas in the unit were strictly off limits. Any prisoners not busy at work were packed into the re-educational-work room, where they quietly watched television.

At moments like that, I felt redundant. Unable to make sense of why all this was being done, I imagined a surreal scene. A commission was on its way to the colony. The camp was purged of all its prisoners. We disappeared, vanished into thin air. The head of the camp proudly showed off his domain. He led the visitors through the rooms, showed them the empty barracks with neatly made beds, the rows of bedside tables all visible, but not a single convict to darken the mood of the honoured guests. Ah, sheer beauty! The stuff of dreams for any head of a colony!

Well, the staff there had no need of us! We were superfluous. That was why they had a visceral hatred of the inmates, not considering them human.

30

THE OPEN DAY

I was surprised to learn that in two weeks' time they were holding an open day in the colony. But there were no plans to send the convicts home for the weekend, nor did they even intend to move us beyond the camp grounds. Although the law does allow for that: by way of incentive, the camp authorities can grant a prisoner home leave. In practice, of course, it does not happen. Why take action when you can just as soon sit idle? I saw a man who'd served seven years of his sentence when, just a few months before his release, his father died. That prisoner fell at the feet of the head of the camp, begging to be allowed home for three days. He was lucky enough to live in that same Vladimir Region, almost in the neighbouring village. Nothing was stopping the camp head from doing a charitable deed – nothing but his own sloth and the tacit instructions of the Federal Penitentiary Service. The prisoner never did get the chance to bid farewell to his beloved father ...

The main objective of the open day (or 'parents' day', as it was also called) was to show the prisoners' relatives what a good life we had in the camp. The event was put on for that express purpose. Guest lists were compiled. The prisoners could only invite close relatives: their parents, wives and children. After a rigorous search, the guests were led into the camp. The tour was conducted by the deputy chief political officer under the beady eye of the operational officer. You could enter the barracks and see the bunk where your relative slept. Or you could visit the dining room and sample some prison glop specially prepared for the occasion. The visitors, dressed as they were in civilian clothes, were a particularly strange sight for the prisoners, who were used to seeing only men in uniform. For a time, the camp ground to a halt, all movement was prohibited, and the prisoners were herded into the barracks. Nonetheless, the guests could not escape the gaze of the curious convicts. All the windows of the barracks were lined with hundreds of watchful eyes observing the guests. The tour ended in the library, where everything was set out for a party. The large room was filled with tables and chairs where the guests could sit with their relatives and drink tea with something sweet bought at a canteen specially opened for the occasion. The prisoners were brought in after a search. For them, the event offered an extra chance to see their loved ones, whom they could only meet on a limited number of visits. During the tea drinking, an amateur band made up of prisoners played and sang. I never took part in those types of events and strictly forbade my wife from coming to the colony for the open days. I could reconcile myself to her staying two or three times a year in the room for extended visits, but to let her walk about the grounds of the camp was simply too much.

One time we were taken out of the barracks and lined up in the local zone. Around eight wayward teenagers had come to visit our barracks, accompanied on their tour by some operational officers. These boys were from a children's home. Judging by the perplexed and even fearful look on their faces, the lesson sank in and had a good effect. I thought back to my own childhood with a smile. Right until my last moment of freedom, nothing in my life had foreshadowed the twist of fate that awaited me ...

31

ALL OF LIFE'S A THEATRE

Every year, a talent contest would be held in the camps. Each prison colony under its own steam would put on a show, and the premiere would be attended by the latest commission. They judged the acting skills of the inmates and picked the winners. In Vladimir Region, a crystal owl would fly from camp to camp – a trophy for the best stage production. While preparing for the latest performance, the deputy chief political officer of the colony would dream of winning that owl. Our camp's deputy chief political officer was being replaced. The old one had committed some grave offence or other and, just a few years off from retirement, he'd willingly resigned, relieved not to be joining us behind bars. The new deputy chief political officer was Alexei Chudin. One of the few decent men I met in the system.

A notice appeared on the doors to the dining room: 'Those wishing to take part in the talent show should register with the club manager.'

I read between the lines: 'Actors are needed for this Russian serf theatre.'

I made the acquaintance of the club manager. Roma G. had been sentenced to fifteen years for murder. In the camp, he was responsible for staging popular entertainments and managing the camp's theatre. Leaving aside the fact he'd killed a man, Roma was not a bad fellow. On the outside, he had played the guitar a little, and inside, he became something of a minor star. For the delectation of all manner of guests and commissions, he would sing on the club stage for practically days on end, whether the occasion demanded it or not. In his time off from singing, Roma would write play scripts with the help of the other prisoners. The themes for the performances were determined by order of the Vladimir Region Federal Penitentiary Service. The decision came from on high that our current year would be the Year of the Family. No sooner was it said than it was done! The play was promptly dedicated to the Year of the Family. For these purposes, an ensemble was put together. Roma intended to put on a breathtaking show that would bowl the jury over. Unlike the choir, a good number of prisoners were keen to earn a commendation for their role in the play.

As I showed potential talent and could memorise sizeable chunks of text, I was promised an additional reward: a month's rest in the sanatorium. Without a moment's thought, I consented. That was how my dizzying career as an actor took off. Every day, come rain or shine, after finishing my shift in the industrial zone, I gloomily trudged to the club for rehearsals. A handful of men from our unit signed up. The action of the play jumped about between the past and future and bore no relevance to the chosen theme. Misha K. landed the role of a mythic warrior. I couldn't look at him without bursting out laughing. With a cardboard helmet on his head, he scarcely managed to squeeze into the caftan made of faux-leather material ripped for the occasion from a door or the seat of an old bus. He was wielding a wooden sword, which in his big hands looked like a child's toy. I looked no less ridiculous. Playing a part set in the Napoleonic Wars, I was given a mockery of a uniform sewn from old curtains and a cardboard cap that barely stayed on my head. The female roles were filled by the pariah prisoners, the untouchables, drawn from the entire camp. They were playing the part of society ladies. Dressed in wigs made of tinsel and cassette ribbon, wearing fake bosoms and holding fans in fingers all blue from tattoos, it was a ghastly sight. Despite us having real Chechens in the camp, the role of the Chechen terrorist went to Daniyar, who'd been convicted for murdering a Tajik. But how can you have a beardless Chechen? Especially when he's a terrorist! Beards and moustaches were forbidden in the camp. Who cared what the Russian Federation Criminal Code had to say if the head of the colony himself had declared: 'No beards!'? The Code, in fact, states in black and white: 'The convicts are allowed a neatly trimmed beard and moustache.'

Art requires sacrifice. Daniyar wrote the following petition to the head of the camp: 'Given my role in the talent contest, I ask you to grant me permission to grow a beard.' To my surprise, he got this statement signed by the head of the unit, the operational officer, the security officer, the head of the re-educational department and the deputy chief political officer. The head of the colony's signature came sixth! I saw the letter with my own eyes. Daniyar would walk proudly down the avenue, and the officer on duty would ask him sternly: 'What's this, Citizen Convict, violating the rules are we? Walking about unshaven!'

'You're mistaken, Citizen Chief!' he'd answer, pulling his document from the pocket of his baggy trousers. 'I have permission!'

The premiere was attended by the bigwigs from the Vladimir Region Federal Penitentiary Service, women from some culture-themed institution who were included in the jury, and the press. The hall was filled with prisoners from quarantine who'd been promised that the louder they clapped, the more time off marching.

The performance, which reminded me of my trial, was a total flop. We took the second-to-last place among all the camps in Vladimir Region. The head of the colony reluctantly authorised the promised rewards for all the participants in this disgrace. As pledged, I was granted a rest in the sanatorium, and I waited my turn for a change of scenery.

32

A MISERABLE BIRTHDAY PARTY

The days flashed past, as alike as twins; the weeks flew by, amassing into months. I was still in the same old unit, the same industrial zone, the same sewing workshop. Sometimes, during a cigarette break, I went out with the men to the smoking room to chat with the prisoners from the other workshops. Once, the head of the workshop, a captain, came rushing over, took stock of all the prisoners imperiously and turned to me: 'You've been smoking rather a lot, Pereverzin!'

'No, I'm a non-smoker,' I replied.

'Well, then, do up your top button!' he said and walked off on his business.

I went back to my workplace to trim caps. The next day was my birthday, and I planned on celebrating.

My mood was not festive; in fact, far from it. I felt heavy of heart. Zuyev took on the organisation of the event and looked after refreshments. On the rearranged stools, a spread appeared: sweets, cigarettes, huge jars of *chifir* and instant coffee. The barracks was celebrating. I was showered with birthday best wishes and cards. Birthday greetings in the camp centred around just one wish, the thing everyone dreamt of: an early release. This was the fourth year in a row I was receiving such birthday greetings. The prisoners in our inner circle came over to the VIP zone in our aisle. There was Kolya M., a friend of Zuyev's and his partner at the sewing workshop. Any friend of Zuyev's was a friend of mine. Kolya was a wizard with his hands, highly skilled at sewing. Smiling beatifically and with a childlike candour, Kolya announced his dream and desire: 'Volodya, I wish you were lying about totally legless somewhere on the outside.'

'Kolya,' I said. 'You see, I don't actually drink!'

Unable to wrap his mind around this idea, he asked incredulously, 'What, not at all?'

'Not as you'd understand it,' I tried to get my meaning through to him.

I wished it could all be over as fast as possible: the birthday, which I wasn't enjoying in the slightest; the whole crazy prison sentence. I rounded off the celebration with the traditional curses heaped on the judge and the investigators of the Prosecutor-General's Office.

The day was drawing to an end. I glanced at the time and, with a sigh of relief, realised it would soon be lights out. The next day I would have to show my face at the industrial zone and relive all those birthday greetings. A mug of *chifir* was passed around the group. The prison tradition was for all the men to drink in turn from the same mug. I'd hated that universal ritual right from the start of my time in prison, and, suppressing my revulsion, I took the mug, turning it so as to find a spot untouched by the other prisoners' lips, before drawing a sip of the bitter drink. Later on, at such gatherings, I'd have the luxury of drinking from a mug of my own, without offending or hurting the feelings of the other prisoners who looked upon my habit as a strange little whim.

The foreman gave me a magnificent gift: he filled out the paperwork for my rest in the sanatorium.

33

HOLIDAY CAMP

I collected my things and moved into the sanatorium. The chance for a change of scenery cheered me no end: I could sleep my fill and have a break from the regime imposed on us, all the endless searches and inspections.

For a while, I was happy. The sanatorium was the pride of the colony, a special kind of oasis. You could bring any commission you liked there and show them how the authorities take care of their prisoners. The two sleeping areas, each with twelve beds, couldn't accommodate everyone who wanted a place, and only select and honoured prisoners ended up there. I had been terribly lucky. There was a small gym and a shower where you could wash each day. You could sleep as long as you wanted in the daytime. What more could you ask for! There was a small kitchen with a fridge and a stove where you could cook food, should you have any. Here I saw a miracle of miracles, an unheard-of luxury in these parts: a Samsung washing machine.

Everything here (including the washing machine) was run by the caretaker, Sergei M. He had an undeniable flair for organisation and was always busy working on his various brainchildren, which bordered on the crackpot. One moment he'd decide to build a fountain on the grounds of the sanatorium, the next, a monument in the fountain. His ideas were happily taken up by the camp staff and implemented by the prisoners – using their own cash. In this place, everything was paid for and repaired with the funds of the prisoners resting there. Sergei beadily kept things in order. The washing machine operated non-stop, and I kept on waiting for it to break down from the ruthless exploitation. Don't mistake this for product endorsement, but that moment never came. The washing machine worked night and day, serving the local elite. Not only the residents of the sanatorium washed their things there, but also some other prisoners: well-connected ones who'd wormed their way up the system – the library administrator and the manager of the medical unit. I gazed in delight at my snow-white sheets, washed at last, and couldn't wait for bedtime. There wasn't a hope of finding a plain ordinary blanket cover: for some entirely obscure reason, they were forbidden in our penitentiaries.

In the kitchen, I drank tea and talked with the guys from the automotive garage. They were frequent guests at the sanatorium. Their slave labour was rewarded with regular stays in that institution and also with food supplies from their guardian, the head of the operations department. Plain ordinary buckwheat, pasta and chicken – the ultimate dream of any prisoner – formed their daily diet. They were content and satisfied. So were the camp authorities. It was a cosy set-up. In the garage, you could repair cars for yourself and for the right people at rock-bottom prices; in the sewing workshop, you could sew yourself a tailor-made suit. A certain captain named Pugin, the terror of all the prisoners and a well-known wrestler who went about with his top buttons undone, had no qualms about turning up in the industrial zone with an old, cracked wooden plug from a bathtub and ordering a prisoner to make a duplicate on the lathe from some stainless steel.

My stay in the sanatorium was overshadowed by the arrival of an especially important commission. A group of journalists arrived in the colony, including a reporter from *The New York Times* and some other foreigners. This was a world-shattering event for the prison camp, and the management was making special arrangements to receive the party. What matters above all in our Russian state? That you avoid bringing shame on yourself, window-dress reality and pass yourself off as better than you are. The deputy chief political officer handpicked the prisoners to be interviewed and prepped them with answers to questions they might be asked. To my relief, I was ordered not to go within a mile of the journalists and, on pain of death, not to talk to them. When the journalists wandered into the sanatorium, I leapt aside and only just managed to dodge a camera that happened to be pointing my way.

'No be afraid!' I heard in broken Russian ... The journalists were walking about, gazing at everything with interest and hearing lavish tales told by the prisoners about how good life was in this place. Listening in on them, you felt like asking, 'So, my friend, if everything is so splendid in here, need we bother releasing you?' One specially selected prisoner (who worked in the experimental sewing workshop where they were mastering the art of fulfilling new orders while simultaneously catering to the private interests of the men running the camp) was gushing about how high the salaries were. He was the only one of 1,500 prisoners on a model salary of 10,000 roubles, which was a huge sum for the camp.

The journalists took a shine to the sanatorium, where they were regaled before their departure with tea and sweets (bought, naturally, with the prisoners' own cash). The contented journalists left our marvellous penal colony, and the camp management sat back and waited for the glowing articles. And sure enough, they began to appear! To the great joy of our jailers, *Moskovsky Komsomolets* printed a long report on the beautiful life in Melekhovo. There was also an article in *The New York Times*. The only downside was it was written in English. I was summoned to the main office and asked to translate it.

'The colony inherited the best traditions of the Gulag,' I rendered the author's words verbatim into Russian. 'The prisoners live in overcrowded, unrepaired barracks built in the 1930s of the previous century.'

The deputy chief political officer then said something so ridiculous that I was unable to stifle a laugh. 'Would you believe it! So how did he find that out, then? We showed him all our finest spots, led him around our showcase units ...'

He became noticeably rattled and embarrassed. He quickly pulled himself together and said, 'Just forget this happened, don't tell anyone.'

I nodded my assent and gave a verbal pledge of confidentiality; then, barely suppressing my laughter, I went back to the sanatorium.

34

ESCAPES AND CATS

One more misfortune was lurking for me during our evenings in the sanatorium. The sleeping section had a TV, which the holidaying prisoners would watch late into the night. All sorts of interminable drama series and war movies would help the prisoners kill time. As for me, I had almost no leisure time. Realising that in a month I'd be returning to trimming caps in the industrial zone, I tried to put all my free time to good use. What interested me were the gym, the shower and books.

Mightily fed up with the muffled sounds of the television, I finally managed to drift off.

The moment we woke, we realised something serious had happened. The industrial zone was closed, and they weren't taking the prisoners to work. The entire police force ran into the colony. Full alert! We couldn't work out what was happening. Rumour reached us that someone had escaped from the camp. Someone from Unit 3.

'Could they be looking for me?' I wondered.

It all became clear. They were looking for Nikolai K., sentenced to twenty-four years for double murder and robbery. I knew Kolya well. Originally from Belarus, he'd moved to Russia a long time ago looking for work. As a boy, he'd done gymnastics, and he was remarkably toned and lithe for his thirty-five years, without a gram of excess fat. He already had a daring escape from the Naro-Fominsk court in his past. When he was brought to the court, he'd thrown a concoction into the guard's eyes – some whitewash he'd scraped from the wall and mixed with salt. He banged the two other guards' foreheads together and vaulted over a two-and-a-half-metre-high fence topped with barbed wire. And he was gone. Traversing the forests and swamps, he reached Moscow, where, within a few days, he was caught.

He was the first and last man with whom I almost got into a fight in the unit. In my first few days in the unit, in the wash area, he clearly decided I looked like a victim and said, 'A pity I never ran into you on the outside!'

'It's not too late, we can have it out right here and now,' I replied. 'What are you doing hiding behind the pigs?'

Before it had a chance to erupt, the conflict was quickly doused by the surrounding prisoners, and Kolya and I ended up conversing. In our unit, Nikolai had a sideline in repairs. He repaired everything: walls, doors, locks. He refastened door handles that had fallen off, painted things, whitewashed the curbs. He mended the prisoners' shoes. He could attach the soles from a pair of old sneakers onto some prison boots, and the other way around. His deft hands could fix anything. In short, Kolya was the go-to guy in the unit, and he was in everyone's good books.

When Kolya received permission for an extended visit from his common-law wife, he set off for the visiting room. Roll calls were held there twice a day, in the mornings and evenings. The prisoners would come out of their rooms and line up in the corridor, where a policeman would check no one was missing. The rooms there were all different: some were a little better, some a little worse, some larger, some smaller. Kolya got a lovely room with a view over … freedom. And below the window of the guards' room was a small courtyard where they would reload their weapons. In the dead of night, Kolya smashed down the grille, dumped his unlucky wife and hotfooted it out of there. Presumably to keep a lid on the story, at first they tried catching the escapee using the forces of the Federal Penitentiary Service. This time, Nikolai did not make it too far. A fake story was put out that Kolya had been caught on the spot, that he'd literally fallen from the window right upon the heads of the vigilant policemen. In reality, he'd managed to reach the camp's pigsty, where he was apprehended by an entire company of guards. Their dog had led them down the right trail at the right time.

The sanatorium courtyard flanked the courtyard of the main office, and so I took up a strategically advantageous viewing spot, from which I avidly observed the events. I saw the pale and teary-eyed woman who had come for her failed visit to Kolya. She was taken into the main office for questioning. A short time later, they hauled Kolya in there too. He had clearly been given a good pasting. At the moment of his escape, he'd done three years of a twenty-four-year sentence. For the attempted escape, he was given three years more. So his term was starting again from scratch.

But the most interesting part came the next day. After the incident, the management of the camp could not carry on as though nothing had happened. They had to take some sort of action! There was no way of bypassing the next round of inspections and delegations, where they might ask, 'So what measures were adopted following the escape? What did you do?'

After rousing us with the alert call, they put together a team of prisoners working in the repairs team for the colony. Brandishing angle grinders and armed with welding machines, they cut through and destroyed all the training grounds throughout the entire camp. The sliced up sections of pull-up bars, parallel bars, homemade dumbbells and barbells were loaded onto a tractor and driven away from the camp grounds. On that day, the reception point for scrap metal in the village of Melekhovo overfulfilled the quota for the year ahead – obviously, until the next escape came around. Having carried out the first stage of their plan, the management of the colony embarked on part two, which was every bit as important. Besides the prisoners, all kinds of other creatures lived unofficially in the colony. The pigeons, magpies, rats and mice did not draw the attention of the management. But as for the cats …

There were gazillions of cats in the colony. They were loved by the prisoners, who were disenchanted with humankind. Some of the inmates became so attached to their little companions that when they were released, they took their beloved cats with them to freedom. For the prisoners, cats could sometimes be their only love and their last comfort. The convicts cherished and pampered them in every possible way. The cats could move freely around the camp, crossing from one local zone to the next, and, fed lavishly by the prisoners, they lived much better than the men did. I often envied the old black cat called Bruiser who lived in our unit. Bruiser would lazily stretch his legs out in his sleep whenever the top brass entered the barracks. He didn't need to stand up and greet every inspector – the sergeant or warrant officer constantly wandering around our barracks. He could do anything he liked.

All the units, all the workshops, all the buildings in the colony had their own pride and joy, and sometimes more than one. Almost without exception, the cats were given human names. Every Tuesday and Thursday morning, at the door to the dining room, a great big beautiful cat called Senya would greet the prisoners. On those days, eggs were served for breakfast, in accordance with the dietary intake requirements set by the Research Institute for the Russian Federal Penitentiary Service. To the sheer delight of the prisoners, who were giving him the last of their rations, the cat guzzled the eggs, shell and all, in huge quantities. Despite his size and appetite, Senya was an underdog in the cat hierarchy. In the countless battles over turf and for the love of the few lady cats around, Senya would always be slow off the mark. Old Bruiser from our unit was the recognised leader.

A high-priority directive came through from the main office: 'All the cats in the colony are to be counted, listed and registered.' A time frame of three days was set. Too bad if you missed the boat. Any cats without registration would be exterminated. 'How nice they won't be shot by firing squad,' I said acidly. Although, as it turned out, an even worse fate awaited those unregistered cats. They were gathered into a big sack and driven out of the grounds by a jailer with the military rank of an officer. History is silent on what happened next to those poor animals. Danger also lurked for the cats that remained in the colony. An officer in the industrial zone with the rank of captain, who enjoyed kettlebell lifting in his spare time, would amuse himself in the camp by hunting for cats. He would turn up to work with a slingshot, load it with steel ball bearings and, rapt with pleasure, lob shots at the cats, rejoicing at each one he bagged. A year of his service was deemed the equivalent of one and a half years of ordinary service, as was the case for soldiers in war zones.

The caretaker for the sanatorium wrote a petition addressed to the head of the camp: 'I request that you give a black cat going by the name of Bullet leave to remain in the sanatorium of the penal colony.' The petition was endorsed by the operational officers, security officers and re-education workers. Similar petitions came pouring into the main office from all the units, as well as from the social club, the bathhouse and the medical unit. The foreman of the cap-sewing workshop, my former boss from among the convicts, came up with a rationale for needing to live with his beloved cat: 'In the interests of preventing the caps from being destroyed or damaged by mice, I ask you to permit the abovementioned workshop to keep a cat by the name of Barsik.' Some time later, I would see Barsik proudly strolling about the cap-sewing workshop with a collar bearing the inscription: 'Tomcat Barsik. Sewing Workshop No. 3. Caps Department.' Barsik was unable to read, and he lived by his own feline code.

From time to time, he would deviate from his assigned duties as mouse destroyer and spray the finished products with his scent.

After Nikolai's escape, the number of cats in the camp plummeted. But not for long. Unfettered by anyone or anything, the cats soon multiplied and recovered their numbers. In under six months, there were more cats in the colony than there had been before, and the collars were quickly forgotten about. Or at least until the next breakout of the next convict. At the behest of the prisoners, the training grounds were restored.

35

MY RETURN

What with this chain of events, my month in the sanatorium flew by as if it were a day, and I returned to Unit 3, which by now felt unfamiliar. Nothing had changed there. It still had the same old faces, the same head of the unit. The same crazy regime. I could not fathom why they wouldn't just let the men take a short nap or lie-down on the bed.

The latest of these pointless measures brought me back to reality: the inventory. 'It's as though they were waiting specially for me!' This preposterous idea flashed through my mind, only to be discarded in an instant. After wake-up, a horde of disgruntled staff burst into the barracks. Many of the men had just come off their shift and were getting ready to go home, but a command came from the main office to carry out an inventory. The procedure was utterly pointless and idiotic, a waste of time and nerves for both sides – staff and prisoners. The disagreeable and distressing operation stretched on the entire day. The prisoners glumly gathered all their stuff and went off to the local zone. Everything was hauled out of the barracks: bags, mattresses, personal belongings. The building stood empty. Whatever remained in the barracks was thrown out and destroyed. Before we could go back in, we had to go through a search. The tables in the re-educational-work room were carried outside, where the camp staff inspected and counted out the prisoners' things. The numbers of underpants, socks and T-shirts were checked. Anything over the limit was confiscated. Surplus towels and sheets went flying into the specially brought sacks. Any plastic tubs received in packages or parcels also got chucked in the sacks. It was my turn. I heaved my bag of tins and jars up off the ground and placed it on the table. The abundance and variety of foods blew the mind of the inspector – a young sergeant who clearly had little desire to work or study.

'Why do you need so many of these?' he enquired.

'I eat them,' I answered.

He dreamily sorted through the cans. He can't have been familiar with the Penal Code, otherwise he would have led me off to have the bag weighed. A prisoner is permitted to have no more than 50 kilograms of food. The sergeant moved on to my personal effects. A plastic lidded tub that I used for making porridge with boiling water drew his attention. His hand was already reaching out for his spoils. But my knowledge of the said Penal Code cooled his hunting ardour. I was thoroughly acquainted with the list of forbidden items that a convict is not allowed to have. Food tubs were not mentioned among them, and I politely informed him of the fact. The sergeant was young, lazy and not very smart. I did not pick up on any aggression from him, though he seemed in a hurry to be rid of me. But he had still not inspected everything. We turned to my personal effects. His attention was arrested by three fluffy towels.

'Pereverzin, what do you need three towels for?' he asked.

My answer confounded and completely deflated him: 'One towel for my body, a second for my face, and a third for my feet.'

Pausing to think for a moment, the sergeant said: 'Pereverzin, look, I need to take something off you! Can you give me something yourself?' he asked in a pitiful voice.

Signalling my consent, I benevolently threw a dirty towel upon the altar of the prison system and gathered up my bags. To my great fortune, I had got off without any losses; I had been very lucky. You rarely encountered men as kind as this sergeant.

The other prisoners spent a long time cursing and bemoaning the losses they'd sustained. They had met with rather more zealous and predatory officers, and they'd been relieved of cherished belongings.

I often felt like asking the staff of the colony: 'Why? What are you doing all this for? What is the point of all these measures?'

It was strange that they could muster the energy for such time-consuming and arduous folly. What would it matter if a prisoner had one more towel than was prescribed, or one extra T-shirt in his bag?

It was only as this irredeemably ruined day of rest drew to a close that normal life resumed in the unit. The iron beds were made up and the bedside tables refilled with our simple clobber. Zuyev and I sorted through our things and went off to celebrate my return to the unit. Soon it would be dinner, and we needed to make sure we finished our feast before heading off to the scheduled activity. Going to the dining room was compulsory; if you stayed in the barracks, you'd get a sanction straight away. The guards on inspection duty would make the rounds of the barracks and flush out those violating the regime. I tipped a can of green peas and a tin of mackerel bought at the prison shop into the plastic tub I'd saved. This culinary masterpiece was crowned with some olive oil from a food parcel. Zuyev didn't want to freeload, and he gently turned down the meal. Sipping on his *chifir*, he smiled and said to me, 'Just remember, Vova, this place is a summer camp.' In his twenty-nine years behind bars, Zuyev had travelled the length and breadth of Russia, and he knew what he was talking about. Mordovia and Chelyabinsk were the two places that still made him shudder.

Feeling contented, we lined up in the local zone and went off to the dining room. That day it was macaroni for dinner, a very popular dish in the camp. Zuyev happily demolished two portions, one for himself and one for me. Our diet was not particularly varied. By prison standards, the food in this colony was perfectly acceptable. The harsher the regime, the better the food was. Broken grain and pearl barley cooked with a lard-and-shortening blend were the key components of our diet and a trusty source of vitamins. Potatoes and pasta were also served, but less often. They gave us a rather decent loaf, baked by the prisoners in the prison bakery. A bit of meat or fish was added to the soup pot in the prescribed quantities, and some barley, pasta or cabbage would be thrown in. The resulting dish slapped together by the prisoners could not rightly be called soup. In a word, it was swill.

36

HOW I BECAME A GOOD JEW

After dinner, the entire unit returned to the barracks in formation. It was these moments I loved. The two hours we had until lights out. Time to yourself. You could sit and read, watch television, drink some tea. As ever, you were not allowed to do the one thing you most wanted: to lie down or sleep. Zuyev brewed some tea, and we were calmly talking away. Umed Ch. was walking about nearby, convicted for murder. He would often ask me if he could read various newspapers and magazines. I never turned anyone down. One day, Umed requested that I get him a Koran, which I did. In my next parcel, the wished-for book arrived, and I selflessly handed it over to the true-believing Muslim. Umed tried to edge into our conversation, making some remarks. The prisoners were feeling angry and irritable after the inventory.

The slightest spark was at risk of flaring into open hostilities. The conversation became high-pitched, with raised voices, and then it seemed to die down. But I had merely to leave for a few minutes before Roma Y. came running towards me.

'Hey, Zuyev and Umed have gone to the changing room to have it out,' he yelled to me as he ran.

'There'll be trouble if I don't break them up in time!' With this thought, I took off and ran to the scene of the kerfuffle. I opened the door and saw a knot of human bodies. Without pausing to think, I pulled the knot into two and grabbed Umed. Zuyev stood and breathed heavily. Hot on my heels came the orderlies from our unit – convicts working for the camp management. In our unit, they were peas in a pod. All of them were doing time for rapes and murders, and they were all members of the Section for Order and Discipline. Each was worse than the next. The police came running in after the orderlies. If I hadn't split them up, who knows how the brawl might have ended. The faces of the parties to the fight betrayed signs of the recent scuffle. We were led under escort to the main office for questioning by the operational officers. I told them I hadn't seen any fighting, that when I entered the changing room, I'd just found the prisoners chatting calmly. Zuyev and Umed tangentially confirmed my story, and they let me return to the barracks. The operational officer later showed me the letter of explanation Umed had written, where he confidentially told the management what had been the cause of the conflict: 'Zuyev and Pereverzin were discussing how good it would be to down a bottle of vodka and slit the throats of half the unit.' I was speechless …

Zuyev and Umed returned to the unit ten days later, after doing a stint in solitary. For several days, Umed refused to look in our direction and wouldn't say hello. We got on with our lives and also acted as though he did not exist for us. One day, out of the blue, I was approached by a go-between – a prisoner who worked out with me at the training ground. After hemming and hawing a bit, he said, 'Umed asked me to pass on to you … He said, "Tell Volodya that he's a good Jew."'

I did not immediately understand what he meant. But it took me a second to realise it was a compliment I'd never received in my entire life. I've been a good Jew ever since.

On one of the weekends, an educational event was held at the social club. All the prisoners were shown a film called *Russia with a Knife in Its Back*. Along with some Russian Orthodox literature, the film found its way to the camp via the church that was based in the colony's grounds. The church had been built by the prisoners' hands and at their own expense, and it was named after the canonised Alexander Nevsky – who was, incidentally, a rather dubious man. There was the molten lead he poured into the mouths of his fellow Christians – those who dared to speak out against the Tatar-Mongols, and the way he crawled on his knees to prostrate himself before the Mongolian khan …

But that's all by the by; let's get back to the film. Its creator, Konstantin Dushenov, was convicted for this film under Article 282 (inciting ethnic hatred) and sentenced to three years in an open penal colony, with the film itself being deemed extremist. The film was a smash hit in the camp. It was shown a number of times, but then (and I had a hand in this) they pulled it. But it managed to bear fruit, because the ideas it was propounding fell on fertile ground. I feel I must cite a few lines from the film. 'Abramovich's net worth increases every minute by 5,000 US dollars, while at the same time, every minute in Russia, one Russian dies. Meaning the death of each Russian brings Abramovich 5,000 dollars.' The film contained an infinite number of such 'logical' inferences; in fact, it was entirely built upon them. I won't go into all the things the prisoners came out with after watching this film, but trust me, some particularly aggressively minded inmates (doing time, as it happens, for robbery and murder), suddenly realising the root cause of their woes, planned on resuming their old habits after their release, but solely along ethnic lines, and they loudly proclaimed these intentions, vowing to kill off, one by one, or perhaps even en masse, members of the Jewish faith.

I lived cheek by jowl alongside these men, sharing a room with them, and I overheard their talk and their comments. One day I could stand it no longer and politely asked one zealous anti-Semite from Lithuania named Prizhevoyts, 'Do please tell me precisely what the Jews have ever done to you.' The man glazed over, thinking hard for a long time before offering the following: 'They own all the gold in the world!'

They didn't like Jews in this place. Nor did they have any love of Muscovites. It is always convenient to blame someone else for all your troubles. I was constantly stuck in the same room as these guys, in the same barracks, and I had to mix with them. There were large numbers of men in the camp with that type of world view – people who would happily drop an atom bomb on Moscow if only it could improve life in Vladimir Region.

I had always been far removed from racial tensions. I was born in Moscow in 1966. My mother's name is Zoya Sergeyevna Koryukhina, a native of Ryazan Region; my father, Ivan Ivanovich Pereverzin, originally came from a remote village in the Altai Territory. I spent my childhood and youth in blissful ignorance of the existence of the race question, devoting absolutely no thought to it, despite belonging to the predominant group, the majority ethnicity. At a more mature age, having reached the correct conclusion that scoundrels, rogues and bastards come from no single ethnic group, I was surprised to discover that, in absolute terms, when it came to the number of vile and rotten deeds, including those against our own selves, members of the dominant ethnicity were unparalleled.

Two boys were playing; one of them was my friend's son. They played for a long time, getting on well. Suddenly the elder boy said to my friend's son in a hushed tone, 'You know what? I hate the Jews.' To which the other boy answered proudly: 'You know what? I am a Jew.' Their friendship, thank heavens, did not come to an end.

I consider myself Russian Orthodox, but not once did I step inside the church we had in the camp. To go to that church, first you had to register with the orderly in the unit. He would make up the lists and deliver them to the main office. The lists would be approved by the heads of the operational and security departments. Next, the prisoners would be searched, then lined up and led to the church, and when the service ended, they were taken back to the unit in the same way.

37

GOODBYE, UNIT 3

I had been in Unit 3 for over a year. My time in quarantine was long forgotten, although every day I saw the prisoners marching by. Having mixed with the prisoners living in the other units, I drew the conclusion that the only places worse than Unit 3 were quarantine and the Strict Conditions of Detention Unit. Bulletproof, as the head of the unit, Major Kuzmichev, was known to the inmates, dramatically darkened the already bleak picture of life in Unit 3. During the month he was away on holiday, the prisoners lived in joy and harmony. No, there was no change to the daily regime. Just as before, the inspectors were forever coming into the barracks, and you couldn't lie down, let alone sleep, on the beds. But the atmosphere became noticeably better, and we could breathe more easily. The man in the officer's uniform was gone; he was no longer walking about, watching over us, trying to find something to pick fault with. Some of the prisoners made fun of the major in their own style, deliberately leaving their unwashed, worn-out socks under the mattress. 'Why bother binning them myself?' they said cockily. 'Kuzmichev can come and take them away.' He did indeed come around with a sack and filled it with things carelessly left by the prisoners on their beds. Some of the snatched items could be retrieved from his office, if you wrote out a letter of explanation and submitted to his lecture.

I could not understand the point of him being there at all. What functions and purpose did he serve? In my opinion, he did nothing but untold harm. Why not get rid of all the clueless staff, who were in the majority, and raise the salary for the men who were halfway decent? As for chaps such as the head of our unit, they needed their own heads examined, rather than being tasked with re-educating others … I was always intrigued to know what they were like on the outside, beyond the barbed wire, in their free time. How did they behave out there, dealing with ordinary people? Our particular specimen was unmarried and lived with his mother in the city of Kovrov.

Right now, as I write these lines, I feel pity for that poor fellow. But when he wrote out that calamitous sanction, thwarting my chances of parole, I experienced contempt and loathing towards him. I was enraged and stung by the fact that my release depended on that man.

For a long time, I had set my sights on a transfer from Unit 3. During my stay in the sanatorium, I managed to make the right connections and get to know the local elite – the caretakers for a number of units. Artur K., the caretaker of Unit 1, doing time for murder, suggested I move into his unit. They wouldn't allow Zuyev in there, as he was on the escape list. I was loath to part with Zuyev, but, realising that life would be a nightmare for me in Unit 3, I accepted and wrote an application.

The crew for flagstone and breeze-block production lived in Unit 1. A place there had become free. I passed the interview with the foreman, a young, ruddy-cheeked guy who spoke with a slur. Vasya warned me straight away that all the guys in his team worked equally hard and no one was cut any slack. I agreed to everything, just to get out of Unit 3. There was one bright side: the work was seasonal. In the winter, there was no demand for our product, and so for December, January and February, the workers got to sit in the unit and keep themselves occupied. I could always find something to do, and I was delighted at the prospect.

Artur sorted everything out in the best way possible. He was on friendly terms with an operational officer, Major Vlasov, whom he visited every day. The major asked Artur, 'So, is Pereverzin really planning on working there?' And upon receiving an answer in the affirmative, he endorsed my application. He knew I would be in dependable hands, under the supervision of his agent, and every word I uttered would be relayed to the main office. My application made its way to the desk of the head of the colony, who, without looking, put his signature to the operational officer's endorsement.

On one of the days during drill, I did not hear my surname. To my great delight, my registration card had been sent to another unit. Major Kuzmichev was agitated and he tore into the main office. For some reason, he was reluctant to part with me. But it was too late. The paperwork for my transfer had been signed; nothing could be done. The operation for my transfer had been handled with the utmost secrecy. If word had got out to the head of our unit or his helpers from among the prisoners, there would have been no escaping his dirty tricks, and I would have been forever stuck in Unit 3, categorised as an inmate on the escape list.

For a while, I was happy again. I was sorry to part with Zuyev, but there was nothing I could do about it. We would sometimes see each other and talk. But for now, we drank tea and packed my things. We said our goodbyes. At the lower end of the local zone, an orderly from Unit 1 was waiting for me, and he helped me carry my bags to the barracks.

38

THE GOOD GUYS FROM UNIT 1

The grey three-storey building stood right next to the camp stadium, where all kinds of sporting events were held. The stadium with its high fence was a strange sight to behold. The metal fencing, patched up in some places with sheets of iron and in other places with steel reinforcing rods, separated the stadium from the rest of the camp grounds. The stadium was entered through huge iron gates. The stadium's ground surface was just as squalid as its fencing. Originally of concrete, it had been chewed up by time and the elements. The innumerable potholes were filled in here and there with gravel or asphalt, yet this did not save the prisoners from the risk of injury during each new round of fun and games. The ruins of a huge tumbledown workshop looming out of the industrial zone completed the sorry picture. It gave you the impression that hostilities had once broken out on the grounds of the camp, apparently culminating in a victorious blitz by enemy aviation, bringing this unknown war to an end. I thought of the German prisoners of war who built the camp. Not much had changed here since those days.

The stadium took up a large chunk of my life. We exercised there to music each morning. Three hundred prisoners in black, crouching and swaying their arms to classical music at the break of dawn, made a strange and memorable impression. Twice a day, there was roll call in the stadium. The prisoners were lined up and counted to check no one was missing. Three times a day, the prisoners would queue up there according to their units and march into the dining room.

I went into the building. There was one unit per floor. Unit 1 was based on the ground floor, Unit 9 on the first floor, and on the second storey was Unit 16, where the inmates who worked in clothing manufacture lived. The orderly Sasha, whose nickname – or, rather, whose 'handle' – was Grouch, gave me a tour of the unit. It is worth noting that in the penitentiaries, nicknames were the preserve of the cats and dogs; the men doing time had only 'handles'. Not that this altered anything materially. Compared with Unit 3, this place was a five-star hotel. I saw a clean washbasin, supplied with hot water, there were proper white toilets … I already liked it here.

A small young guy, Grouch was a habitual offender, which was how he came to be in a strict-regime camp. He was doing time for an offence that was uncommon in these parts: theft of metal, for which he earned the handle 'Metalhead'. Nature had endowed him with tremendous physical power. Grouch could swing around the pull-up bar without stopping, and he could do an impressive number of pull-ups. In his youth, he had performed 130 giant swings in one go. He had trained his balance by going on fairground rides for hours on end. He climbed along a cable from a nine-storey building to a neighbouring five-storey one, just for kicks. At the various festivities for Shrovetide, he used to take part in the contests and make a clean sweep of the top prizes. Grouch could effortlessly shimmy up the maypole and bag the richly deserved awards. He ought to have joined the circus or become a cosmonaut, but instead … here he was. Positioning some pliers between his teeth, off he went up his beloved power poles. During the crime reconstruction, Grouch proudly showed off his prowess to the astonished policemen. It took him twenty-five seconds to tackle one pole. He climbed it, cut through the wires and came back down to earth. He had even set a personal record: 3 kilometres of wire in the space of a night. He couldn't do it without doping up, though. Grouch flat out rejected drugs, preferring natural substances: neat surgical spirit with spring water. As luck would have it, his mother worked in a pharmacy. He would down a glass, and off he'd go. He'd walk one block, wind his booty up into a spool, hide it in the forest and head back to dose himself back up. Then off to work again. And repeat all through the night.

I came to the unexpected and agreeable conclusion that the guys in this place were a bit nicer than in Unit 3.

I was offered a place of honour on a lower bunk by the wall. Now I no longer had to sleep on my side to avoid accidentally banging into the face of a sleeper on a nearby bed squashed up against mine. The bed above me was empty – nobody there. I had a bedside table all to myself, where I could store my stash of goodies. Among my neighbours in the same aisle, I spotted a familiar face – my new boss, Vasya the foreman, convicted under the single most popular article in the camp: 105, part 2 (murder). Vasya was a good lad. He plied me with tea and heaps of food. Born late in his parents' lives, he was the darling of his parents and elder sister. The endless procession of parcels and packets arranged by his father never faltered. His dad was a gamekeeper in the local forests and he was well-connected. The head of the Vladimir Regional Federal Penitentiary Service was crazy about hunting, and he became a regular client of the gamekeeper. In exchange, Vasya was to get parole (and fully deserved, too), pending which he was granted the chance to eat homemade stew made from game killed in the hunt.

The working season had not yet begun, so I whiled away the time in the unit. Books and exercise were what appealed; I began warming up and coming back to life after Unit 3. This unit had the same regime, but without the craziness that had featured in my previous residence. The head of the unit was a major, and, due to the cutbacks in the armed forces, he clung on to his job in the prison system while waiting for his pension. He was a nice enough man, respected by the prisoners. Neither the inmates nor he himself overstepped the mark.

Gradually, I got to know the numerous occupants of the barracks. All of them worked. The bakery workers had settled in the aisle next to ours, toiling night and day for the good of the entire camp. Opposite them was where the repairs team slept; their workers tackled (sometimes as emergencies) the countless breakdowns in the camp. Things were always malfunctioning, left, right and centre. The taps would run dry, or the lights would go out, or something else would fail, and all at the same time. There was never an idle moment for those guys.

These were my happiest days. I made daily visits to the training ground. The pull-up bar, the parallel bars, the barbells, the dumbbells — all of them were put to use. I worked out until I was ready to drop. All my problems faded away, and I began planning for the future. Sport helped me to survive.

I made the acquaintance of Dima. This twenty-two-year-old bruiser, who was 2 metres tall, gathered all the weights into a pile and effortlessly lifted the gigantic barbells. He had been into weights while living on the outside, where he was fond of pumping iron. Brought up by his grandmother in the countryside on a wholesome diet, he adored soured cream and milk. Nature had graced him with height and brawn, yet it had also made him none too smart. The village where he lived had just a single amusement arcade, and Dima had decided to raid it. Donning a mask and arming himself with a baseball bat, he went off to do the job. Straight away, he knocked out the guard and took all the cash. There were slim pickings, something like five thousand roubles. It was a wonder that Dima, with all his muscle power, had not finished the poor guy off. A good thing too, for both of them. The hunt for the culprit was soon over. In a couple of hours, they had tracked Dima down to his home. Only one man in the village had matched the description.

Dima worked in the automotive garage for the camp and was faring reasonably well.

39

A GALLEY SLAVE

Vasya introduced me to the other members of our friendly crew. They were birds of a feather, all of them convicted for murder.

Sergei K., from the same town as Vasya, had shot his opponent with a hunting rifle. Ilya, too, had snuffed someone out while drunk. I felt somewhat small in front of these guys with my 'stolen thirteen billion'. At forty-four, I was the oldest. As soon as spring arrived, our product would be back in demand. I still had no idea of what lay ahead and remained in blissful ignorance, enjoying my stay in the unit with my head in the clouds. But that was soon to end.

Before the snow had managed to melt, our foreman began receiving the new season's orders. It seemed the management of the camp had special plans in mind for us. Tomorrow we would be taken to work.

It was my first working day. We had wake-up, then workout – in other words, morning exercise. Followed by breakfast. Then we were posted to work.

One convict filed a complaint with the Supreme Court contesting the legality of the internal rules and regulations obliging the prisoners to do daily exercise. The Supreme Court responded: 'In compliance with the UN Convention on Human Rights, every convict enjoys the right to engage in sport. Exercise is the realisation of that right!' The guards would vigilantly monitor compliance with this 'right'. Should you refuse, you'd be beaten up and thrown in solitary. Each morning, during exercise, I'd see someone from the camp management lazily pacing about the stadium and monitoring compliance with our right. There was one young lieutenant who was particularly vicious. He studied us closely to ensure we had every button done up and our collars pulled down over our jackets. I was quite sure that beyond the camp's grounds, the man behaved as meekly as a lamb, that the moment he took off his uniform, he would be someone you'd barely notice.

I have observed so many times that the smaller the dog, the louder its bark. Sometimes you run around Bitsevsky Park and, catching sight of a big dog such as a sheepdog or a Rottweiler, you unwittingly slow your pace. But the dog won't even sniff the air, it won't glance in your direction. A small dog, however, will yap and chase after you for ages.

In our penitentiaries, you found not only small dogs, but big ones too, the sort that could do serious damage to a person. The men in those places metamorphose in the strangest ways. Our former head of the camp, Novikov, a lieutenant colonel by rank, ordered his serf, that is to say one of the prisoners, to paint an enormous portrait. The inmate was rather good at painting and, under the sage direction of his master, he depicted the latter in a general's uniform on a white horse and holding a girl in his arms. The girl was the head of the camp's daughter.

In each unit, there were boards on the walls offering prisoners information on various topics. The addresses of human rights organisations and of the oversight body for compliance with the law in penitentiaries were of greater interest to the local employees and were intended for the visiting commissions. No complaint could leave the camp walls without the knowledge of the operational department. Browsing through the board's notices, I was surprised to learn the Vladimir Regional Federal Penitentiary Service had an officer responsible for upholding prisoners' rights. That officer was a full-blown colonel who had a particularly apt name: Vasily Sekret. In all the five years of my stay in the Vladimir Region, I never did unravel the secret of what that colonel was busy doing.

The prisoners lined up in front of the industrial zone's iron gates, which I had never passed through. The work-assignment orderly, an ordinary prisoner entrusted with the role by the management, made up lists of employees and handed them over to the policemen. The latter would call out the surnames, shifting your registration card to the appropriate place. The card always followed you. Each prisoner had a card. It was simple and reliable, with no computerised records. The same system they'd used a hundred years ago and the one they will probably always be using. Just before the gates, there was a search. The sleepy policemen checked to see if you were carrying anything you shouldn't be.

In some camps, work was assigned to the sounds of a prisoner orchestra. They played 'Farewell of Slavianka' or some such stirring march. Thank heavens Melekhovo had not hit upon the idea.

I set foot in the area for the first time. It was how I imagined Stalingrad must have looked after the great battle. There were huge ramshackle workshops. In Soviet times, a branch of the Vladimir Tractor Factory had been based here. The workshop where they made the windings for electric motors stood abandoned. You could still see the dusty motors; nobody had stolen them yet to sell as non-ferrous metal.

Total disorder and chaos reigned here, and not only in the workshops, but also, to quote the great author Mikhail Bulgakov, in their heads. A major with the rather apt surname of Oshibkin – meaning 'error' – was in charge of the place.

A former plating shop had been put at our disposal. An uphill road led to it. Along the way there, you saw the barbed-wire fences dividing the camp from freedom. You saw the forest. The fungi-filled areas attracted droves of mushroom pickers, and I could just imagine the glorious view they saw when, hunting for the next cep, they came to the edge of the forest and set eyes on our wonderland. I could see why they didn't allow convicts on the escape list into the industrial zone.

The vast, unheated space with its leaking roof made an ominous impression. Thirty metres above us was the ceiling, filled with swallows' nests. The swallows would soon be returning to the building and flying around happily, cheering us with their chirping. The workshop was divided into two parts. In one half, there was the small-scale production of metal goods. Officially, metal lockers were manufactured here, but unofficially, the men were making portable barbecues. It was a rather attractive barbecue: a stainless-steel case that could be instantly transformed with a flick of the wrist into a grill for kebabs. This exclusive product was in constant demand. Time and again, I would see men in uniform leaving our workshop carrying little metal suitcases.

Our side of the workshop was filled with enormous heaps of sand and gravel, which were regularly delivered by a ZiL dump truck that could easily fit inside the workshop. Near these heaps stood a cement mixer, and a vibrating table for paving slab production lay at the end of the workshop. The open space meant you could fit 230 breeze blocks and 1,500 plastic moulds for paving slabs of various shapes on the floor of the shop. This was the work area for our operation.

It was still dark, not yet seven in the morning, and, despite our various morning procedures, I had not yet fully woken up. But the working day had begun. The morning started with a warm-up. We changed into some old work clothes in a small room and went to get cement from the warehouse, where the materials we needed were kept under seven locks and seven seals. We began loading the tractor. Eighty sacks, each one weighing 50 kilos, went into the cart. On top of that, we threw in some sacks of dye, plus a sack labelled 'Plasticiser. Toxic'. Vasya climbed into the cart, took the sacks that the three of us were bringing to him and stacked them up. I humped twenty-eight bags to the tractor. It wasn't far, just 15 metres metres or so. But each sack had to be carefully picked up, hoisted onto your back, carried over and then dumped into the tractor. Done twenty-eight times, at fifty kilos a go. Totalling almost one and a half tonnes. The tractor drove into our workshop, where we repeated all these actions in reverse. I had to shift the same one and a half tonnes of cement. There was no shirking; everyone was hard at work. Outside, I quickly became coated in cement dust, some of it settling in my lungs. I could feel my body perspiring, despite the cold. I tore off my padded jacket.

That had been our gentle warm-up. Now we needed to fill the cement mixer with water, gravel and sand. We carried everything in pails made from empty 40-litre paint tins. You brought two pails of water – that was another 80 kilograms. One of us took a shovel and began filling the pails with gravel and sand. Together, we all shovelled the crucial ingredients into the precious receptacle and turned on the machine. While the cement mixer was working, we took a rest. The mixture was ready. Stop! Beneath the cement mixer lay a tray to catch the cement. We quickly scooped the mixture into the wheelbarrow with our shovels, then took it to the machine that produced breeze blocks. This apparatus was state of the art! It was designed to make four whole breeze blocks at a time. You poured in the slurry, started it up, lifted the twenty-odd kilo counterweight, and, after a minute of rattling and mechanically shaking the cement, you lowered and then raised it again. The lead weight would press the half-finished product out of the mould. And back to the wheelbarrow. This left you with four breeze blocks that looked like sand pies from a children's sandpit.

But there was an art to it: the sand pie could fall apart if the mixture was a little on the thin side, or the other way around – a touch too dry. It would break up if the counterweight was raised too quickly or too slowly. My hands soon got the hang of it, and all my sand pies stayed in one piece. One and a half wheelbarrows of cement went into every four breeze blocks. You loaded it up, brought it over, unloaded it. Gradually, the empty space of the workshop was filled with freshly made breeze blocks. The slurry in the cement mixer would quickly run out. So, it was back to your spade, pails, water, sand and gravel. I lost count of the quantities I had wheeled over and tossed in.

A ten-minute break. We could have tea. The management indulged its slaves by generously allowing us to use a kettle element in the workplace and drink tea that we'd brought along. Lunch was coming up. 'Just one hour to get through, and then the end of the shift will be close!' I thought with relief. Before stopping for lunch, we managed to produce around thirty more breeze blocks. The piercing whine of the siren interrupted our workout, and we went to lunch. I was starving and instantly polished off a serving of slops. Both the soup and the main course disappeared. Not a crumb of our bread was left. Everything was crammed into twenty-five minutes, during which time I began to come back to life a little.

We returned to the workshop. The relentless production cycle resumed. The sound of the machinery rang in my ears, even when it was turned off. Every ten minutes I glanced longingly at my watch. Thirty minutes, twenty minutes, ten minutes to go till the end of the shift. Hurray! It was three o'clock! In the workshop next to ours, we could have a quick shower and change our clothes. My first working shift had ended, and I returned to the unit more dead than alive. The next day I would be dealing with paving slabs.

Despite Vasya's assurances that I would wake up in agony, I felt fine when I rose. I was fascinated to know what hidden resources the human body held, and I wondered how much my own body could take …

The next morning barely differed from the previous one. We had wake-up, workout, breakfast. Then we were posted to work. I was glad that today we'd have no warm-up – there was enough cement to last over a week. The breeze blocks would dry out for a few days, before being taken away on the third day. In the meantime, we had to produce as many facing tiles and paving slabs as we could. This work required more deftness than the production of breeze blocks. The gravel had to be strained through a special sieve, and that was what we were doing.

The rest of the technique was similar. We filled the cement mixer with the buckets. In went sand, gravel and water, more gravel, more sand. My eyes went funny from the constant trips with the pails. We made up the slurry, adding the toxic plasticiser and dye. The finished mixture was shovelled into the wheelbarrow and carried to the vibrating table. Plastic moulds were laid out on the table and greased with waste oil delivered to us in unlimited quantities from the local automotive garage.

Then the motor was switched on, and the table began to vibrate with a gentle shiver, compacting the mixture. The deep moulds were used for the paving slabs, while the shallow ones, 2 or 3 centimetres deep, were where we made the facing tiles. We filled all the moulds and put them aside, leaving them to dry out for a few days. By the time we had filled all the moulds, the breeze blocks were dry. While we made a new batch of breeze blocks to replace the ones that had gone, the paving slabs were drying out. The slabs were laborious to make: you needed to pull each brick carefully out of the mould, and the mould itself had to be washed and oiled. The whole process was interminable; before you could finish, it was time to start all over again.

There was tremendous demand for the paving slabs. It looked like they'd decided to pave the entire camp with them. The breeze blocks too were snapped up in no time. For the next batch, the head of the workshop, a lieutenant, asked us to make a special effort, as this lot would be going to Novikov, the former head of the colony – that same man who had commissioned the portrait of himself perched atop a white horse. We weren't sure quite how we could try any harder, short of spitting into the cement mixer. The idea occurred to me of slipping a note into the concrete or stamping the finished brick with something – the word Yukos, say. We turned out the batch with gusto, following the production technique to the letter. The facing tiles were enormously popular too.

The month flew by in a flash, and I received my first pay: 800 roubles. With fury and resentment, I found out we had not met the production quota, which had been artificially inflated. Our wages came from the cost of each breeze block; we got 4 roubles per block between us. The camp management sold those breeze blocks to the outside world at 37 roubles apiece. A tidy profit margin! Through the use of slave labour, the management were making a killing. It was an endemic problem that blighted the entire system like a contagious disease. What's more, the Federal Penitentiary Service officers, who loathed the prisoners and did not think of them as human, were living entirely off those very prisoners. Take away the prisoners, and it would be the end of all those spongers who knew no other life!

I suggested a redesign of our scruffy operations: we could move the cement mixer closer to the vibrating table and the water source, making it possible to fill the drum with a hose. Our foreman, Vasya, did not like this idea, and my suggestion to go myself to the head of production, Major Oshibkin, was interpreted by him as an attempt to go over his head and take over as the crew's official leader. Vasya slogged away with the rest of us, and I too kept up with the pace, sometimes working even harder than the others. Sergei, who was from the same town as Vasya, told me about the foreman's suspicions. I reassured the young and ambitious Vasya, telling him truthfully that I wasn't interested in forging a career in the crew and I was ready to do whatever he said without grumbling.

We carried on working. It might have been possible to slow down the pace, produce fewer tiles, but Vasya kept urging us on. What drove him? Excessive ambition, the desire to curry favour? I never did fathom his motives. Sergei was extremely put out by Vasya's behaviour. At one point, we were sitting quietly and calmly pulling the facing tiles out of their moulds. It was a fiddly job. You had to pour hot water into a bath, where the prepared moulds were laid out. Then, holding the mould beneath the water, you had to bend the plastic gently and pull out the tile. Sometimes the tiles would break. Vasya decided to run an experiment, and he shortened the drying time. The tiles broke in Sergei's hands, one after another. The foreman decided he'd give Sergei a good scolding. From that moment, everything went into slow motion. Sergei leapt up and grabbed a shovel. He brandished it. Vasya barely had time to stand up straight before the shovel began descending towards his head. At the last moment, Vasya managed to dodge it, and the shovel whistled down with a whack on his shoulder. Sergei took aim for the next blow. I saw myself as if from the outside, jumping onto Sergei. I mustered enough strength to wrest the shovel from him and hold him down. Just as the scene was reaching its climax, the sanatorium caretaker, Martyn, turned up at the workshop along with an orderly. They had come for the facing tiles and witnessed this bloodcurdling sight. The uninvited spectators froze with their mouths agape.

Everything that had been building up suddenly erupted. The endless humiliations, the abuses, the marching, the prisoner transport had all taken their toll. The man snapped; he couldn't take it any longer. I myself was terrified of cracking up like that. God alone knew all the tensions that had built up inside me. The disgraceful and unfair trial; losing my father; the monstrous sentence ... You were constantly bottling everything up. You held in all your anger and outrage; you stopped yourself saying what you wanted to say. Over all those years, so much of everything piled up, ready to come crashing down like snow in an avalanche ...

There were many who could not believe that 'Khodorkovsky's accomplice' himself, Yukos's chief moneyman, who had stolen billions, was humping about with breeze blocks and paving slabs. Some of the staff in the camp would come over to gawk at me. Satisfied with the sight of the dirty convict all coated in cement dust and sand, they went off on their important business.

40

MANUFACTURING ERROR

After the incident, Sergei was transferred to Unit 3, and a new prisoner joined our crew. We continued our heroic feats of toil. Saturdays and Sundays were our days off. I got to know the industrial zone. Just past the gates, at the entrance, was a vast sewing workshop, the paths to which were paved with the fruits of my labour. Peering inside the building, I saw countless prisoners hunched over their sewing machines. They seemed unusually small in the vast 30-metre ceilinged space and reminded me of ants. This was where they sewed everything the system needed – uniforms for the police and the prisoners. In the middle of the shop stood a tower with a guard inside; he was watching over the sewing prisoners. Opposite our huge hangar was a workshop producing footwear for the police and inmates. A hundred metres further on, you could see a joinery shop, where window and door frames and other forms of woodwork were planed.

Beneath an awning near our workshop, there suddenly appeared a strange piece of machinery. It had a certain beauty and elegance even. Numerous steel hooks stuck out in rows from the 3-metre-long iron appliance. I began keenly studying this unidentified object, wondering what purpose it served. It was clearly not a UFO. My mate Misha, a prisoner from Unit 9 who worked as a foreman in the sewing shop, revealed the mystery. Misha was a Muscovite graduate, an engineer, and he told me the following story. It turned out Major Oshibkin had come up with the idea of manufacturing socks and stockings in the camp, for which a knackered old hosiery machine was bought in Ivanovo. They travelled there, purchased it and brought it back. But they could not get it up and running. Alas! The machine simply did not want to knit socks or stockings. Perhaps Melekhovo had an unconducive climate, or something else was playing up. The idea was soon abandoned, as was the machine itself, and every day I got to feast my eyes on that wonderful specimen of industrial design.

Misha shared another story with me. He was once asked to wire up some equipment. Misha drew a diagram, knowledgeably explaining what was to be done and what had to be bought. He said the main thing was that he needed 10 metres of copper wire for a certain section. The major decided to save money: instead of copper, he bought aluminium wire.

It all went up in flames: the wiring, the machine, the entire room. Oshibkin, the former head of the unit and educator of the prisoners, who was destined to run the prison manufacturing, escaped unharmed.

In that place, you were truly living in another dimension, in a looking-glass world. And everything going on around you seemed like one big error.

41

DEAD SOULS

The camp carried on living in its looking-glass reality. Suddenly I found out the senior work co-ordinator was being thrown in solitary. The work co-ordinator is a prominent figure in the camp. He performs a lot of useful jobs for the staff of the colony and instead of them. In return, he's entitled to live in staff accommodation, where he keeps records of the camp's sizeable population and their movements. He is allowed a television, a cassette player, an electric stove and a kettle. Our work co-ordinator enjoyed all these benefits, which were unheard of for ordinary prisoners, and rightly so – he was overloaded with tasks. He could even have got away with a mobile phone, banned in the camp on pain of death. But then something out of the ordinary happened. There were many staff positions in the camp available for prisoners. A number of them remained vacant. Quick on the uptake, Kostya officially filled these posts with certain prisoners, who began receiving a salary without actually working. Kostya regularly picked up his share of the proceeds at the prison shop in the form of provisions.

The operational officers uncovered the gang of fraudsters. One of the accomplices had been unhappy with his share and kicked up a fuss, and word of it reached the operational department. The wrongdoers were caught. Kostya was ousted from his job, given a long, hard beating and thrown into solitary.

I was taken aback by the wording used on the order to place him in solitary. The document unequivocally announced he was being punished 'for brawling'.

Prisoners who did in fact brawl, and it happened frequently in the units, were sent to solitary with the phrase 'for smoking in undesignated areas'. One inmate, a guy who built barbecue grills in the workshop next to ours, was put in isolation for 'obscene language and altercation with the camp authorities'. This was how they worded the transgression of that prisoner who had dared to prepare and sample some home brew.

I never did understand why they couldn't just call a spade a spade. It was obviously symptomatic of the sickness that had swept over the entire system. Who said the system could never reform you?

In that place, they gave you a first-rate education in lying, deceit and hypocrisy.

I did not regret for a moment escaping Unit 3 to find myself in manufacturing. Despite the many downsides, I saw the positives too. The atmosphere in the unit was much better, and the regime was a little less rigid. Having forbidden the prisoners from doing everything under the sun, the camp authorities sometimes allowed them a little breathing space. After roll call, from 4.30 to 5.30 p.m., the prisoners were secretly allowed to lie on their beds.

Following another hard day at work, I sat in the aisle, sipping tea and chatting peacefully with Vasya. He was a kind and hard-working guy, but his passion for drink had been the ruin of him. In a drunken haze, an argument broke out in which Vasya put the matter to rest by fatally stabbing his opponent. He no longer remembered what they'd been arguing about, or perhaps he didn't want to say.

You could toil like a galley slave in the industrial zone, be a model prisoner, have a clutch of commendations, and yet none of this mattered a jot. At the request of the prisoners, I personally wrote large numbers of requests for parole, and then watched as they were turned down for no reason. The camp would intercede on behalf of the prisoner, who was willing to do a brief stint and who had commendations for his labour in his file. But no! The judge would stare at the paperwork and ask, 'Why didn't he take part in any amateur performances? Why no singing and dancing?' And he'd turn down the application! I saw the tears in the eyes of a grown man who had spent many years slogging in the bakery for long hours on a monthly wage of 2,000 roubles. The work was hellish – the intense heat, the sacks of flour, the trays of bread. It was not for the faint-hearted. Oleg was denied parole on the grounds that he had not had any commendations for taking part in amateur performances.

'What on earth?!' he hissed through clenched teeth. 'I work shifts, night shifts. Where can I find the time for amateur performances? What more do they want? Bastards!'

42

THE DAILY GRIND

I ploughed on with life in Unit 1. To give Artur his due, he never asked me for a thing and didn't try to extort money from me. He told me he'd had strict orders from an operational officer not to take any humanitarian relief from me, although it was a common enough practice in the camp. As I had a stake in improving the unit's living conditions, of my own accord I offered to buy the unit a fridge and TV set. We managed to pull off the purchases while maintaining the illusion I had nothing to do with it. My job was to arrange the transfer of the necessary funds to a certain prisoner's relatives, and they would, for their part, arrange the delivery of the goods.

A rosy prospect glimmered before me. There was a hope I might change my profession and field of work. No, the library and school were still off limits, but I had a chance of becoming a maintenance worker. My saviour Artur had enjoyed a meteoric rise in the colony, becoming manager of the camp. He was now responsible for looking after the residential zones. Repairs, whitewashing and painting fell under his remit. Since everything was constantly breaking down, Artur became a much-needed and sought-after prisoner for the camp authorities. His task was to manage the convicts, in the process making life easier for the prison bosses. Artur was in charge of the camp's maintenance section. It was the duty of the workers assigned to the section to unload a truck full of paint or tiles intended for the repair of the barracks, or one packed with my beloved sacks of cement. To dig up a burst pipe and bury it again, clean away snow, repair the roof of the library, fix a worn old door coming off its hinges, cut down an old tree threatening to fall on the prisoners' heads, lay some paving slabs – to name just a few of the tasks. The storehouse with maintenance supplies also fell within Artur's domain. He put his faithful sidekick Winnie on warehouse duties. Not a single nail or tin of paint would leave the place without his say-so. Artur was a man of first-rate organisational skills and tireless energy. No building escaped his notice; he could show you with his eyes shut where and what to clean, grease or repair. Under different circumstances, he would no doubt have made an excellent foreman.

Artur did a lot of kind deeds for me, and I accepted his help. We continued getting to know each other. Every day, Artur went to his supervisor in the operational department as if going to work, bringing him a daily pack of cigarettes and a chocolate bar. What they talked about remains a complete mystery. There was just one occasion when Artur couldn't resist bragging to me that the operational officers told him they were surprised at how, unlike Foma, the caretaker of Unit 3, he had managed to see eye to eye with me.

'What total idiots they are!' I thought gloomily to myself, for the umpteenth time.

Life in the unit carried on as usual. The unit had a new caretaker. Artur's place was taken – and he had a helping hand in this – by Roma Gurbo, the club manager, a man I knew well. He was happy to give up his bothersome role in the club and find a replacement. Roma was a decent and amiable guy, with an appealing nature. Once he got a taste of power, he didn't overstep the mark, and he remained unchanged as an ordinary prisoner. Many people in his situation let it go to their heads, went over the top and stopped thinking of themselves as inmates. Much of what happened in the unit depended on the caretaker. Any initiative of his, no matter how bad, would find support from the staff of the camp. Banning or confiscating something new, or thinking up yet another nasty measure against the prisoners – all such powers rested in the hands of the lucky incumbent filling the role of unit caretaker, or senior orderly, as it was officially known. Later, I would see monstrous examples of the personality metamorphosis undergone by convicts handed power by the colony's staff. But at that time, I simply plodded on with serving my huge sentence. I lived from one weekend to the next, from one parcel to the next, from one visit to the next. I did a lot of reading and reflecting on things. No one at any point ever managed to make me change the way I thought. I always remained a free man inside.

Time marched inexorably on. I was getting regular commendations for my diligent work and participation in all sorts of re-educational activities. It occurred to me that I could try to get moved to improved conditions of detention. Prisoners enjoying such conditions carried on living in the same barracks, but they were entitled to more frequent visits and packages and they could spend more in the prison shop. A commission in the camp, which met regularly in the main office, looked into such questions. Serious issues were determined there. The commission would also decide whether you merited parole.

The colony's head chaired the commission. The heads of the educational, operational and security departments, along with the heads of the units, made up the other members.

I was called to the main office, where I waited my turn. Unlike the other men, I wasn't too worried – in fact, it didn't really matter whether I got this or not. I already had enough visits, as my wife couldn't come more than four times a year, and I'd also solved the problem of parcels and packages, swapping cigarettes for parcel rights with the other inmates. It was the prisoners awaiting their parole decisions who were really anxious. Whether your parole request would be given the green light, whether the camp would support your application was being decided there and then. They read out your character references, took into account the number of commendations. All of the camps required a standard set of documents, including a letter from your future place of work! How was a man who had done six years for murder supposed to get a job lined up while still behind bars? What kind of insanity was that?! This sheer idiocy thrived and was actively nurtured. The leadership of the camps fanatically insisted on receiving such letters, realising all along they would be fictitious. It did not enter the heads of the Federal Penitentiary Service to play a role themselves in helping their wards find employment. Apparently, they had more important tasks on their hands.

My turn came round, and I stood in front of the men in uniform. My old friend Major Kuzmichev, the head of Unit 3, had somehow wormed his way into the commission.

'Unskilled worker?' he asked in disappointment as he fiddled with my personal file. And he added with a sneer, 'So then, Pereverzin, this is the best you're capable of?'

'It's the best you're capable of!' I snapped, unable to hold back. 'If I'd been convicted of boring old murder or rape, I'd have been working in the library or school for ages by now!'

I did not pass the commission's assessment that day. My application was refused.

People ought to serve the law, not their higher-ups, as is the custom in Russia. If only everyone carried out their actual duties, how much better life would be.

43

THE GREAT MIGRATION

It is how we like to do things: a law exists on paper, and yet life carries on as usual, blithely ignoring that law. Suddenly there comes a clap of thunder or a new face at the top, and everyone promptly falls into line. Until the special instructions arrive from above, the law remains mere words on paper.

I won't drift off into a discussion of the Russian Constitution, a marvellous document in theory.

Let's take Article 80 of the Russian Federation's Penal Code, which states: 'Persons given their first custodial sentence must be held separately from those who have been previously incarcerated.' It is worth noting the article has stipulated this for a very long time. But to no avail. Who cares about the written word in Russia? We have plenty of fine-sounding proclamations that are not adhered to. There are a thousand fawning interpreters of the rules and laws who read between the lines, and to accommodate their masters will pretend that an egg is actually a tomato and a coffee cup is an iron.

The head of the Federal Penitentiary Service, Yury Kalinin, paid no attention to this little detail; he was busy with more important matters. On his watch, four prisoners died upon arrival at their camp in Chelyabinsk Region. The moment they stepped off the train, they allegedly attacked the camp's staff, for which they were given a severe beating. The official version has it that the colony's staff acted legitimately in self-defence, and their only fault was failing to provide medical assistance to those same prisoners they had beaten up. The story made it into the papers, and Kalinin was forced to quit his post and change his field of work. So he became a member of the Federation Council, Russia's upper house. And now fortune is smiling upon him again. He is a distinguished person, graced with government medals and decorations, and he has become head of human resources at Rosneft. When the now sacked Alexander Reimer took over from Kalinin as head of the Federal Penitentiary Service, it would appear Reimer thought it over and decided there was no harm in complying with the previously enacted law. And so they got the ball rolling – or rather, set the wheels in motion. Thus commenced the great migration. Stolypin cattle cars and prisoner trucks took off across Russia, transferring prisoners from one camp to another. First-timers were taken to the left, while the rest of the prisoners, the veterans, went to the right.

How dearly I would love for a similar story to happen one day with our marvellous constitution. If only a new chief would rise to power, or, at worst, an old one would come to his senses, and he'd have a read, say, of Article 2 of the Constitution, which states, 'Man, his rights and freedoms are the supreme value. The recognition, observance and protection of the rights and freedoms of man and citizen shall be the obligation of the State.' And from that point onward, the Constitution would be strictly adhered to, and we would all suddenly become equal before the law, and it would no longer be the case that some are more equal than others, and Russia would at last become a truly civilised, democratic state.

So they issued the order and set the deadlines for the transfer of prisoners. For a long time, we lived in limbo while the Vladimir Regional Federal Penitentiary Service decided which camps to keep for the first-timers and where to send the veteran inmates. I had almost started packing my bags when, to my relief, I learnt the first-timers would continue serving their sentences in Penal

Colony No. 6 in Melekhovo village. The camps in the villages of Pakino and Vyazniki, in our same Vladimir Region, were picked out for the old-timers. It was a particularly emotional moment for the men. As I've already mentioned, our lifestyle in the camps was shaped not by any particular law, but rather by how despotic the local leadership was. Rumour had it the prisoners lived well in Vyazniki, where there was some degree of self-governance. Whereas the village of Pakino had earned notoriety among the men. It was where the most obstreperous convicts were sent for ideological correction. Photographs would later appear in their personal files of these former heavyweight criminals smiling as they held brooms or with their veins slashed or their stomachs cut. They said it was the region with the highest crime detection rate in the whole of Russia: 110 per cent. Their system for beating out testimony ran so smoothly and efficiently that they could have several men who didn't know each other confessing simultaneously to one and the same crime.

The camp began compiling the lists for the prisoner transport. On Tuesdays they sent people to Vyazniki, and on Thursdays to Pakino. Many of the guys became nervous. To be yanked away from a familiar place is unpleasant at the best of times, but even more so when you're behind bars and a transfer could spell disaster. Your more or less comfortable life in the camp could shatter in an instant. This was particularly true for certain inmates. I saw Slava, the orderly for Unit 3, rushing full tilt into the main office. His name had shown up on the list of prisoners heading to Vyazniki, which for him was tantamount to a death sentence. Slava personally, of his own accord, had treated his fellow prisoners abominably, ratting on them to the head of the unit. Sometimes he would see an inmate resting briefly on a bed after a hard day's work – he'd fly straight into the office of the head of the unit to report the guy. Major Kuzmichev would be out of his office like a shot, dashing to the scene of the crime. The two of them worked as a team, hunting down and catching offenders. Why was Slava doing it? What was driving him to shop those prisoners? Did it make him feel important or special? Convicted for rape and murder, Slava was an orderly and a member of the Section for Order and Discipline to boot; if he ended up in the camp at Vyazniki, where the authorities had less power, he knew he'd be in trouble. The prisoners would hold him to account for his past behaviour and he'd face a terrible reckoning. Slava flung himself at the feet of the operational officers, begging them not to send him to Vyazniki. In the end, he was taken to the strict-regime camp in Pakino, where he landed on his feet. And so the system created its loyal cadres. Such convicts would do the management's bidding; they'd sign any document put in front of them or give any testimony.

Many of my fellow prisoners in the camp were preparing for the move. Valera Gerasimov, known as Winnie, a good-hearted lump of a man who had shot three people dead at point-blank range, held little kitten Yashka to his chest, showered it with kisses and whispered something to it. I caught his words: 'So, little fellow, how are you going to cope without me?'

They were taking my loyal friend Andrei Zuyev away. He came to say goodbye. 'You are a good man, Vova. Thank you for everything,' he told me.

A new order came through: the migration was to be sped up and completed before New Year's Eve. The prisoner trucks were packed to the gunwales, with thirty or forty convicts crammed inside each one. In return, we had an influx of newcomers. The camp welcomed them rather inhospitably. Nothing had changed since the day of my arrival. It was the same brutal reception, complete with the broom or snow-shovel rite – the same old methods of persuasion. There ensued a torrent of complaints against the camp, and word got out to the press. Somebody had the bright idea of inviting the television cameras in and showing the world how new prisoners were received in the colony. No wonder our camp had won the regional prizes for amateur dramatics. The reporters filmed as a prisoner truck drove up to the camp gates. The new arrivals were promptly bundled into solitary for a few hours, where they were hidden from prying eyes, while in their place a flock of extras carrying bags taken from quarantine appeared, performing the part of the newcomers. The men jumped deftly from the truck, putting on a show of mirth and merriment. All that was missing was a red carpet and the traditional bread and salt.

44

THE FIRST MIRACLE

Zuyev was leaving, Winnie too. Artur, despite his previous conviction, would be staying in our camp as a highly prized specialist. Nothing changed in my life. I was now a worker in the maintenance crew. Each morning I went to work, where every now and then I had to unload a truck or haul something from one place to another for the sake of appearances. Artur did not overburden me with work, and I could just sit in his room and read books. I had reached my pinnacle of happiness in the camps. It would never get better than that.

Five years remained of my sentence. There were constant reminders of the fact. Twice a day, at morning and evening roll call, we had to call out the start and end of our sentences, and the dates were written on the tags attached to our beds. At the time, I lived in hope of a miracle – and then suddenly it happened. Amendments to the Russian Penal Code. They changed the sentence length for the offence I had been convicted of: Article 174.1, laundering the proceeds of crime. At the time of my trial, they could hand you from ten to fifteen years for that article. In the newly revised Penal Code, the sentencing range was reduced to between seven and ten years. This was no small matter. First, the article was downgraded from the category of 'very grave offence' to 'grave offence', which meant switching me from strict-regime custody to general-regime, and thus moving me to a different camp. But, most important of all, they would now have to reduce my sentence to bring it into line with the new law.

At first glance, the sums here seemed simple enough. I had been given ten and a half years under this article, meaning six months over the minimum custodial sentence. Therefore, you took the minimum sentence in the revised law, i.e. seven years, and added on six months. That gave seven and a half years. So according to the law, my sentence now needed to be reduced by three years. It was what the law stipulated. But then, by law, I should never have found myself in the particular camp where I'd spent the past five years, so I was under no illusions. This time, though, a miracle occurred! My lawyer petitioned for the sentence to be brought into line with the amendments to the Russian Penal Code, and the judge in the Kovrov Court reduced my sentence by two and a half years. This really was remarkable. It was like throwing the dice in a board game and all at once leaping several squares ahead, moving two and a half years closer to the long-awaited freedom. There were now just two years and a bit left until the end of my sentence. The prospect of parole came into view, and I had all the essentials for it, earned with blood, sweat and tears: a good character reference and commendations.

Here I was, already packing my things and preparing for the prisoner transport. I knew there were two general-regime camps in Vladimir Region. One was designated for veteran convicts; it lay on the outskirts of the glorious city of Vladimir. And the other, reserved for first-timers, was located in the town of Pokrov, between the swamp and the factory where Alpen Gold chocolate was produced. Our gentlemen jailers were in no hurry to abide by the law, and so they deported me to General-Regime Colony No. 5 in Vladimir City. I was bursting with the rosiest of plans.

'General regime, easy as pie,' I thought dreamily, as I happily packed up my things. Mindful of my past experience, I filled just two bags. I got rid of the rest of my plentiful belongings, bequeathing a rich inheritance to Artur and Roma. The blissful thought that I was leaving Melekhovo was throbbing through my head, while my soul sang for joy. I strode down that well-trodden avenue for the last time, with the bags in my hands, and headed towards solitary, where I awaited my last search in this camp. 'What are you looking to find?' I asked the sergeant. He did not answer, but instead half-heartedly glanced through my things. Cereals, nuts and dried fruit, books and papers, clothing, toiletries, my tracksuit and trainers – this was the simple clobber I'd stuffed into the two bags.

After the search, I found myself at the processing point, where a prisoner from Unit 16 awaited his fate – he was being taken to hospital. We were totally different people, and yet we were of one mind on a certain matter: our attitude towards the camp management. He was happy to be taking a brief break from Melekhovo, while I was delighted because I was quitting the place for good. I laughed for joy. The laughter would soon run out though.

An empty prisoner truck approached, and we were signed over to our armed escorts. The two of us fitted with relative ease in the large cubicle. The drive to Kovrov railway station was bumpy and luckily didn't take long – around an hour. I could hear the sounds of the station and took in its smells. The truck drove onto a deserted platform. We were loaded into an empty Stolypin-style cattle car, where we had a compartment to ourselves.

'Practically first class,' I thought, and just then I heard the guard's voice: 'Get ready for a search!'

Another inspection. Our journey from Kovrov to Vladimir took about an hour, and that was how long the search lasted too. The guard did not have time to finish looking through my luggage before the train came to its destination. The railway station at Vladimir greeted us with the din of commuter trains and long-distance trains. I relished inhaling the smells of the station and those long-distance trains, which awoke pleasant childhood memories. On the deserted platform, the usual prisoner truck plus surly escort were already waiting for us. The frenzied barking of dogs straining at the leash and guards with Kalashnikov rifles brought me back to reality: this was no weekend jaunt to the countryside.

The battered old prisoner truck trundled creakily along an unknown road, halting at endless traffic lights. Our first proper stop was the hospital. We drove into its grounds, and my fellow traveller said goodbye and left me. I'd heard many a horror story about this place: the corpses of convicts dumped under the stairs; operations that did not correspond with the diagnoses … Prisoners have a habit of exaggerating, but in this instance, after my taste of prison medicine in the camp, I felt sure the tales I'd heard were true.

The next stop would be mine: Vladimir Regional Federal Penitentiary Service General-Regime Colony No. 5.

45

GENERAL REGIME

The metal gates creaked open and we entered the grounds of the camp.

I jumped nimbly out of the prisoner truck with my bags and heard the command: 'Squat on your haunches, cap off, hands behind your head, face down.'

I put my bags on the ground and did as I was ordered.

'What's this? Going to the market with all this stuff?' came an unfamiliar voice.

I said nothing.

'Your surname, conviction, sentence – and your place in the criminal world.' Out of the corner of my eye I could see men in camouflage uniform, armed with batons, pacing around me imperiously.

I gave my name, conviction and sentence. It was an unusual criminal offence for these parts and a long sentence for a general-regime camp: eight and a half years. The unknown man holding my bulging personal file asked, 'Right, and what is Article 160?'

'Embezzlement,' I told him reluctantly.

'Must have been a big theft to land you with such a sentence,' the guard pursued the matter.

Not wishing to get drawn into conversation, I answered vaguely, 'Must have been.'

'And your place in the criminal world?' The guard continued to probe, swinging his baton.

I knew that one wrong word – for example, suggesting you followed the thieves' code – could lead to a flurry of blows raining down on you. If the guards overdid it, they would draw up a report saying you fell down the stairs, or you'd attacked them and they'd acted in self-defence, and a dozen well-fed snitches would gladly confirm it, putting their signature to every word.

'A *muzhik* – an honest con,' I replied, which squared with the reality of my prison life.

He was happy with this answer, and they led me to a room for searches and the processing of newcomers. It was a large room, lined with tiles. A few prisoners had been brought in ahead of me, and I saw some hefty, naked guys standing splayed against the wall with their arms raised. Their palms were turned outward and their legs wide apart. It was an uncomfortable pose to hold; you wanted to move your legs back. I saw a man in plain clothes wielding a rubber baton who was watching closely to ensure the prisoners experienced discomfort. He was lavishly showering them with blows. Nikita Krashanov was the quarantine caretaker, a former member of the underworld and previously the criminal leader of a general-regime colony in Kaluga Region. He had it good here, probably didn't feel like a prisoner at all. Several employees in uniform rummaged eagerly through the prisoners' things. The contents of their bags were shaken out onto the desks, falling to the floor and flying all over the place. For me also there was no escaping the same fate, and I too studied the wall tiles from close up. My legs and arms spreadeagled, with my palms facing outward, I tried to listen in on what was happening. I heard the crackle of my jumbo laundry bag and the clatter of things tumbling out. The guards were rough and careless with my baggage.

'Hey, he's been keeping a diary!' I heard a voice behind me saying indignantly. They found a notebook with my writings in, which I would never set eyes on again. They saw note-keeping of any kind as a threat to their own security and wellbeing. Clearly, they were driven by a hidden fear of what might happen if all their low-down tricks and misdeeds suddenly came to light.

The search quickly turned into outright robbery. Our jailers were not troubled by any scruples. I lost several ballpoint pens, some vitamins, T-shirts, cigarettes and hand cream. Officially, only my tracksuit and trainers were seized. The local despots treated the sportswear I'd received in a package at Melekhovo as prohibited items. I looked in horror at my things strewn about and upside down, the jumble of documents I'd packed up so neatly and lovingly before the journey. I stuffed my things back in the bag and followed the quarantine caretaker.

On the other side of the door was a washroom that you could not even dignify with the name of showers. A few hot and cold taps, some plastic tubs, though not enough to go around. Grabbing the chance, I mixed up some warm water in a tub and tipped it over me. Then I rubbed myself with a towel, got dressed and, accompanied by the half-prisoner, half-policeman Krashanov, went into the quarantine room. The convicts who'd arrived ahead of me were already there. There was a hall with boards on the walls, a small dormitory for twenty men and a room for eating – this was our living space for the coming week. I was relieved to learn that convicts were kept here for no more than a week before being dispersed among the units. Another search awaited me, this time conducted by inmate Mukhin, the orderly for quarantine, who did a more enthusiastic and thorough job than any policeman. The son of a traffic cop who had been sacked – like father, like son – Mukhin was an inveterate junkie sentenced for theft. He turned out to be more honest than the men in uniform: this time, none of my things went missing, and he merely asked me if he could have a tube of toothpaste. Our time in this place was killed by workouts, daily marching, constant cleaning of the already spotless areas, memorising the internal rules and regulations, and sitting dumbly in the dining room.

As a seasoned prisoner, I had set aside a biography of Pasternak that would be of little interest to anyone else. It was written by Dmitry Bykov, one of my favourite authors. That book saved me. Opening it up and turning the pages, I was instantly transported to those times and felt myself a tiny part of the events described. But reality brought me back to the quarantine block. There were ten of us. One of the convicts who'd arrived that day, Mikhail Maryin, went over to join the quarantine orderlies. The son of a lieutenant colonel in the KGB, Maryin was a second-rate businessman, owner of a motor depot in Vladimir, convicted of being an accessory to larceny. His story was that he'd been set up by his deputy, who stored hot cars on the grounds of his business. Chances are he was guilty as charged; he, for his part, was in no doubt of my guilt. Mikhail was to enjoy a meteoric career in the camp. Having made a good impression in quarantine, he quickly became the senior orderly for Unit 1, in other words, the manager of the dining room, replacing the previous one who was released on parole. One day, he had a good moan to me about his lot, almost holding back tears: 'Do you realise how hard I found it at first to make myself beat up the prisoners? I'm willing to do anything the management asks! If they tell me to kill, I'll kill! I'll do anything for the sake of my family, for my kids, who are waiting for their beloved dad to come home.'

Misha soon acquired a taste for it and made excellent progress in the art of prison torture. Apparently, somewhere deep inside of him lurked a dormant sadist, lord and serf, all in one. Behind barbed wire, the lord in him awoke; the sadist stood up tall, straightened his shoulders and proudly performed his heroic exploits. Misha authored and executed the system of corporal punishment practised in Unit 1 under his charge. He sauntered about the unit with a lazy gait and aristocratic airs. To my eyes, though, with his well-stuffed and shiny face, he looked more like a Nazi collaborator from a war movie. The saddest thing about this story was that, as a man of means, Mikhail could just as easily have achieved the desired result and won these rewards without the need to ruthlessly exploit and humiliate the other prisoners, simply by making a certain donation, which he ended up making in any case, to pay for his high office.

On my third day, I was summoned to the main office; I was taken there by the caretaker of quarantine, Krashanov. They ushered me into the office of the head of the operational department and offered me a seat. My escort, clearly also intending to park himself on a chair, was shown the door.

After six and a half years of a relatively quiet life, I now had a visit behind bars from some top-level guests. One was an operational officer for the Vladimir Regional Penitentiary Service; the other two were from the FSB. I was struck by their bungling ignorance. The conversation opened with a question.

'How did you pull off the shortening of your sentence, Pereverzin?' asked one of the strangers, who let me know he had an economics degree. All doubts about his affiliation with a certain department now vanished.

The guests were visibly irritated and unhappy that my sentence had been reduced. The question was asked in such a tone that you'd think I had stolen from them personally their entire salaries – several months' worth, or a year's worth, even.

I wanted to have some fun and answer, 'You want to know how? I arranged it with President Medvedev, he approved the amendments to the Penal Code, which led to my sentence being cut short.'

I knew perfectly well that these were the kinds of men who did not get jokes, and humour would only end up needling them. So I played it safe, politely explaining about the amendments to the articles I was convicted under. I tried to say a few words about the Yukos case, mentioning that innocent people were behind bars because of it, but I ran into a brick wall. Not in terms of misunderstandings, simply as a result of pure ignorance.

'Well, you shouldn't have plundered the state, then,' the plainclothes gentleman with the economics degree said. 'First he robs Russia, then he goes running to Strasbourg,' he said, summing up his perspective on the world.

Suddenly the FSB officer showed a keen insight into my thinking.

'So, you're off to Moscow, then, as a witness? You've got bored of sitting here, itching for an adventure?' he asked.

I didn't reply to his remarks and silently stared out the window. The conversation was over.

Krashanov was burning with curiosity and asked, 'What did they want?'

The cleverest answer I could come up with was: 'They asked about you. They were interested in what things are like in quarantine, the state of affairs. They asked if the prisoners in here get beaten up.'

For a moment he blenched, tail between his legs, before he remembered that everything he did was carried out on the orders of and with the blessing of the colony's officers. And he slipped back into his usual state – namely, a pompous sense of his own superiority.

46

UNIT 2

I spent five days in quarantine before I was assigned to Unit 2. This turned out to be pretty much the worst unit in the camp. The only place worse still was Unit 1. The pointless and preposterous rules and regulations degraded the convicts and blighted their lives, making them unbearable. I'd never seen anything as bad as this. What went on here reminded me a good deal of quarantine in Melekhovo. Another search followed – this time, the orderly for the unit, nicknamed Vampire, examined the contents of my bags. Looking back, it all seems hard to believe. It was simply beyond imagination. The overcrowded dormitory, with shaky twin bunks placed so close that I couldn't even squeeze sideways into my sleeping space. One little bedside table to be shared among four men. Our personal things were stored inside boxes left over from 20-kilogram packages; only your toiletries were allowed in the bedside tables. The orderly inmate kept an eagle eye on the observance of the rules, with daily checks of the contents of our bedside tables. We could access the boxes with our belongings three times a day, after queuing in line. The night before, we would sort out the rota for making the beds. Blink and you would miss the chance to wash. Each morning began with the orderlies yelling wildly, 'Everybody up! Move it! Faster! Exercise time!'

After the workout, we washed ourselves and made the beds. Time was limited, and everyone was rushing and pushing, spurred on by the orderlies. We had to be quick and vacate the dormitory by a certain time so we could sit dumbly and in silence for an hour in the re-educational-work room. No talking was allowed: on the other side of the wall, the local grandee, Seryozha Zhukin, was sleeping in a separate room. Nicknamed Beetle, he had been convicted for actual bodily harm. His sleeping session was policed by the orderlies. Anyone breaking the silence would be severely punished – with a beating. Zhukin had been a drug addict on the outside; behind bars, he deemed himself a top athlete. Seryozha pumped iron all day long and popped steroids supplied by the operational officers as if they were candy. He tirelessly honed his skills on the punchbag, on the orderlies and on prisoners who had done something wrong. He had no idea what it meant to wait for the latest parcel or package. As a reward for his services, the operational officers personally brought unlimited bagfuls of groceries into the colony for him. The only thing not allowed was drink and drugs. Beetle, however, had little need for packages, as he was already dining splendidly. His friend, colleague and crony from Vladimir Prison's 'pressure cell', Vinogradov, alternatively known as Fanatic, was now manager of the dining room and provided Beetle with a hearty diet and a constant supply of food. There was a personal chef, a prisoner preparing food for the police from ingredients stolen from the prisoners, and he did his job exceedingly well. The stolen food was enough to go around – feeding the colony's staff and orderlies alike.

This was how the system begot its monsters. Puffed-up men with a pompous sense of their own superiority, incapable of doing a day's work, whose routine was to boss people around left, right and centre, men who beat up their own kind with impunity, were ready to commit new crimes upon release.

Meanwhile, we, the ordinary prisoners of Unit 2, were made to spend our time sitting on the benches in the re-educational-work room. The unit implemented Article 106 of the Penal Code in full measure. Every inmate had to work a minimum of two hours a week on improvements to the grounds. The notion of 'improvements' was interpreted broadly and freely by the prison lawyers. It included unloading groceries delivered to the prison shop as well as unloading logs and planks in the industrial zone. Our remit also included unearthing burst pipes and digging up the soil along the security strip in the exclusion zone. Our two hours per week turned into a full eight-hour day of unpaid toil.

Many of the prisoners were happy to grab any chance to get out of the unit. Indeed, the unbearable atmosphere in the unit was created with that purpose in mind. We could only go to the toilet strictly one at a time and with the permission of the orderly, so a queue would build up of those needing to go. In the time off from sitting in the stuffy room, twice a day you could go outdoors for a smoke break. After six in the evening, we had an hour of personal time, when you could get on with your own business and go for a walk around the small local zone.

From the window of the re-educational-work room, you could see the watchtowers, a barbed-wire fence and freedom. After the prison scenes in Melekhovo, this view from the window was paradise for me. In the distance, you could see the highway, the famous 'Peking Road', connecting Moscow and Nizhny Novgorod. Watching the distant cars go past became my favourite pastime.

I got acquainted with new people. Some time later, one of the orderlies confessed to me he'd been ordered by the caretaker to keep his eye on me and listen in on all my conversations. Another inmate, Denis Rozmarilo, who loved to chat with me, would be summoned to the caretaker's office and forbidden to interact with me. Realising I would not be able to stand it for long in this place, I counted the days left until parole and my transfer to Moscow as a witness for the defence in Khodorkovsky's trial. The lawyer had already filed a request for my parole, and I was waiting for a decision. The judge had no formal grounds for refusing me parole, and I'd set my hopes on a positive result.

'The thing is for it to come through before I leave for Moscow!' I told myself optimistically.

I carried on chatting with the prisoners and found out some interesting things about the camp and the unit. Convicts who'd been sentenced to serve in an open penal colony were being kept here illegally for weeks on end. They waited, existed, endured, not daring to complain. They were afraid. Our unit was a safe haven of sorts, a place where convicts from the other units could defect to, those who had lost at cards or were in some kind of trouble. This was also where they moved prisoners who had got up to no good in other units – as a punishment. I automatically fell under the latter category – of prisoners who had erred. In reality, my only sin was the fact someone some place wanted to curry favour.

This place was certainly no Melekhovo; it was a separate state with its own rules and laws. Each morning, we were greeted with live music. A brass band made up of prisoners belted out the national anthem; it was the pride and joy of the head of the camp. Scrawny old Colonel Nikiforov, who turned up to the colony each day in his BMW X5, cut a strange figure. I got the impression he didn't have the foggiest what was going on in the colony, which was run by his deputy, Alexander Rybakov. Nikiforov, meanwhile, was content to listen each day to the medley performed by the orchestra for his delight and delectation. At 3 p.m. and 5 p.m. the orgy of music would commence. The repertoire ranged from the famous criminal song 'Murka' and the comedy-film classic 'If I Were a Sultan' to the upbeat war song 'Victory Day'. Try as they might, the musicians could not hit all the right notes or keep the right rhythm. There was always someone lagging behind or rushing ahead. The drum would leap out of the musical fabric, then the trumpet would, and then the fanfare trumpets. I was shocked at what I heard.

The penal colony lay within the city limits and had at its disposal vast industrial premises and a huge pool of manpower ready to work practically for free; it made for a very profitable set-up. The sewing workshop, the automotive garage, the joinery shop and the production line for packing combat rations ensured a good number of prisoners were kept in employment. Among the items produced by the joinery shop were children's playground equipment (swings and playhouses) and bedside tables for prisoners. Those wretched bedside tables, knocked together from chipboard then given a lick of grey paint, were the epitome of crudity. And yet they were rather pricy: 12,000 roubles. At least that was how much they were sold for to the nearby general-regime penal colony in the town of Pokrov, Vladimir Region. Operation Bedside Table was conducted by the Vladimir Regional Federal Penitentiary Service and it yielded a tidy profit. Given a rough outlay per bedside table of around 800 roubles, those prison entrepreneurs were making a killing.

47

I, TROUBLEMAKER

Notwithstanding all the loading and unloading and the other pointless chores, time in the unit dragged interminably. My hopes for the future were soon dashed by the head of the unit, Lieutenant Belikov, who held out a sheet of paper for me and said nonchalantly, 'Sign here for this infringement!'

The world went dark before my eyes.

'What's this? What infringement?' I said in perplexity.

'It's all written here.'

I read the sheet. 'It has been decided to impose a sanction on convict Pereverzin for initiating a conflict and using expletives during his admission to the penal colony.'

My jaw dropped. I felt no anger, no irritation, and all I could muster was: 'But that never happened!'

'I don't know anything about it. You need to take it up with Rybakov. And be thankful you were shown this paper at all. Otherwise you'd have gone to court and only found out about the infringement there,' he told me. It was something that happened often in the Russian prison system. You'd submit a parole application, only to discover, once you were in court, a whole heap of sanctions that had been slapped on you. In place of your signature on the paperwork there would be the signature of a colony employee, with the remark: 'The convict refused to sign.'

The head of the unit was a bit of a dimwit, and more than once he asked me, 'Pereverzin, so who had it in for you?'

A lieutenant of the Interior Ministry's internal services, Yevgeny Belikov had joined the prison service to dodge serving in the military. The lazy young fellow couldn't be bothered to put himself out. Dumping your workload on the prisoners was a very common practice in the camp. From first thing in the morning, the prisoner-orderly would be found sitting in the lieutenant's office, in the unit's block, doing all his work for him. Dima acted as his secretary and waiter all in one. He was the head of the unit's right-hand man – and also his left-hand man. He was the one who wrote up and filled out all the documents and numerous forms. The head of the unit had merely to sign the prepared documents, and at times, he didn't even do that. Dima would often perform the procedure for him, so as not to disturb the man in uniform, who was, in his own way, also serving a sentence, although of his own free choice.

To say this new-found sanction upset me would be putting it mildly. Like a granite boulder, it blocked the path to my long-awaited freedom; it was the ruin of all my plans and hopes. So I decided to fight back. I wrote an appeal to the oversight body for compliance with the law in penitentiaries; I tried to have the sanction overturned in court. My lawyer carried out his own investigation and learnt a lot of interesting things about me. It turned out the sanction had been imposed on the strength of a statement by inmate Mukhin, the quarantine orderly, whom I'd only seen once I had reached the quarantine block. This account, however, claimed the following: 'Upon arrival in the colony, convict Pereverzin insulted Mukhin in the washroom, calling him names, using foul language and trying to pick a fight.' The operational officer who wrote up the document had let his imagination run riot: 'The police came running over and tried to calm him down, but they were unable to do so. Pereverzin ignored their appeals and continued in his troublemaking.'

Attached to the statement were reports by the colony staff confirming what had been written.

Well, blow me down! My head was spinning from what I'd read. It felt as though I was losing my mind.

Or could I be suffering from amnesia or a split personality? Did I kick up trouble and then blank it from memory?

Even the lawyer, who had known me for years, repeated his question: 'Are you quite sure none of this happened? Could you maybe have lost control?'

'No, it simply did not happen,' I insisted again.

By this point, Mukhin, the author of the statement, was being released on parole. My lawyer, who had a background in law enforcement, tracked the former inmate down and met with him.

'But I never wrote that,' Mukhin said, as he looked in amazement at the document written in his name. 'And that's not my handwriting, it's Krashanov's.'

I still cannot make sense of why they did it. All the operational officer needed to do was to tell Mukhin to write the statement, and he'd have done it in a trice!

My lawyer recorded Mukhin's testimony on camera and took a handwriting sample for analysis. The experts confirmed the statement was written not by Mukhin but by some other person.

48

JOURNEY TO MOSCOW

Khodorkovsky's trial, for which I was announced as a witness for the defence, was in full swing in Moscow. Any day now, I would be summoned to court and transported to Moscow. I was waiting with bated breath.

That summer, the peat bogs were on fire, and smoke enveloped our camp. Rumour had it they were discussing the idea of evacuating the convicts. After giving it lots of thought, they decided to leave us all where we were, at their own risk and peril, and to hope for the best, in true Russian style. The worst that could happen was the inmates would be poisoned by the smoke – no great loss. There were top-secret instructions on what to do with the prison population if unforeseen events broke out – disasters or wars. What to do with the prisoners during hostilities, for example, if the enemy was about to seize some patch of land including a strict- or general-regime prison colony. There were numerous directives for just such a scenario (and for plenty of others besides).

I waited each day to be transported to Moscow, listening to the announcements hailing from the rattly loudspeaker.

'Ivanov and Sidorov – get your belongings and go to the office, you're leaving,' I would hear, and I carried on waiting for my turn.

One evening, the orderly came over and told me my name was on the list. I had to be in the office with my belongings by 6 a.m. the next day.

'Hurray! It's happening at last,' I thought, packing my things. I took only the bare essentials so as to travel light. In the morning, after wake-up, with just the one bag, I was escorted by the orderly to the office. Despite the unearthly hour, the sun was beginning to warm up. The drowsy guards quickly went through the motions of inspecting my things, before putting me in the caged pen. I did not have to wait very long – in around twenty minutes, the truck came for me. I was handed over, along with my bulging personal file, to the armed escorts.

'Your conviction, your sentence?' I heard the usual questions, which I answered, before climbing into the vehicle in a buoyant mood. The prisoner truck acted like a shared taxi. There were some passengers already in the compartments; I sat down and joined them. These guys were heavyweight criminals, on their way from a closed prison to the strict-regime penal colony in Pakino. The floor was cluttered with their things. A television set, a cassette player, clothing. I knew they would look back later on the closed prison as the high point of their years behind bars in Vladimir Region. Nothing good awaited them in Pakino. We introduced ourselves. When the standard questions came up – who I was, where I'd been doing time, what the set-up was there, which men I'd crossed paths with – I had plenty to say. It was the usual conversation among prisoners. By now it had become hot in the truck, and I was thirsty. I began to feel car sick. The guys asked me for a smoke. Barely two hours had passed when the truck drove into the grounds of a camp and stopped. One at a time, the guys jumped out and unloaded their baggage. I jumped out last. The guard verified our personal files, and he pulled me to one side. Another prisoner truck was waiting for me. Its destination was the Vladimir city railway station. I said goodbye to the gang, wishing them luck.

New companions awaited me in the new truck. None of these men had yet been convicted, and I made quite an impression on them in my black prison clothes and with my eight-and-a-half-year sentence. The journey to Vladimir took around an hour; it was over in a flash. I was met by the familiar station, where a Stolypin-style cattle car awaited us. We transferred to the train. There were six of us in the compartment, with one bunk per man. Luckily for us, the trains to Moscow were not overcrowded. After the search, I settled on one of the top bunks and tried to remain motionless. Each time you moved, there would be streams of sweat. It was August 2010. I didn't feel hungry or thirsty. The clacketing of the wheels lulled me, and I drifted off into sleep. The rhythmic rocking of the coach evoked pleasant childhood memories: summer holidays and journeys to the Crimea. I remembered the little stations where you'd pop out and buy an ice cream; I could taste the snowy, cloying sweetness in my mouth.

The train came to a sudden halt, jolting me out of my bliss. I didn't want to come back to this compartment and face the mugs of my fellow travellers; I wanted to retreat into my dreams. The train began moving and I returned to the present. We were approaching Moscow. A prisoner truck was waiting for us on a faraway platform of Kursk station. We were transferring again. Drenched in sweat, I climbed into a cubicle. It was dark already, and the Moscow streets were empty. The entirely ordinary prisoner truck whisked us off to the prison. I recognised Matrosskaya Tishina. Once they had unloaded all the convicts in the courtyard of the main building, I was taken to the special block, to the prison within a prison, Detention Centre 99/1. I got the feeling I was bonded to this prison for life, and my personal file most likely contained some special note to that effect. In the intervening four years, nothing had changed in that place. It had the same guards, the same regime. I caught myself actually feeling glad to see them all. The search went on for several hours. Not one scrap of paper, not one bag escaped their notice. My property was all carefully recorded. It was already late, two or three in the morning. I was issued with bedding and a mattress and put in a one-man cell. I laid the mattress on the iron bed and tried to sleep.

After breakfast, I was moved to another cell, which held a couple of freshly detained men of educated appearance. Dima and Stas were under investigation and had been charged with financial crimes. To them I was a seasoned old-timer, and they hung on my every word. I received a warm and friendly welcome. They fed me and plied me with tea. Dima took off and gave me the garment that I later wore to Khamovnichesky Court: a white sports jacket bearing the words 'BMW Sport racing team'. I spent two days in this cell. It was not quite the usual crowd for me. Normally I was put in with murderers.

And that's just what happened. I was transferred to cell No. 610, where Khodorkovsky had once stayed. This time, I found myself in the company of two lads. One was just a kid; he'd been charged with assaulting and killing security guards in a cash-in-transit heist. The other was a hit man working for the Kurgan gang. We soon found common ground. Andrei V. originally hailed from Kurgan, and he'd worked hard and dirty. He had a good number of murders under his belt. After the gang was smashed, he spent thirteen years on the federal wanted list. He was living under a false name, using a fake ID, in a different city. His arrest was a sheer fluke. His past was enough to land him multiple life sentences. Andrei struck a deal with the investigators: he had to sign a special document, after which he'd be granted special status. If you helped the investigators, you'd get no more than two-thirds of the maximum sentence for the gravest offence. According to the Penal Code, the maximum sentence he could get was twenty-five years. So Andrei was facing around eighteen. He was strong-willed and focused, with a fighting spirit. Hard as nails. We got into lots of long conversations.

'Andrei, what did it feel like to kill people?' I asked.

'It was war,' he said coldly. 'They killed our lads, we killed theirs.'

I ate my fill, caught up with sleep and recharged in this prison. I was getting ready for my court appearance and writing a speech. Strange as it sounds, I did not prepare any questions with Khodorkovsky's and Lebedev's defence team, let alone discuss the possible answers. Everything was crystal clear as it was. There was no need to be imaginative.

On the morning of 31 August, a guard came for me, and I climbed into a brand new GAZelle van bearing the inscription 'Police' on its flank. I had never travelled in such comfort before. I sat in the cubicle opposite the door and looked through the window. The view was exhilarating and made my head spin. Just a few metres away, I could see cars, the faces of unknown drivers hurrying about their business. Right before my eyes were the streets of Moscow. The trip from Matrosskaya Tishina to Khamovnichesky Court took about an hour. We drove down the Sadovoye Koltso ring road, then passed the Kiev Station forecourt, crossed the bridge and went along the embankment. I saw the illuminated Evropeysky shopping mall with the ice rink on its roof. Such scenery had faded from memory, and what I saw entranced me. I remembered how right here, in this very spot, I had sat at the wheel of my own car, and I couldn't believe it had really been the case. It felt as though everything would return to how it was, if I could only reach out and touch it. But almost two years stood between me and freedom.

The van drove briskly into the courtyard, and under the escort of several policemen I entered the courthouse. I waited in the spacious basement for my hour to come. And come it did. Handcuffed to a policeman, I went into the packed courtroom. I saw several familiar faces. Khodorkovsky and Lebedev were sitting in the aquarium. It was a good occasion for a first meeting with my 'accomplices'. While working at Yukos, I had never spoken with either of them. I was led to the witness stand and the examination began. I told my story. Years of my life raced past: Menatep Bank, Cyprus, Yukos. I described in detail the time I got the job at the Yukos subsidiary in Cyprus; I explained how the job offer came from Michel Sublen, the financial director of Yukos, an American citizen. I talked about the administrative work, about finding offices for the company, about the auditors. I remembered to mention that I'd never made a single payment and was not even authorised to handle the bank accounts. Not that it had stopped them from convicting me for Article 174.1 (laundering the proceeds of crime).

My account did not tally with the prosecution's narrative, and this clearly irked the prosecutors. Lakhtin became visibly nervous. My story graphically illustrated the flimsiness of the trumped-up case. Through my personal example, the absurdity of the charges and the idiocy of the so-called evidence became all the more apparent. The case continued to fall apart at the seams. The people in uniform desperately wanted to put a brave face on a bad matter, and they tied themselves in knots to justify their existence. I poured petrol on the fire by talking about how they put pressure on me during the investigation, offering me a suspended sentence in return for bearing false witness against Khodorkovsky and Lebedev.

'Just make a confession; say that you knew Khodorkovsky and Lebedev, you were given instructions from them, and you'll be free as the wind,' I said, recalling what the investigators had told me.

Upon hearing these words, Prosecutor Lakhtin flew into a fit of hysterics and demanded my questioning be stopped. But the examination continued. The judge couldn't deny Lebedev and Khodorkovsky the right to question me. Although when he came to deliver the verdict, he would do his black deed in defiance of all the arguments of the defence and the testimony of the witnesses.

The prosecutors became hot and bothered as Lebedev began putting questions to me. A brazen lie came to light, trumped up by the staff at the Prosecutor-General's Office. Lebedev read out extracts from the indictment against him: 'Platon Lebedev, while in his workplace, appointed the member of the criminal gang Vladimir Pereverzin as company director of the Cyprus-based Routhenhold Holdings Limited.'

I was shocked at the sheer effrontery of the investigators, and I said bluntly this was a barefaced lie.

It was high time the prosecutors themselves be arrested, charged and hauled into the cage in our place.

I managed to call Prosecutor Lakhtin a paid liar for good measure, before a break in the session was announced, and I was led to the dungeons. I went down to the courthouse basement, where I spent a long time pacing from corner to corner in an extremely agitated state. I wanted to strangle the investigators and prosecutors. The lot of them.

Each witness was examined by both sides – the defence and the prosecution. The defence had finished questioning me, and I was waiting for the prosecutors to begin. I was handcuffed again to a policeman and led to the courtroom.

'The prosecution has no questions for the witness,' I heard the prosecutor say. They didn't know how to get rid of me, and no doubt would have gladly burnt me at the stake.

I didn't want to leave. I still had more to say. In fact, I had a surprise in store for the prosecution – but they were already leading me out of the courtroom.

People stood up and applauded me. That moment will always stand out vividly in my memory.

Our criminal case formed the backbone of Khodorkovsky's second trial. Our case was also to destroy it.

That evening, I returned to the cell utterly drained and went to bed. I stayed two more days in the prison – until they ordered me to leave. The idea of going back to Vladimir, where clashes with the camp authorities awaited, held little appeal. A sinking feeling of anxiety and overwhelming depression hit me hard. I silently packed up my things for the journey.

This time I parted with the prison for good. After one last search, I was taken for processing. An hour later, the prisoner truck drove me to the station. The train carriage was jam-packed. Another search followed, then we took our seats in the compartment. There were not too many of us – around ten men. The train began to move. The prisoner transport was delivering convicts who had just been sentenced. I was the only seasoned prisoner among us. All the guys were first-timers on their way to a strict-regime camp. They were heading for Melekhovo. My stories about that camp would come in very useful to them, and we spent the whole journey talking. The trip was exceptionally calm and peaceful. We were led out to the toilet one at a time and given boiling water for tea. We were blessed with good guards, who were from Vladimir. It was the guards from Kirov and Mordovia who had a bad reputation.

In Vladimir, to the sound of barking dogs, we were crammed into a prisoner truck and driven from one prison to the next. The party of brand-new arrivals was dropped off at the Copeck, the transit prison in the city of Vladimir, where the prisoners would wait before continuing their journey. Then I was personally delivered to my destination. The prisoner truck drove through the gates of the camp, and I reluctantly got out of the vehicle. They already knew me here and were waiting for me. I was greeted by some guards, the officer on duty and an operational officer. Nearby stood Beetle, the unit's caretaker, who walked me back to the unit.

'And so ends my journey,' I said with a wistful sigh.

49

STORM CLOUDS GATHERING

After my return from Moscow, events began moving at a frightening pace.

I was summoned to the main office, where a prosecutor and judge had come for my parole hearing. I eyed the judge with curiosity. She was a young, beautiful woman. She made it clear I wouldn't be released on parole while I still had an unspent sanction. Everything boiled up inside me.

'What do you mean? I've spent three years running, jumping, toiling like a galley slave, and I've earned a heap of commendations and thank-yous, but now because of a forged sanction I'm being deprived of liberty? Does one sanction outweigh all of my prison-life past?'

It seemed the answer was yes.

The system had failed to reform me. I had not lost faith in people or given up on justice. I'd been convicted cynically and brazenly, in total defiance of the law, and I was hoping for some crumb of justice. I wished a little drop of justice could fall my way.

The lawyer asked for the hearing to be adjourned, and this was granted. We were waiting for the lawsuit against the prison camp. I knew that opposing them would be difficult and dangerous. The management behaved differently in each colony, and personality was ultimately the deciding factor.

I was aware of the abundant reprisals against the prisoners, the beatings. The case of Alexei Pashunin, a native of Stavrov, sent shock waves through the camp. After a chat with our unit's operational officer, Ilya Kulikov, young Alexei fell down the stairs, smashing himself up and dying. Well, he may have infringed the camp's rules, and maybe he was even doing time for a crime he'd actually committed, but that was no reason for such a violent end. After lights out, he'd gone missing from his bunk, which made the camp employees very cross indeed. They found him in another barracks in another unit, where he was peacefully drinking tea with a guy from his home town. The furious staff dragged him into the office and had a lengthy 'chat' with him. Soon after, Alexei was transferred for re-education to Unit 2, where Lieutenant Kulikov also had a compelling precautionary 'chat' with him, following which the poor chap fell down the stairs. Naturally enough, everything was corroborated by the prisoners' statements and the prosecution service's investigation held after the accident!

If you take a look at the statistics for the Vladimir Regional Federal Penitentiary Service, you can only marvel at the number of inmates falling fatally down the stairs. It is enough to make you wonder what is going on and why they don't repair all those flights of stairs across the entire system.

Storm clouds began gathering. I was not allowed to make calls, though I noticed the unit caretaker had his own mobile phone. A local lawyer visited me twice a week. He came for the sole purpose of checking I was alive, healthy and hadn't 'fallen down the stairs'. I stuck rigidly to the insane rules and tried to show enormous restraint, which, believe me, was not easy. You were living in each other's pockets, keeping company with the prisoners and spending all your time together. Time began to drag endlessly and heavily. Once a week we had what couldn't rightly be called showering or bathing. I am at a loss for words to describe this cleansing procedure. Ablutions, perhaps, or lavations. Time was limited. The number of taps with hot and cold water was too. The only things not in short supply were the tubs we used for quickly splashing ourselves and our clothes. I saw with my own eyes how the men would put on their just washed, still wet trousers. Laundering and drying things in the unit was a huge problem, and one that was artificially created. Once a week we had a mandatory 'educational activity': marching with singing. 'Oh how I long for Russia, Oh how I yearn to go home, So long since I last saw mother!' the prisoners yelled as they stomped noisily.

One prisoner shared his story with me. He had been summoned in the night for a talk with the caretaker and the operational officer Kulikov. They had beaten a confession out of him. The camp would receive regular bulletins on crimes that had been committed. To solve a case was a point of honour for the operational officer, and it would also earn a financial reward. They offered Sasha a deal: he was to confess to a theft he hadn't committed.

'It won't add much to your sentence in any case, and then later we'll release you on parole,' the officer assured him.

According to the locals, you could find senior operational officer Lieutenant Kulikov on the weekends at the Vladimir market, where he had a job on the side selling roses.

Our appeal against the infringement was dragging on. First, the judge went off on holiday, then she fell pregnant and left again – this time on maternity leave. A new judge was appointed. I was counting the days. The atmosphere was heating up. Each time my lawyer visited, he had to go to the head of the camp or his deputy to sign the paperwork. The camp head, Colonel Nikiforov, had no qualms about making overt threats, demanding I play by his own prison rules: 'Wants to lock horns, eh?' he asked my lawyer. 'Ah, but we'll stitch him up with five new infringements!'

271

There was a wide and varied arsenal of tools for putting pressure on a prisoner who'd decided to fight the system. You could be approached by the heavyweight criminals and asked 'nicely' not to make complaints against the camp management, as it would only make the situation worse for everybody. In a 'red' prison unit, though, the arsenal of tools was different. After a chat with the infamous Lieutenant Kulikov, the orderly known as Vampire suddenly turned against me. Before, he had been fond of acting clever in front of me and showing off how much Nietzsche he'd read, but now the twenty-three-year-old kid was insulting me in front of others and trying to goad me. It was plain who was behind this. Realising where the verbal clash was heading, and aware it could not carry on much longer, I knew I would soon have no choice but to punch him in the face. The consequences of doing so were not hard to guess: a written report, a statement, a reprimand – or even a new sentence for assault.

I wrote to the head of the colony requesting a transfer to a safe place. They put me in solitary, where I spent ten days alone. It was a big improvement on staying in the unit. I was left in the company of my thoughts and the abundant rats that lurked in the waste pipes of the cell. I plugged the opening of the squat toilet with a bundle of rolled-up old sheets wrapped in polythene bags. One time, I was careless enough to scrape the leftovers from my plate down the toilet. In doing so, I lured the entire rat population of the solitary block into my cell. I distinctly heard their squeals and scrabbling. They were chattering and communicating with each other, and perhaps they were trying to tell me something too. The rats were gnawing and pushing up the bung from below, trying to pay me a visit. Once, I dozed off in the afternoon on the wooden floor and was woken by rats brushing past me. A young rat couple was cavorting on the floor of the cell in the shafts of daylight, flicking me with their long tails. Outside the window, I could hear the live music so beloved of the head of the camp: 'If I were a sultan, I'd have three wives …'

272

During this enforced solitude, I thought a lot of things over and managed to clear my head and regain my composure a little. An operational officer came into the cell and showed me an order issued by the panel to transfer me to Unit 1, which provided services for the canteen. The camp staff had convened, thought it through and this was their decision. Of course, why not send a highly educated man who was having issues with his health to serve up slops? Offering him a job in the library would hardly be appropriate!

'If you refuse to transfer to the unit, you'll have to stay in solitary,' the officer warned me and waited for me to decide.

'They've left me with no choice, the bastards,' I thought, and I reluctantly agreed.

'Let's go!' I said and took a step forward.

50

A GALLEY SLAVE AGAIN

At first glance, the unit created a bleak impression. Misha Maryin, whom I knew from quarantine, was now the unit's caretaker, and he made an immediate demand: 'We need you to refuse to work! Write us a letter stating you refuse to work and then go back to solitary, or else you'll find yourself on dishwashing duties!'

I chose the latter and became a galley slave once again. My working day lasted from wake-up until lights out, with fifteen hours spent sopping wet. Dishwashing was the toughest job of all; it was where slop-servers who had done something wrong were sent for punishment and where men not fit for anything else ended up. Our team had three punished wrongdoers, counting me, and two regular dishwashers. It was unanimously decided by the crew that I should get the easiest role: rinsing the washed dishes and carrying them over to the serving counter. But even this job was not plain sailing. Through the serving hatch that separated the washing area from the dining space where the prisoners ate, we were bombarded with plates, ladles and vats. The conveyor belt would not stop for a minute. There wasn't one second of peace for us. The men were in tears – literally crying. For a poorly washed vat or ladle, you faced punishment: a clout with the stick used for stirring the food in the pots. The stick was more like an oar in shape and size. This punishment would be inflicted on the spot by the manager of the workshop, the caretaker of the unit, Misha, and the senior cook, Dima. Although often the punishment was deferred until the evening, when the job would be done with a vengeance in Maryin's little office. Dima would clasp the prisoner's arms while Misha flogged the fellow with a bendy plastic tube specially kept for the purpose.

The most terrible part was that any delegation visiting the camp and visiting this particular unit would get a negative answer if they asked a prisoner in front of others whether they were abused here. And if you asked a prisoner on his own, with no camp staff present, only a few would resolve to tell you what was going on. It was only the convicts on the outside who were ready to confirm everything.

'These delegations come and go, but you still have to live in this place,' came the sinister whisper that would nag darkly in the heads of those still inside.

There are various approaches you can take towards these people: you can judge them, label them as this or that, take the line that 'if they allow themselves to be treated like that, then they deserve it'. Here it is worth stopping for a second to reflect on what is happening and ask yourself the question: how can a society consider itself civilised if it tolerates such abuse? What kind of people will such a 'school' be churning out?

I watched what was happening around me in horror.

'Not long to go now; I just need to stick it out a bit longer, make sure I keep my cool,' I told myself.

I wrote another grievance against the camp's employees. The Labour Code was not being adhered to, wages weren't being paid, the working hours exceeded all the limits. We kicked up a stink, filed complaints at all levels. My lawyer wrote a letter to Reimer, the head of the Federal Penitentiary Service of Russia, demanding I be transferred to another colony.

The camp leadership did not plan on backing down, and they responded with another sanction, slapping a reprimand on me. Twice a day, our unit had roll call. The bell would ring, the prisoners would run out from their workplaces, line up in the yard outside the dining room, and upon hearing their surname, call out their name and patronymic, whereupon they would head back to their workplaces. For one particular roll call, the bell was not rung. The orderly dropped in on all the workshops except ours and secretly led the whole unit into the yard for inspection. The officer on duty, Captain Tryastsin, patiently waited for the entire unit to line up. Everything had been agreed in advance between him and Lieutenant Kulikov, who was the brains behind this performance. Meanwhile, we were busy washing dishes and were unaware a trap had been set. We only realised something was up when the orderly ran screaming into the washing area and informed us the unit was assembled and waiting only for us. To maintain appearances, the sanctions were imposed on all the members of our crew – me included, naturally. The prisoners whispered about it for a long time and were stunned by what had happened. One of them commented candidly: 'Wow, look how many men they had to use just to give Pereverzin a sanction!'

I myself was shocked by what had happened and was waiting to see what would come next. My partner in the crew, Lyosha, confessed to me that a few days before I'd joined them, he'd been called over by the caretaker Maryin and asked to pick a fight with a newcomer who would be entering the unit. There was no shortage of candidates for the role of agent provocateur. I was living in a constant state of alert. I opened up some safety razors and armed myself with the blades. Then I tied a thread to one of the blades, and I reliably hid it in my lapel badge. If you gave the thread a tug, the blade would slip right into your hands. I hid another blade in my boot and a third one at the head of my bed. No, I wasn't planning on hurting anyone in the slightest; this was purely for my own safety. It was a tried and tested prisoner method. In order to stop violence and abuse directed against you, you needed to turn the situation around by slashing some part of yourself – for example, your veins. I was already feeling an oppressive atmosphere: there were conversations, hostile glances. Another partner in the crew and a neighbour on the bunks, Vanya, later told me how after lights out he was taken to the caretaker for a chat and was asked about my plans.

All the convicts who were careless enough to talk to me would face the same fate. I had merely to exchange a few words with someone for the poor fellow to be hauled off to the caretaker for questioning.

Maryin wanted a chat with me too.

'Look, do you really need all this? Just stop stirring up trouble among the guys, withdraw your complaints, and you can enjoy a peaceful life in the unit!' Misha tried to reason with me, alternating between promises and threats. 'Rybakov's patience will snap, the guys will take things into their own hands, and then there'll be no helping you,' he continued.

Hardly an evening went by without the yells of prisoners being punished. One night after lights out, they were beating someone brutally. The poor fellow's screams were so loud that they were drowning out the stereo in the caretaker's office playing at full volume.

'How come they aren't afraid of accidentally killing someone?' I wondered.

The next day, Roma Sh. did not get up for roll call. He lay on the bunk, unable to move. Nobody took him to the medical unit, though, as that would have meant filling out forms. If he died, they could always write he'd fallen down the stairs. And if he lived, there was little danger he'd file a complaint; even if he did, he couldn't prove anything. Misha Maryin bragged to me about the services he carried out for the operational officers. He had personally sussed Roma out, as the latter was serving up the special diets to the inmates. They caught Roma in the act of slipping a mobile phone from one unit to a prisoner from a different one.

'You total bastard!' I said to Maryin, unable to bite my tongue.

Roma recovered and he took my place in the dishwashing team. Meanwhile, by some miracle, I managed to get seen by the doctor, and I was transferred on medical grounds to another job, no less vital: the vegetable-cleaning section, or vegetable-chomping, as the prisoners called it. The main task was peeling potatoes. To ensure I didn't fall behind the others or relax my pace, they gave me my own personal vat for the peeled potatoes. I quickly learnt the art of peeling and worked as fast as the others. I alone from the dining room managed to win an eight-hour day. I got my own personal notebook for recording the hours I'd worked, which I solemnly signed after each shift. I didn't fit in with the team, as once I'd done my eight hours, I would head off to the barracks and sit on a bench there, while the rest were forced to complete the quota for me.

Suddenly, the opportunity arose to visit the prison shop. There was nothing much I needed, and I treated it as a chance to stretch my legs. As our names were called out, we left the heavily guarded local zone, formed a line and set off towards the store. Only a lucky few could go to the shop; most of the poor fellows didn't have the funds in their accounts. But even this small group of inmates was watched like a hawk by the caretaker's loyal orderlies lest they run away. And that really did happen. From time to time, unable to take any more humiliation and torture, one of the slop-servers would escape from the dining room. They would flee to the camp or the main office in the hope of finding help there. But, alas, they were always sent back. Later, when I first encountered my persecutor, Mr Rybakov, the deputy head of operations, he proudly told me, 'Units 1 and 2 are my babies!'

I asked him, 'But why have all this abuse of the men?'

To which he answered philosophically, 'How else can you force them to work?'

This prison shop had a similar selection to the one in Melekhovo. I bought some tea, coffee, sweets and cigarettes. Much of this was not for myself, but for my fellow prisoners. The guys did not have tea or cigarettes. They would share one cigarette between two or three men. By handing out cigarettes, I inadvertently incurred the wrath of the caretaker Misha. I was amazed to learn that only he had the right to dispense gifts among the inmates! On the evenings of the days when the shop was open, he would give the prisoners cigarettes supposedly bought at his own expense, but in reality purchased with money stolen from the inmates themselves. At the orderly's command, the prisoners would chant in unison to the smug and glistening caretaker, 'Thank you, Lvovich!'

The caretaker's responsibilities were indeed onerous and indispensable. Besides needing to feed the prisoners, he also had to provide meals for the camp's employees – naturally enough, by cutting back on the inmates' food. Who would notice if two or three kilos of meat went missing from the huge cauldron of bubbling slop? The meat brought to the camp was past its prime and came from the state reserves. Once its shelf life had expired, it was sent to the undemanding customers of the colony. Unofficially, the dining room had a designated cook for the camp's management: a prisoner who made meals for the staff. If some delegation or the top brass was expected, the food vats for the staff would be hidden far from prying eyes. And so they kept the lid on their secret. The moment the delegation was gone, though, the revelry would begin. Living it up at the prisoners' expense, eating and drinking till you burst! Here you had your own personal takeaway restaurant. The dining room would take orders from the camp employees! The menu was nothing special, but the demand for a free lunch was strong and stable. From morning to night, come rain or shine, the waiter – also an inmate – would be lugging bags full of cooked dishes to the operational officers, the guards and all other takers. The system ran as smooth as silk and did its founding fathers proud. Who would keep sight of the fact the inmates were meant to be served buckwheat and pasta twice a week? Once a week was more than enough! Or why not feed them cereal mush, which most of them refused to eat? And then all the food saved could go to the camp staff.

True enough, from time to time, there was the odd mishap. Once, some crushed glass was found in the meatballs served up to the operational officers. Try as he might, Misha Maryin could not find out who was behind it. So they punished everyone. Just to be safe, all the men who might have done it were beaten up, but still no one confessed.

The date of the court case against the camp was approaching. Misha Maryin, acting as a go-between in the negotiations, called me in for yet another chat. He tried appealing to my conscience, attempting to make me see reason.

'The entire unit is having a rough time because of you! The guys have had their sleep cut back, the Article 106 men are being forced to work! Come on, now, think about this, withdraw your grievance from the court!' he harangued me. 'You've got enough problems already! Think it through, you're a grown man! There's nothing I can do here, I can't help you. You'll fall down the stairs and that'll be the end of it.'

The next morning, the caretaker took me to see Rybakov himself. A tall young man with the rank of captain, he explained his position to me clearly and coherently.

'Either withdraw your complaint or you will face problems.'

He couldn't keep himself from asking, 'I wonder how much cash you forked out in Melekhovo to get those references and commendations?'

The captain saw the whole world through the lens of his own notions, and he could not conceive that I might have earned everything through my own hard work.

51

HARA-KIRI

Realising where everything was heading, and not doubting for a second the credibility of the threats I faced, I'd made up my mind a long time ago. I wanted to live, but I wasn't willing to withdraw my complaint from the court. So what could I do? I needed to do whatever it took to be removed from that loathsome camp. I'd heard the inmates tell many a story about men slashing their veins, ripping open their stomachs, cutting their throats. The prisoners would maim themselves just to get out of the camp and into the prison hospital. The more exotic methods – swallowing needles or nails rolled in a ball of bread – weren't an option. Although, of course, they were guaranteed to work. Once you'd gulped it down, only an operation could save you. I agonised for a long time over what to choose, and, after thinking long and hard, I made a tough choice. I was troubled by the idea of what my son would think if the attempt were unsuccessful – or rather, too successful. I did not want to be seen as a suicide case. Every step of my plan was mapped out.

It was evening roll call. A dull winter day, with some sleet falling. As they waited for the bell, the prisoners calmly paced about the small yard. Once the bell rang, the inmates would line up and the inspection would begin. I quietly walked among the prisoners and pretended to follow their conversation. In reality, I didn't hear what they were saying; I was lost in my own thoughts. Under my buttoned-up jacket was naked flesh. I had unfastened my uniform so it wouldn't mess with the plan. The cold wind nipped my skin. In my right hand, I held a razor blade between my fingers. I had another in my breast pocket, just in case. The bell rang out. Each prisoner had his place in the row. We fell into line and waited. My heart was pounding wildly; I could barely breathe.

'Ivanov!' yelled the officer.

'Pyotr Nikolayevich,' the prisoner replied, and he stepped forward.

I heard the names: Nikolayev, Lizochkin, Panin …

It would be my name next.

'Pereverzin!'

'Vladimir Ivanovich,' I yelled, stepping forward, counting my paces.

One, two – turning my back on the inmate-on-duty, I moved away from the line, unbuttoning my jacket.

Three, four – I stared in amazement at my bare stomach and the blade in my right hand.

Five, six – the blade slid into my belly like a knife through butter.

The first cut was the hardest part – it didn't go in deep enough – but also the most important. After that, a wave of adrenaline washes over you, and, numb to the pain, you enter a frenzy.

My plan had been to slice open my abdomen, spilling my guts out with the words: 'So you wanted my blood? Here, you bastards, enjoy!'

Then it felt as though I was watching it all from outside myself – from some place above and to the side. The stunned faces of the prisoner-orderlies, their mouths frozen in a scream. They all came surging towards me, surrounding me, swooping in from all sides. I didn't have the strength – nor, perhaps, the desire – to resist, and I just wheezed out in a faint voice: 'Freedom for political prisoners!'

My injuries were not grave enough, and everything remained as before. My insides were the same, as was my plight in the camp. True, they moved me to another unit – Unit 11 – with better conditions.

I was left with the scars on my stomach as a memento of that eventful day.

My enjoyment of the improved standards in the new unit was cut short. The letter to Reimer requesting a transfer to another colony had worked. Once again, I had a journey ahead.

As we parted, Captain Rybakov addressed me: 'Why did you have to file a complaint against us? Not nice! Look, it wasn't our fault! We personally couldn't give a damn about you, it was Moscow that called and asked us to put the screws on you!'

At first, I couldn't believe that someone in Moscow would take such an unhealthy interest in me.

52

THE SWEET SCENT OF VANILLA

The prisoner truck was chock-full of convicts bound for the general-regime penal colony. We were on our way to the town of Pokrov. A mood of jokes, laughter and fun reigned in the truck, which seemed as though any moment now it might collapse.

Bitter experience had taught me not to lay any plans or harbour any illusions. Rumour had it this was a 'black' camp – controlled by the criminals – and things there were laid-back. Though you could always get a tough reception. There was no telling what to expect. I was travelling light, carrying just one bag. After all the adventures and robberies, the number of my belongings had plummeted.

All the camp's workers would assemble to meet the new arrivals. The door of the prisoner truck would open, and you would jump out to face a line of guards. Without any shouting, in a flash you realise that you had to run past them. The quicker you ran down the line, the fewer whacks you got. I received three rather nasty blows from a rubber baton. On my spine and sides. We were lucky: this was a gentle reception. We were led to the punishment cell, where the admission procedure began. One at a time, the men were taken away to be searched. Having gone through hundreds of searches, I saw no excesses in this one. It was just a regular search, which was already a good sign. They marched us across the entire grounds of the camp towards the quarantine barracks. From the various zones of the colony, thousands of curious eyes were turned on us, trying to pick out friends or men from back home.

The bleak quarantine building greeted us with cold, draughts and mosquitoes. It took me a while to realise what the bumps on my face were. Mosquito bites! Outdoors, we were facing the late January weather. At night, in an attempt to block out my neighbours' snoring, I put in earplugs and ceased hearing the relentless buzz of the winter bloodsuckers. This camp was surrounded by marshes, and mosquitoes were a serious scourge. They were everywhere, haunting the half-flooded basements, utility rooms and industrial zone. Making no distinction between different ranks of men, let alone their uniforms, the mosquitoes attacked their sources of nourishment incessantly, treating staff and convicts as equals. But when the wind blew from the west, the colony would fill with the scent of vanilla and chocolate. A hundred metres from the camp was a factory producing Alpen Gold chocolate bars.

Chaos and havoc prevailed in the colony; there was virtually no work, and the convicts were left to their own devices. The camp was considered a 'black' one and lived by the thieves' code. A real criminal boss oversaw the place. Each barracks had a boss of its own. Then there were the endless bosses for the industrial zone, the medical unit, the prisoner kitty, the quarantine barracks, all watching that the prisoners kept to the code. The set-up suited everyone: it meant the camp stayed comparatively calm and orderly. The staff of the colony could get away with doing nothing, just turning up for work and pocketing backhanders for doling out commendations and paroles. The prisoners were saved from doing idiotic correctional tasks and could quietly serve out their sentences.

The moment we entered the quarantine barracks, we wrote out a note listing who we were, where we came from, what units we'd been in. I had worked in the dining hall and said so on the note. According to the local rules, that made me one of the pigs, a gruel server, a rat. No self-respecting convict could share a table with me. While in quarantine, I became a leper. Just an hour earlier, in the presence of these barely literate guys, listening in on their conversations, I had wondered in horror how I could bear to endure their company. And yet now it was they who were rejecting me, though I had suffered at the hands of the pigs far more than the lot of them put together. I was dumbstruck. The worry and stress consumed me. I stopped eating, began starving myself.

'Don't get us wrong, Volodya,' one lad told me. 'We've got nothing against you. But we'll get grief if we go against the rules and share a table with you.'

After a while, things turned around, and I struck up excellent relations both with the management and with the prisoners. Prison life is so full of subtleties, and often you stand a much higher chance of restoring justice in the criminal world than in the ordinary one. It might not shock you to hear that seventy per cent of Russians have no faith in Russia's law-enforcement agencies or its courts.

We were in quarantine for nine days, following which we were summoned to the main office to be assigned work. I went in last and introduced myself, giving my surname. Two men sat in the room: an operational agent for the directorate of the Vladimir Regional Federal Penitentiary Service, Captain Fomin, and the political-education officer for the camp. They already knew who I was and were expecting me.

'Well, then, Pereverzin, will you be lodging complaints against us?' asked the agent.

'So far, there's been nothing to grumble at. But if you mess with me, I'll lodge complaints,' I levelled with them.

They were suffering from staff shortages, and the political officer suddenly suggested I work at the school. He assigned me to Unit 3, a 'red' unit for prisoners who collaborated.

After the events in the Vladimir camp, I had acquired a stellar reputation as a troublemaker and lodger of complaints, and the police were afraid of contact with me.

They didn't give me the job officially, as then they would have had to offer regular commendations, which they'd been strictly forbidden from doing. They were free, though, to heap infringements on me. They could send me to the punishment cell to their hearts' content, or issue official sanctions or warnings. But no commendations for me! Someone quickly removed from my file the commendation issued in error for my involvement in the comedy contest, where I was both director and actor, playing multiple roles at once.

One day, the major who headed the education department (a man so drab and toothless that you barely noticed his absence – or, indeed, his presence) asked me, 'How are your relations with the President?'

I choked in surprise, and, slowly hammering out each syllable, offered the neutral statement, 'Things are fine between me and the President.'

The major couldn't resist spilling the beans and shared with me a state secret. 'We got a call from Moscow warning us that Pereverzin's release into society would be undesirable.' I could picture it clearly in my head. A deputy chief of some department in the Presidential Administration calls up the godforsaken prison camp in the town of Pokrov. The local chief, upon hearing the words 'Presidential Administration', leaps to attention and salutes the unknown caller, awaiting orders. He lavishes the caller with honour, though in this place, honour has long since vanished from sight.

The days went by, gathering pace and merging into weeks and months, bringing my freedom closer. Rather than sitting about in the unit, I started calling in on the school, where I met the head – Nadezhda Gafarova, a born educator. Sometimes I marvelled at the patience and wisdom with which she transmitted knowledge to her adult students, who were not always the most grateful of people. School being too grand a word for it. For a long time, the chilly, unheated classroom became my retreat too. I organised an English language club. To my surprise, people came from every corner of the colony. I was inundated with men hoping to learn English. I was given textbooks and audio courses. The men were arranged into groups, and I got started. News had still not reached the deputy chief of security. The story of the English language club had passed him by, and when he found out what was going on right under his nose, he was livid.

'We cannot have an enemy of the people teaching English!' he said in outrage. 'He'll win them all over to his side.'

In Melekhovo, I had been an 'enemy of the state', so I responded calmly to the news that I was now deemed an 'enemy of the people'.

I had to meet personally with the deputy chief of security, Captain Stepurin, which led to us striking some kind of deal. Our pact allowed for me to serve my remaining term quietly and peaceably, without lodging complaints against the management, in return for which they would leave me alone, let me get on with life and let me teach English to the prisoners. I was around two years away from completing my sentence, and I accepted these terms.

Realising that I had no prospect of parole, I decided to put my remaining time to maximum use – by getting into shape. In our unit's local zone, under my strict guidance, the convicts erected a training ground. A pull-up bar, parallel bars, bench, barbells, dumbbells – we had everything we needed to get started. School, sports and books engaged my every spare moment.

The penal colonies follow a hard-and-fast rule: the more freedom the convict enjoys, the worse he is fed. In this camp, they fed us abysmally, and what they gave us in the dining hall was utterly inedible. I had to switch to dry rations. Rolled oats, buckwheat flakes and rice flakes, nuts and dried fruits became my main diet. I was receiving regular parcels. Warrant Officer Valentina, who worked in the visiting room and handed out parcels to the prisoners, was sweet-natured, polite and chatty. She would examine the contents of my packages with curiosity. I was surprised to learn from her that whenever I picked up a parcel, she would immediately be visited by agents who would record the contents as she described them. Once a month, the agents would write a report on me. Valentina was replaced in the parcel room by her colleague Lyuda, who was her polar opposite. When she saw that my parcel contained a book written in English, Lyuda wailed like a siren. 'In our colony … in our colony, we allow only Russian literature!' She would say this, stuttering with rage, and solemnly hand over the confiscated book to the agents. John Grisham's *The Innocent Man* lay for a month in the agent's office before the major handed it over to me. 'We had to check it, you see. What if it had contained some hidden coded message?'

In the strict-regime camp in Melekhovo, where I had regularly received similar books, nothing like this had happened. Indeed, it was a strange thing to hear in a colony where one in three prisoners had a mobile phone.

After the book, Lyuda entirely switched her attention to the magazines *Men's Health* and *GQ*, which underwent brutal censorship. She ruthlessly ripped out all the pages where she saw the merest hint of bared female flesh.

The zeal of the staff in the visiting room knew no bounds. After putting relatives who had come for an extended visit through the degrading search procedure, the vigilant female warrant officers would demand certificates from a gynaecologist and a local physician confirming they had 'not had sexual contact with infected persons'. By the time the loved ones had jumped through all the numerous hoops and made it to the visiting room, it would be evening. I decided to protect my family from these abuses and refused extended visits in this camp.

53

COMEDY CONTEST

From time to time, I had to turn away from my own activities and engage in creative work. Our camp was a 'black' one, and among the prisoners observing the thieves' code, performing on stage was deemed beneath their dignity – not the done thing. Absolutely nothing could persuade the inmates to attend the club, not even a commendation. The men in this camp had much shorter sentences than those in Melekhovo, and many quietly served out their full two years while abiding by the thieves' code. The camp management, nevertheless, still had to account for themselves. They had to show they were enlightening and re-educating the convicts.

One day, the head of the education department approached me and asked, 'Have you ever been abroad?'

'Yes,' I replied.

'Could you write a script for a comedy sketch?' he asked in a pitiful voice.

An order had come through to hold a comedy contest among the prisoners. The contest would be dedicated to Diplomats' Day. I could not stifle a laugh. Which idiot thought this up? They have entire research institutes at their disposal, and they proudly call themselves 'penologists'! The number of parasites we have in

Russia never ceases to amaze me – people maintaining a façade of work. They'd do less damage if they did nothing at all.

I graciously agreed, and threw myself into the job. The comedy contest had to be run as though there'd been a competition between the camp's units and we were now holding the finals to find the winners. I had five prisoners at my disposal. I was acting as the scriptwriter, director, compère and a member of several of the teams. We had the bare minimum of scenery. Running ahead a little, when my sixteen-year-old son watched a recording that somehow miraculously survived, he asked, 'Dad, what is this rubbish?' But at the time, I decided to amuse myself and I wrote a script, thinking up scenes for three teams. I repeat: there *were* no teams, just as there was no contest. We had only a handful of prisoners, including me, tasked with creating the illusion of a competition.

From here, on the outside, it does of course look rather pathetic, but at the time, I quietly chuckled to myself and even felt proud of my efforts, all the while aware that I might end up in solitary, because the recording would be sent to the Vladimir Regional Federal Penitentiary Service. To this day, I still find it funny. Two of the sketches were not all that interesting, but the first one was rather good. The action was filmed inside the camp's library. Here is how it went.

Compère (yours truly): 'In the face of stiff competition to reach the closing round of the competition dedicated to Diplomats' Day, two teams have made it through: the Hurricane team whirled into the final, literally sweeping away all the rivals that lay in its path, and the Tortoise team, which has slowly but surely pushed ahead, following the principle "slow but steady wins the race". Your attention please, as the final battle begins ...'

The action takes place in an improvised foreign ministry prison camp. The words 'The General-Regime Pokrov Town Penal Colony's Ministry for Foreign Affairs' flash up on the screen. We see several prisoners – the staff of the Foreign Ministry – sitting around drinking tea. A high-ranking ministry official waltzes into the room (again played by me, as I left the relatively speech-heavy roles for myself) and he says, 'That's enough tea drinking! Do you have any idea what's happening in the world?'

'What do you mean? What's happening?' one of the staff replies.

'Do you realise the Earth revolves around the Sun, and not the other way around?' I ask.

'No way!' the same prisoner says in surprise.

'Oh yes, it's true,' I continue. 'In fact, we're living in an age of scientific advance, of nanotechnology and innovation. Ever heard, for example, of the City of the Sun? It is also known as Strasbourg!'

'City of the Sun? Strasbourg?' the prisoner repeats pensively.

'Yes! And we urgently need to establish diplomatic relations with it! Who will be the ambassador?'

The prisoners look at me in bewilderment and dismay. I take in everyone present and my gaze lingers on one of the employees: 'Aha, Vasily, we'll make you ambassador!'

Vasily glances around, frightened and lost for words.

'Yes, you're Ambassador to Strasbourg,' I conclude, and it sounds like a curse …

Scene change. The action shifts to France's Ministry of Foreign Affairs, as signalled by the relevant poster. We see the office of the minister, who (apologies for the lack of modesty, but played by me again) is sitting at his desk, pretending to look through some papers. A few people enter the office hesitantly. They shift from foot to foot, nudging each other. One of them begins speaking in a mix of broken English and Russian: 'Hello, friends. Vee come from a distant land' – initially I had the idea of giving him the words 'a wild, dark and distant land of lawlessness', but then thought better of it. 'Vee vont friendship, diplomatic relations!'

To which the French minister replies in my voice, 'I am very glad to see you here. We have been waiting for you for ages! I would like to ask only one question! What about human rights in your country? Human rights?'

The diplomats from the distant country exchange puzzled glances, clearly unable to understand the conversation. Then the minister switches to broken Russian and says with an accent, 'Rights, human rights!'

The ambassador from the faraway land replies with a sigh of relief, 'Ah, Wrights! Herman Wrights! No problem – I know the man!'

The curtain falls.

At first, I thought of ending the scene with a portrait of the Russian president, but I ditched that idea, because the camp staff might catch my sarcasm. As it was, they didn't understand a thing – or else they didn't watch the recording …

And that was how some of the better days of my incarceration were spent. Even at the time, it gave me some pleasure, and it still puts a smile on my face now, as I write these lines.

54

ENEMIES ALL AROUND

I was not destined to find peace while in detention. I now acquired a terrible new enemy: the deputy head of operational work for the Vladimir Regional Federal Penitentiary Service, Colonel Anatoly Deykun. The terror of all the prisoners and policemen, the young colonel loved to drop in on the camp. He enjoyed frequent visits, and always made a point of favouring me personally with his attention. The entire camp knew that whenever Deykun came to the colony, the first place he'd head would be Unit 3, to pay me a call. He made no secret of visiting Unit 3 for the sole purpose of seeing Pereverzin – and he declared the fact loudly. Deykun loved rifling through my things and nosing about in my bedside table. He would lift up the mattress, pull the sheets off, peep inside the pillowcase. Sometimes he wasn't averse to lying down on my bed. As he did it, I wanted to ask him, 'Trying it for size, are you?' I was sorry not to have a mobile phone with a camera. What unique shots would have circulated online, bringing the colonel to a sticky end. I wonder how he is coping without me. Perhaps I should send him a package with my old prison garb.

If you're wondering if the man was crazy, I can confidently tell you: he was a bona fide maniac!

Deykun was as gleeful as a child the time he arrested me and put me in solitary for ten days. He personally discovered two flimsy mattresses and two blankets on my bed, a gift from a prisoner who'd been released. Caught red-handed, I was solemnly marched to the isolation cell for ten days.

'Hurray, they've freed me!' was how I began my letter to a friend when they finally released me. As I didn't smoke and wasn't hooked on *chifir*, I coped fairly well with solitary. Being locked up in the summer would have been perfectly tolerable had it not been for the mosquitoes; hunting those bloodsuckers was how I spun out the hours in there. The bloody corpse of a mosquito splatted on the white ceiling could have landed me an extra day in solitary, so I had to cover my tracks. Time flies when you're in isolation, and I soon found myself back in my old environment.

For smokers, doing a stint in solitary was sheer torture. And there weren't many prisoners who could go for long without tea, so they had to use their cunning. You wouldn't be entering the cell in your own clothes – you were completely changed into new clothing marked 'solitary'. The only way to smuggle anything into the cell was inside your body. So that was what they did. They wrapped up and sealed their tea and cigarettes in polythene bags before inserting them inside themselves. I saw it with my own eyes. You could also get hold of cigarettes, if you were in luck, during your walk in the exercise yard. Plastic-wrapped packets of cigarettes and tea would come flying through the air – tossed between the prisoners. That was how things worked in a 'black' camp. According to the thieves' code, a prisoner should not suffer while behind bars – instead, he was meant to rest and recharge. The jailers tended to take the opposite view. They were convinced the prisoners should be made to suffer, which was why they tried their hardest to intercept the forbidden consignments, to catch those flinging them and lock them up in solitary.

Despite Deykun's regular visits to our unit, the prisoners treated me sympathetically. I slept in a place of honour, on the bottom bunk next to the wall. The most diverse range of men surrounded me. The convicts in our barracks worked in the bakery, at a construction site and in the dining room.

The senior orderly for our unit, Scarface, was a young guy with a massive scar on his neck. He told me his story. Hailing from a dysfunctional family, he'd had a life of hard knocks and was doing time for robbery. After his arrest, he found himself in Vladimir Prison inside a notorious 'pressure cell', where, under the guidance of the local operational officers, the prisoners created a living hell to put the heat on their victim. No normal person has imagination enough to conceive of the horrors human beings will inflict on their own kind. Anatoly, who had not yet morphed into Scarface, to escape the pressure to confess to someone else's crimes, slashed open his own neck and managed to get transferred to the infirmary. It turned out I too had personally encountered the thugs from that cell in Vladimir Prison. They worked as caretakers in Units 1 and 2 at the general-regime camp in Vladimir. One was Sergei Zhukin, nicknamed Beetle, and the other was Sasha Vinogradov, nicknamed Hooligan. By a strange twist of fate, their third helper in the 'pressure cell', Hare, found no demand for his services as a thug and so switched to the peaceful profession of gruel server. Scarface, in some perplexity, later pointed out to me his unremarkable-looking tormentor. I have to hand it to him – after gaining the upper hand over his oppressor, Scarface would limit himself to delivering a single beating and refrained from taking any further action against his foe. Despite the crime he'd committed, Anatoly had more nobility and grace than many of the crime-fighting police officers.

You'll find a whole range of people serving time in Russian penitentiaries. I would estimate a good thirty per cent of them are innocent. A vast array of circumstances landed them behind bars. There are plenty of out and out rogues and bastards. But the way the system deals with them simply defies description. In this setting, a good man will turn bad, and a sceptic will lose any last vestige of faith and hope for justice. A bad man will turn even nastier. As for men in uniform, I would not let them anywhere near the prisoners, let alone allow them to adjudicate on their parole. They are only fit to guard the outer perimeters of the colony to keep the prisoners from escaping. Psychologists, doctors and teachers – now these are the people who can be of benefit to the convicts. If the prisoner does work, he should earn a point; if he studies, he gets another point; if he goes to a session with the psychologist, let him earn two more. Everything should be voluntary. Once you have amassed ten of these symbolic points and received a reference from the psychologist, go up for parole. If you'd rather not, then serve your full sentence. Keep it simple. No need to concoct anything more elaborate.

55

SPARTAKIAD OF PEOPLES OF THE FEDERAL PENITENTIARIES

From time to time, the staff of the Federal Penitentiary Service could show real imagination. We had another large-scale event ahead of us. The Spartakiad of Convicts from the Penal Colonies of Vladimir Region was approaching. Football, volleyball and table tennis were the three events in which the prisoners would be competing. The right to host the competition was won by the strict-regime camp in Melekhovo. Our participation in the games was compulsory and it was a grave affair. The teams for our camp were hurriedly cobbled together. Not many volunteered. The thieves' code did not allow those prisoners who observed it to take part in such games, so the teams had many positions vacant. The idea of visiting Melekhovo, where I'd spent three years, took hold of me, and I enrolled in the volleyball team. I had never played volleyball in my life. The team captain, Anatoly Scarface, the caretaker of Unit 3, encouraged me: 'The main thing is to get out on the field, for the sake of a tick in your box.'

We had seven volunteers ready to play ball for the sake of a tick. Some footballers and tennis players also popped up. The criminal boss of the camp caved in to the management's urgent request and gave the green light for the observant criminals to take part in the Spartakiad.

Early in the morning, after a hearty breakfast made specially for us, we squeezed into the prisoner truck and took to the road. Under the supervision of a guard, armed with an assault rifle, and a dog, we were relatively comfortable in our cages. The truck barely moved, stopping and starting the whole time. We faced traffic lights, then traffic jams, then the engine simply stalled. Four hours later, we had reached our destination. The truck entered the grounds of the camp, stopped inside the gates, and one by one we jumped out. We were met by the local police, wielding rubber batons.

'Do you realise where you are?' a hulking operational officer said in a thunderous scream that shook the sportsmen.

We were clearly not welcome here. As far as the operational officers were concerned, the whole enterprise was a complete waste of time they could have done without and an all-round headache.

'You won't find your general-regime camp here. Oh, no! You're in Me-le-kho-vo now!' the officer said, hammering out each syllable. 'Understood?' he addressed himself personally to each man.

'Understood,' the confused prisoners replied. They had not been expecting such a warm welcome.

The major noticed me and asked, 'Pereverzin, what are you doing here?'

'I'm visiting,' I answered truthfully.

One by one, we went through a search, formed a line and entered the sanatorium building. Peeling off our black uniforms and donning our sports kits, the entire team came out onto the avenue so familiar from all my marching, then headed for the stadium.

I walked past the local zones, where I saw many familiar faces. The prisoners greeted me with animated shouts, waving at me. I waved cheerfully back. In the local zone for the stadium, the prisoners were flocking to watch the event, and we were free to mingle with them. Besides us, teams had also been sent to Melekhovo from the Vyazniki and Pakino strict-regime camps. In all, there were just four teams. Full press coverage was being extended to the huge and bizarre event. Numerous journalists had installed themselves in the stadium.

The Spartakiad kicked off with the volleyball contests. All eyes were focused on us. The first match saw the teams from Melekhovo and Vyazniki locking horns. They played beautifully; it was a spectacular sight. The wonderful playing was due to the fact that, through some quirk of fate, both teams included Candidate Masters of Sports in volleyball. We were next. I was not agitated in the slightest. I had not even given the impending game any thought. The rules were explained to me just before the match. Volleyball looked an easy enough game. However, once I stepped onto the pitch, I realised it was a much more serious affair than I'd expected. I only managed to return the ball once, and that was a sheer fluke. The ball slipped past my fingers, whacked me in the chest, then randomly bounced towards a member of the rival team, who took the ball, hitting it back. In those minutes, I burnt with shame and wanted the ground to swallow me up. I happily kept count of our lost points as they brought the debacle closer to its end. My playing was not much worse than the other members of our team, who could not manage to return the ball to our rivals even once. An officer for re-educational work in the Vladimir Regional Federal Penitentiary Service offered an outburst that hung in the air.

'Why the hell did you bring these clowns here?' he shouted to the deputy political officer accompanying us, clasping his head in his hands.

One of my friends, a prisoner who'd run to the stadium for a chat, had found out I'd arrived in Melekhovo from another prisoner.

'Volodya is here! He's messing around on the field!' The news spread quickly through the camp. A few minutes after we'd lost our match, I was swapping impressions with my old friends. I had to go out on the pitch again to slug it out for our richly deserved last place.

With football and table tennis, things all went much better. In Vladimir Region, no one could equal our tennis players and footballers, and they swept to victory, taking first place. Passions were running high during the football match. The heads of the colonies (who must have been feeling like Abramovich watching Chelsea play) were yelling wildly in support of their charges. In the final game, our men were up against the strict-regime team from the village of Pakino, where the current head of our camp had formerly served as deputy chief. The lieutenant colonel would rejoice when the glad tidings of our victory reached him!

Despite the complete fiasco in volleyball, in the final team scores, our team took first place; we returned to the colony triumphant!

After we'd had lunch in the dining room, we all piled into the prisoner truck and headed home.

The local prison glop blew the minds of my teammates. In Melekhovo, they fed the prisoners vastly better than in Pokrov. That day, they put on a celebratory lunch consisting of macaroni made in the local bread factory and split-pea soup.

We left with a whole sea of emotions and impressions. My teammates were shocked by how rigid the regime in Melekhovo was. Sergei, who won first place in the tennis tournament, said, 'I'd rather do two years in Pokrov than one in Melekhovo.'

He had a point. But my subconscious mind had banished all the bad stuff, leaving nothing but good memories of the camp.

I wanted to yell, 'I love you, Melekhovo!' I wanted to turn back the clock, return to that carefree – as it now looked – time, when I was blissfully unaware and had no inkling of the trials that would befall me.

Tired but happy, I was back in the barracks by late evening, and for a long time I was unable to sleep, raking through images of the past.

The next morning, the head of the colony himself offered his congratulations to our team of winners.

'Well done, guys, you made my day,' he said, shaking our hands. 'Would you believe it, they beat Pakino!' He could not get over the shock. The idea that his team had won against the camp where he used to work, meaning he had kicked his former boss's butt, gave him no end of pleasure. He fell over himself to heap praise and thanks on us, promising we'd all be rewarded. I would be the only member of the team not to get a commendation.

56

LIFE GOES ON

Everything returned to normal; the daily grind began again. Each new day was no different from the one before: wake-up, lights out, school, training ground – that was it. One ordinary morning, there were no signs that anything out of the ordinary was on its way. But then, at wake-up time, into the colony burst a band of Federal Penitentiary Service officers, including the 'astronauts' – a squad of Special Forces in balaclavas. The rest of these professionals set to work on a gargantuan search. The entire camp was being inspected at the same time. All the units and all the buildings were turned inside out; they sifted through absolutely everything. A vast quantity of personal clothing was confiscated from the prisoners. Sweaters, T-shirts, jackets and other belongings went flying into large bin bags. Mobile phones were thrown in there too. What was the purpose of all this? Why unleash so many officers? The entire operation was utterly pointless, of no use to anybody. Over a hundred healthy men frittering away their time on this nonsense.

'They could be laying roads or working the land,' I told myself.

Why is such a manic war on mobile phones waged inside Russia's penitentiaries? You will, of course, be given a lot of hot air about how they do it to prevent the inmates from plotting new crimes, or intimidating their victims; they will bombard you with stories about mobiles being used 'for illegal purposes'. Perhaps there is some truth in that. But it is not the primary reason at all. The primary reason is that mobile phones allow the prisoners to share information about what is happening inside the camps. That is what terrifies the Federal Penitentiary Service officers most in the whole wide world.

Autumn greeted us with a series of searches and all manner of commissions and inspections. We were expecting a delegation from Moscow. Rumour had it that a Moscow general was on his way. The camp was in a state of tense anticipation – one week passed, then another. Everything was ship-shape in the unit; the bedside tables had been cleared out. Now all that remained was to hide all the prisoners, and the place would be perfect! Finally, the long-awaited commission arrived at the penal colony. The large delegation spent a long time walking about the camp. They looked around, discussed something or other, entered the barracks and then left. Nothing changed in our lives. 'What was the point of their visit?' I wondered.

Suddenly, flames brought some colour into our grey routine. Fires began flaring up in the camp. A blaze broke out in the large manufacturing workshop where the garment production had been muddling along. A short circuit turned out to have been the cause of all the trouble. The fire raged in earnest. I watched as the workshop burnt and the fire engines arrived at the camp. I realised I was enjoying it.

Let it all go to blue blazes! Many of the other prisoners felt the same way.

The workshop burnt to the ground, forever memorialising the local mismanagement.

A week later, the rubbish dump went up in flames. The fire was not as big, but we couldn't extinguish it by ourselves. Several fire engines arrived at the camp, this time managing to extinguish the flames.

Good things come in threes. A short time later, a fire broke out at a checkpoint dividing the residential and industrial zones in the camp. The two-storey building was burnt to cinders.

Havoc reigned throughout the camp. All the cellars were flooded; the sewage system wasn't working. The cold water kept running out. There was no hot water. The pipes were leaking. We had power cuts. I had the impression the camp was in an environmental disaster zone. The nearby bogs complemented the gloomy look. They seemed as if they were sucking in and swallowing up the surrounding space, creating an atmosphere of bleak despair. I could not shake off the sensation that one day the prison camp would sink entirely into that swamp and disappear from the face of the earth.

Sometimes the leadership of the colony would attempt to look after their charges and were even ready to spend money on them. Quite out of the blue, some vehicles arrived with a delivery of bedside tables. It did not matter that we had no hot water, that we were cramped for space, that everything everywhere was breaking down and falling apart, that the roofs were leaking. The important thing was that every man would get a grey bedside table to delight the eyes of the guards.

According to insider intelligence, each one of those 500 bedside tables set the prison camp back 12,000 roubles. The bedside tables were manufactured in the all-too-familiar general-regime Penal Colony No. 5 in Vladimir city, and they cost at most 800 roubles. Operation Bedside Table yielded rather nice dividends for the management of the Vladimir Region Federal Penitentiary Service camp. For a long time, the prisoners took a stand against the newfangled items, but it was an asymmetric contest, and soon the horrid and miserable bedside tables flooded into all the barracks.

In a couple of months, it would be New Year. I was counting down the time till my release. I would break what remained of my term down into chunks and then put them back together in a different order. It seemed to make things easier.

'Now I'll do a month and a half until the New Year,' I figured. 'Then I have another year left, and the longed-for moment will be close at hand. The last three months don't really count.'

In the camp, the run-up to New Year was a disturbing and most unpleasant time. There was one search after another, and security was enhanced. The situation was tense and nerve-racking. Once a week, I'd get a visit from my friend Colonel Deykun. He took an obsessive interest in my belongings and my bedding. I was amazed at the patience of the prisoners in my unit, who did not pick a bone with me or say a word – not even the slightest hint – about the mad colonel's visits. The last time he called in on us, it ended with my friend having his mobile phone confiscated and landing in solitary.

One frosty evening, I was walking around on my own in the local zone, pondering over what had been going on. I had merely to imagine myself for a moment walking in that same spot one year on, awaiting the next New Year, and I felt sick. My patience was already at its limit, and the remaining term seemed terribly long. Time was slowing down.

57

A SECOND MIRACLE

In December, the Criminal Code was amended. Once again, they changed the length of prison term for my conviction. The maximum sentence dropped from ten years to seven. My term was eight and a half years, meaning one and a half years over the maximum. Both logic and the law dictated that my sentence should be cut to five and a half years, that is, reducing it by three years. So it turned out I had already overstayed my sentence. My lawyer filed a petition with the local Petushinsky district court to bring my sentence into line with the new Criminal Code. The date of the court session was set for 17 January. I was stewing and fretting, counting the days to the trial, laying plans. In my case, anything could happen.

New Year's Eve passed in a haze. The day of judgement arrived. The judge reduced my sentence by a year and two months. I had precisely one month left to the end of my term! Once again, as if in a board game, I had jumped several squares forward in one go. The judge was taking no chances, playing safe by leaving me in the camp for another month.

I counted the days. This month would prove extremely tough, the final days stretching to infinity. I hid the joyous news from the other men until the last moment. I was waiting for the decision of the court to take legal effect, and also waiting for it to reach the camp's special unit. Soon the news of my imminent release would be public knowledge. I didn't know what to expect from my jailers. I couldn't shake off the idea that a number of them would wish to prevent my release, and I was terribly nervous. Realising that my words would be passed on to the operational officials, I let the orderly know of my resolute state of mind.

'Woe betide anyone who tries to set a trap for me,' I said in warning. 'I'll give them a scene to remember for the rest of their life! I'll slash myself all over, invite the TV stations and journalists and tell them about all the low-down tricks in this place!'

My message reached its intended audience. A week before my release date, Colonel Deykun came to the colony and called me in for a talk.

'Why do you need to put on this spectacle? You want to play the martyr? We don't need any TV stations or press here! Give me your word that no one will turn up!' he suddenly demanded.

I answered that I personally hadn't invited anyone and it was out of my hands; I had no influence over the free press …

It was 14 February 2012, my last evening in the camp. I gave away my belongings and tried to sleep. But I was wide awake. I was waiting for the morning, when I could wake up, wash, have a farewell drink of *chifir* with the men and set out for home. However, my plans were not to be fulfilled. After wake-up, the head of the unit appeared at my bedside.

'Get your belongings, you're going to the office,' he said.

It was not yet six in the morning; outside, it was pitch dark. I couldn't make sense of where they were taking me. The officer on duty, after confirming my identity, let me out through the double iron doors separating the two worlds. The head of the special unit was waiting for me. She had been called in to work so she could give me all the necessary paperwork. I got a passport, a certificate of release and the money from my personal account. Outside, I was met by the deputy head of security and operational work, an operational officer and a stranger in plain clothes.

'Get in the car,' the operational officer said.

I wanted to flee. I couldn't work out where they wanted to take me. Could they be about to bring new charges? Or were they going to kill me and dump my corpse somewhere? In a panic, my mind ran through the various possibilities.

'Where do you want to be taken? To the railway station or the bus terminus?' the operational officer persisted.

There was nothing for it but to meekly get in the car. Fifteen minutes later, we reached the bus terminus for the town of

Pokrov, where I got out of the vehicle. It was still dark. I was wearing a ghastly looking padded jacket with my name tag sewn on the chest and an equally hideous cap. My feet were clad in synthetic leather prison-issue boots.

'No need to alarm people. Rip the tag off and remove your cap,' the operational officer said in parting. Then he drove off.

I stood there as if in a dream, unsure of what to do. Luckily, I had some cash on me. Frightening away the few passers-by who were around at such an early hour, I went into a roadside café. After I'd bought a coffee and ice cream, it started to sink in that I was a free man. Twenty minutes later, a taxi was ferrying me to meet my loved ones, and we were reunited between Pokrov and Moscow, in a village called Obukhovo. There were tears of joy as we embraced each other. These people had stuck with me through all the years of my imprisonment: my good friend Leonid Belenky, my wife Irina and my son Denis.

My new life had begun.

AFTERWORD

As I write this, more than a year has passed since my release. It is now time to step back and take stock. The years spent in penitentiaries have left their mark on me. Unfortunately, I cannot erase the memory of what happened to me. Sometimes I dream that I'm back in the past. As Varlam Shalamov said, no sane person benefits from prison, but once a man has experienced it, he will never be able to escape from it. You are holding in your hands not just a book, but a piece of my life: the seven years and two months I spent in prisons and penal camps.

The thought of writing a book about my experiences came to me a long time ago, while I was still behind bars. I nursed the idea through all those years; it helped me survive. I had no choice. They came and arrested me, ripping seven long years out of my life. Bringing this book into the world was very hard for me; I had to return to the past and relive sensations that were far from pleasant. But I pushed on through, considering it my duty. I wanted to convey to people the following thought: what happened to me could happen to anyone.

Certain events connected with our case have already become history, but the case itself is not yet over and awaits its dénouement. The most interesting chapter is yet to come.

The investigators and judges received apartments, medals and orders. The lawyers got their substantial fees. Some of the Yukos employees made a killing, milking the situation. The ordinary employees of the company – mid-ranking managers such as me – suffered the most. Vladimir Malakhovsky, Alexei Kurtsin and Svetlana Bakhmina had to spend years of their lives in prisons and camps. There were other employees of the disgraced company who also had it tough. They were sentenced in absentia in Russia, international arrest warrants went out for them and they were forced to live abroad. Not a single country has extradited any of those named in our case. As one, the courts of Cyprus, Spain, Italy and Great Britain recognised the political motivation behind the case. To accuse the courts of those countries of collusion is hardly credible.

The Yukos case is far from over. Multiple claims filed by the defendants await their turn at the European Court of Human Rights. The Arbitration Institute of the Stockholm Chamber of Commerce is yet to have its say. With their illegal decisions taken for short-term gain in order to ingratiate themselves with their superiors, the investigators and judges planted a time bomb under the Russian justice system. All the millions of dollars officially paid by the Russian government to international consultants working on enhancing Russia's image abroad will ultimately be of no avail. The Magnitsky case, the Yukos case, the Pussy Riot and Bolotnaya Square cases – these are all important landmarks and highly disturbing; not just a national disgrace for Russia, but also a potential threat to every citizen of Russia. At this point, I'd like to ask Russian patriots to keep calm and not start blaming foreign agents for meddling in our internal matters. How would you like it if your upstairs neighbour started waving weapons about, harassing his children, causing a rumpus, making a racket and behaving like a thug? And when you try to have a word with him, calling him to order and demanding he follow the rules of human society, he has the cheek to answer: 'Why are you meddling in my domestic affairs?'

The Prosecutor-General's Office of the Russian Federation stubbornly chased after all those ex-managers living abroad, obsessively persisting in sending out warrants for their arrest. A third Yukos case was prepared and lies ready and waiting. Khodorkovsky was convicted of embezzling shares in Tomskneft VNK – allegedly becoming its owner illegally. They cooked up new charges (similar to the old ones, still fresh in everyone's minds) of embezzling the company's entire oil production and laundering the proceeds. They wanted to press those charges, but the hand of the conductor, much to the chagrin of the investigators, froze in mid-air, and there was an unforeseen pause. Perhaps there was a change of heart, or perhaps with a special cynicism they were biding their time to bung a couple more years onto Khodorkovsky's sentence on the eve of his release ... What can we expect from these people? A regime that has taken the straight road to repression and adopted a series of laws allowing them to throw people in jail for dissent is capable of anything. With our state-controlled judicial system, to this day they can bang up whoever they want merely by planting drugs on them or fabricating some charge or other. But what we are talking about here is the *legalisation*, or *legitimisation*, of knowingly unlawful arrests. The *law-enforcement* organs have cast restraint to the wind; legalised criminal gangs are running wild. A sombre picture emerges, bleak and mirthless.

What do I feel right now? Disillusion, pain, grief, sorrow. And yet at the same time, I feel like a lucky man. To my great fortune, amendments to the Penal Code came out, leading to my release. Otherwise, I would have been locked up until 15 December 2013. Over these years, life has changed considerably, and it is not quite clear what comes next for us. What should we do with ourselves? Where should we work? How should we live? The past and the present have left a huge number of encumbrances and restrictions on me and my colleagues. Not many employers want to risk giving a job to a 'political prisoner'. I have already had trouble obtaining a loan from any Russian bank. My criminal record not only prevented me from getting past the bank's 'door policy', but also prevented my appointment to a particular role in one public company. Obtaining visas has also proved a serious problem. I managed to resolve things with the Schengen visa, but the UK authorities still deem me undesirable.

People often asked me if I wasn't afraid to live in Russia and why I didn't move to the West. There were many reasons. Russia was my country, and I didn't plan on abandoning it because of some rogues and bastards. I believed that time would set things straight. But how much time it will take – that is up to us, whether at home or in exile. Sadly, we Russians fail to learn from our mistakes and we fall into the same traps time and again. We survived the Revolution, the war, Stalin's repressions … but now we are returning once again to the 1930s. Things are not as bleak as they seem, though. An unstoppable process of change has begun. The young shoots of protest are no longer so isolated; in some places they are pushing miraculously through the asphalt, and the profuse growth cannot be smothered in concrete using the old Soviet methods. We now live in a new world, in a different infosphere that shapes our reality, and this inspires a degree of hope.

Finally, I would like to thank the two people without whom – it is no exaggeration to say this – I would not have survived. They may have been on the outside, but in reality, they were serving my sentence with me and helping me pull through those seven years and two months. They were my dear friend Leonid Belenky and my wife Irina. I am especially grateful to my lawyer, Alexei Dudnik.

I also wish to thank the people who supported and helped me after my release: Irina Yasina, Igor Pisarev and Boris Galkin.

I would particularly like to thank the wonderful Olga Romanova, the founder of the rights group Russia Behind Bars, who lavished care and attention upon me when I was released, lending me invaluable help and support.

In closing, I'd like to cite a poem by my friend Leonid Belenky.

A Prayer

I beseech you
Every day with all my heart.
Do not forsake me.
Rescue me, shield me, save me.
Look at me:
Kneeling before you,
Rattling my chains,
Beating my brow bloody on the floor.

But eyes shut tight,
Not seeing. My ears are blocked.
I cannot hear your voice.
The Beast howls through the street.
I am lost in darkness.
Deep dark seeps into my soul.
The Devil hurtles towards me,
The door cracks from his blows.

I prayed all night,
My voice and prayers fading.
You're powerless to help.
You'd have come, no doubt, if you could.
But again you are silent.
I suppose you cannot hear.
Hear me, o human!
Once more your God is praying to you.